READING JAZZ

edited by David Meltzer

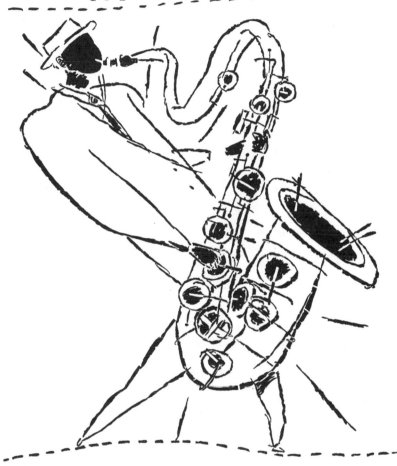

MERCURY HOUSE
SAN FRANCISCO

Published in the United States by
Mercury House
San Francisco, California

United States Constitution, First Amendment: Congress shall make no law respect-
ing an establishment of religion, or prohibiting the free exercise thereof; or
abridging the freedom of speech, or of the press; or the right of the people
peaceably to assemble, and to petition the Government for a redress of
grievances.

Cover art by Ward Shumaker

Mercury House and colophon are registered trademarks of
Mercury House, Incorporated

Printed on acid-free paper
Manufactured in the United States of America

—*Library of Congress Cataloging-in-Publication Data*—
Reading jazz / [edited] by David Meltzer.
    Includes bibliographical references and index.
        p.   cm.
    ISBN 1-56279-038-2   :
    1. Jazz—History and criticism.   I. Meltzer, David.
ML3507.R42   1993
781.65 DC20   92-44561
                                                        CIP

5   4   3   2

CONTENTS

ACKNOWLEDGMENTS

In the process of putting this work together, many friends have been helpful, though I nevertheless went on my own bent way with the project. A provisional list: Clark Coolidge (whose jazz writings deserve to be gathered into a book), Chris Winks (whose enthusiasm, research, translation skills were inordinately helpful—as was his ability to let me rant without blinking or throwing a pie in my face), Duncan McNaughton (whose sympathies and ironies I find irresistible), Larry Fagin (whose archival mania I find enigmatic yet essential), Herbie Lewis (bass maestro and director Jazz Studies at New College of California), the late Wallace Berman and Robert Alexander (whose distinct yet compatible versions of creativity and hipsterism gave me my wings), Kirsten Janene-Nelson of Mercury House (who entered the permissions labyrinth and, I'm happy to say, survived and triumphed), and, as always, for Tina.

—DM

Pre-ramble

Indeed, it is power with which we shall be concerned indirectly but persistently. Our modern "innocence" speaks of power as if it were a single thing: on one side those who have it, on the other those who do not. We have believed that power was an exemplarily political object; we believe now that power is also an ideological object, that it creeps in where we do not recognize it at first, into institutions, into teaching, but still that it is always one thing. And yet what if power were plural like demons? "My name is Legion," it could say: everywhere, on all sides, leaders, massive or minute organizations, pressure groups or oppression groups, everywhere "authorized" voices which authorize themselves to utter the discourse of all power: the discourse of arrogance. We discover then that power is present in the most delicate mechanisms of social exchange: not only in the State, in classes, in groups, but even in fashion, public opinion, entertainment, sports, news, family and private relations, and even in the liberating impulses which attempt to counteract it. I call the discourse of power any discourse which engenders blame, hence guilt, in its recipient. Some expect of us as intellectuals that we take action on every occasion against Power, but our true battle is elsewhere, it is against *powers* in the plural, and this is no easy combat. For if it is plural in social space, power is, symmetrically, perpetual in historical time. Exhausted, defeated here, it reappears there; it never disappears. Make a revolution to destroy it, power will immediately revive and flourish again in the new state of affairs. The reason for this endurance and this ubiquity is that power is the parasite of a trans-social organism, linked to the whole of man's history and not only to his political, historical history. The object in which power is inscribed, for all of human eternity, is language, or to be more precise, its necessary expression: the language we speak and write.*

---

*Roland Barthes, "Inaugural Lecture, College de France," [1977], Richard Howard, trans., from *A Barthes Reader*, Susan Sontag, ed. (New York: Hill and Wang, 1982), 459–460.

This work explores the literary and critical use of jazz during four historical moments of cultural transition. It presents aspects of the ways jazz was mythologized, colonialized, demonized, defended, and ultimately neutralized by white Americans and Europeans. This is about the white invention of jazz as a subject and object.

Like almost all other forms of popular culture—children's literature, comic books, paperbacks, rock 'n' roll, TV—jazz as subject and object creates its own dialectic of acceptance and rejection. It was, from the beginning, an emblem for public discourse; depending on which edge of the ledge you watched from, it was either destructive or redemptive, degenerate or transformative. While the music is the creation of African-Americans, jazz as mythology, commodity, cultural display is a white invention and the expression of a postcolonial tradition.

Conflicting racial perspectives dominate and play into the uses of jazz as subject and object. The perception that jazz is simultaneously primitive and modern circulates through many of the texts. Myths of Eden collide with myths of Progress.

Its structures were developed through performance and restructured through the technology of the phonograph. A great amount of criticism, hagiography, collecting, and fandom is played out by white Americans, Europeans, and now Japanese savants of the art mainly through listening to recorded performances.

In essence, a jazz performance is a real-time utopia, a collaborative effort supporting individual expression. At its highest, it takes nothing but gives an endless cornucopia of improvisation into the air and into the ears of an audience. Contained by a theme, it yields infinite possibilities of invention. It's stand-up composing of the highest order; it's given away. The record is the "text," while the performance is the mythological moment.

Despite the early stereotype of jazz musicians as noble savages or simple-minded entertainers, the making of jazz is (as Wynton Marsalis reiterates whenever possible) the transmission of an intellectual activity as complex as theoretical physics, allied to a core of emotional power and intelligence.

Often the jazz devout tend to simplify (or delimit) the complexity of their prize. Jazz remains (and retains) a set of unresolved problems contended with daily in our postmodern culture(s).

Jazz has been looked upon as a "new and unique" art or form or art form created by African-Americans, yet the mythology and demonology of jazz, its main economic support, is primarily a white male activity. Early modernists used the art of jazz as a tactic to shock the bourgeoisie and separate themselves from the cultural and social pressures of middle-class entrapment.

One enters a utopic sphere, partakes of, retreats from, reflects upon it, then grafts together a communiqué sent to possible converts "out there" in a bourgeois culture needing a jolt, a realignment with an art both romantically primitive and ultra-now new. The readings here are filled with descriptions of the players' savage ("folk") simplicity, and how their pure, direct inspiration intones passionately and effortlessly out of their primal psyches. Given qualities similar to the Romantic poet-hero, the players are "seers," entranced and possessed by powers beyond self.

This is a source-book of forms of permissible racism.

The issue (presence, appearance, context) of racism is inseparable from the history of jazz as practice and culture in relationship to itself and the world outside it.

This is a source-book of permissible (intentional, accidental, unavoidable) racisms.

———

Jazz was the first music I felt expressed me; the first music I felt, in listening to it, was "me," "mine"; this despite (or because of) the fact that both my parents were classically trained musicians. The first music I remember hearing as an infant is chamber music played in the living room: my mother at the piano, father playing cello, faceless colleagues from the Eastman School of Music playing viola, violin. A primary and vivid memory: crawling under the Steinway baby grand, my mother's feet pushing the piano pedals, creak of wood, metal rods damping and then sustaining sound, the music of the piano above me, radiating out and across the piano frame, resonating, enclosing me in its sound, shutting out, diminishing the other string players. You could say that it was "their music" and that part of the heresy of self-creation is an alliance with a music you claim as your own.

In another perspective, "their music" was perceived as a cultural power in post-Depression America; they were replicators and interpreters of music deemed "classic," i.e., a source of cultural authority, "serious music." My father was a first-born child in the United States of Polish-Jewish immigrant parents. My grandparents were garment workers. My mother was raised by her grandparents, essentially by her grandmother. Her grandfather was a railroad worker, a foreman. My father was born and raised in Rochester, New York, my mother in Los Angeles. It was in "their music" that they found autonomy and lives beyond their origins. Both were scholarship students at the Eastman School of Music. She had been a prodigy on the harp. He had started out on the string bass but settled with the cello. Through their music they were not only able to escalate their educations but, through their skills, play the endless odd jobs "serious" musicians endure (and sometimes enjoy) to pay the rent: weddings, dinner parties, receptions, as well as local chamber-music concerts, recitals, and occasional gigs on local radio. (I remember, but no longer own, a white acetate seven-inch 78 r.p.m. disc of my father playing a movement of a Vivaldi cello concerto on the radio; deeply entrenched in a minor key, melancholic, poignant, throbbing incomplete fragment attacked by scratches and eroding grooves.)

We had a wooden radio/phono console and an eclectic stack of 78 r.p.m. albums and singles. I don't know whose records they were, whether some were my father's, some my mother's. But I know that as soon as I was able to, I would plop platters on the turntable and listen to whatever I wanted; listening over and over to an odd mélange of records: Gershwin's *Rhapsody in Blue* played by Alec Templeton, a friend of my parents; Dvořák's Cello Concerto performed by Piatigorsky;

Casals playing the unaccompanied Bach Sonatas—the power and emotional intimacy of his performance created an expectation in me rarely matched (the first virtuoso after Casals to surround me with demands of intelligence and emotional force was Charlie Parker, when I heard him at the Royal Roost); The Rhythm Boys (Bing Crosby, Al Rinker, Harry Barris) with the Paul Whiteman Orchestra (Bix Beiderbecke on cornet), "That's Grandma"; Mildred Bailey, "You Don't Know My Mind Blues"; "The Sergeant Was Shy" played by a small Duke Ellington unit—and a favorite amazement, "Honky Tonk Train," a duo-piano boogie-woogie exhilaration performed by Meade Lux Lewis and Albert Ammons.

One is left to list names and titles to depress others beyond the page without any reference to hearing, the experience of the music; all the names, titles, record-company logos, matrix numbers, books, periodicals, catalogs, web out of an initial moment, the revelation of creation, a transfixing and often transcendent moment one can not retrieve, relive, or experience again. An ongoing realm of moments, of momentariness; a monumental event is alarmed into a brief sequence of being. The rest of it is aftermath, a futile ritual of gathering shadows and snowflakes, a trace of the event, a code of aftermath the initiate plugs into to reconstruct a gone moment.

At the outset, the "history" for me was the record itself, the music proclaiming and announcing each moment. And each moment, for this listener, was the instant of hearing and re-hearing. It was only years later, as a teenager, that I became aware of a history surrounding the music, pervading it. Initially, I constructed my own "meanings" out of the music, whether listening to Coleman Hawkins or caught up in the waterfall of Tatum's virtuosity. (My father told me Vladimir Horowitz listened to Tatum and declared him a genius. Story has it that Horowitz asked, "If Tatum could see, what would he—what *could* he—do?") The records I listened to had, in their randomness, no chronology for me. Older music and newer works were undifferentiated; they coexisted equally. Each record was its own narrative, its opening and closing; as the disc itself, a circular and contained event.

In one sense, I "invented" jazz from whatever sounds, names, images, labels the records provided, out of whatever my kid's brain could grasp from any kind of clue, including the mysterious code of matrix numbers scratched into the inner rim of the disc, spinning in orbit around the printed label. The labels told me stories in Vocalion's gothic type or in the "modern" red Columbia or gold Decca letters on black. The labels with their color codes I later understood to be degrees of ascent or descent. High-culture "classic" middle-brow was top-of-the-line while the low-brow otherness of "race" records was at the bottom. Hefting a disc, checking weight and width, was another tactile act, part of the rite. Some older discs felt heavier, more solid, denser, as if their grooves went darker and deeper.

When I was three or four I answered the front door. I looked up a long body to a black face looking down at me. It was the basso Kenneth Spencer, a friend of my parents, a fellow Eastman student. (A few years later I would see him in *Back to Bataan*, nobly dying as the one Negro in a House-I-Live-In Hollywood army unit.) His voice erupted out of an enormous frame. I'd never seen a black person before. I began to cry. My father interceded, deeply embarrassed, making Kenneth Spencer welcome in our house. Up to that moment I was unaware of the presence of race or difference even though my musical sensibility was being shaped by African-American forms.

(As I am typing this, bluesman Jimmy Reed is playing a gravely out-of-tune harmonica.)

As with the record, what we read or hear is up to us; the source is always elsewhere. How do I describe hearing music when I was four years old or fourteen or yesterday or now? How does the description have anything to do with the music or, for that matter, the music with the writing? How does one write "about" music?

———

"The four historical moments of cultural transition" euphemize epochs of violent disruptions, reversed certainties, shattered truths flying apart within key configurations of power, imploding within tribal units subordinated by power yet wheeling in orbit beneath power's golden belly. Simply: each period of jazz's reinvention or renewal comes after war, revolution, and social upheaval, a clarion of continuity and affirmation, allied with other arts in a refusal to surrender the imagination, the resistant energy of the creative, to the death-affirming brutality of systems of domination.

How is it that the condition of slavery produced an emancipatory art form that remains intact despite the fact of racism pervasive in the United States at the edge of the twentieth century? Why is the subtext of American popular musics African-American—that the shape, sound, and movement of our popular musics are either taken directly from African-American practices or indirectly colonialized? No matter what you're listening to, the music in the air is black. (Country and Western, Rock 'n' Roll, Heavy Metal, Christian pop, however *Billboard* or *Cash Box* slices the action into categories of markets and sales.) ("The air is black" may be the conditon all cosmopolites share as the twenty-first century lurches upon us—the atonality of ecocide, the static of planetary suffocation.)

The soundtrack of global mass mediation and the dance of cultures moving to it; the display of self in emblematic costumes of affiliation; the composted vernacular used to define and redefine cultural relationships; and the *fin de siècle* fantasy-realities of urban surrealism on TV, in film, on the streets, and in the self imagining the self in an ongoing video are deeply embedded with African-American arts and strategies of cultural survival. White fascination with slave culture is complex, a relationship based on its position and authority to determine its uses, mis-uses. Most of the texts reflect this fascination, the creating and re-creating of a romantic other; acts Aldon Lynn Nielsen calls "romantic racism." (Implying a dialectic that polarizes between racism of hate and racism of desire. Also suggestive of the impossibility of Romance; the participatory blindness of either two-way or one-way ardor.)

A "romantic other," a black word-shaped Golem speechless before its inventors.

"Fascination," another key word with roots in magic and magical empowerment. Acts of magic intervention, interaction with (or within) presumed or assumed realities; acts of self-protection, self-definition. *Fascinate* has its roots in *charm, spell.* Even on the dime-store level, there's a clear-cut public perception of black magic being evil and sexually malign, while white magic is seen as "good," helpful, at the service of "true" love.

———

The radio in my bedroom, a small, tan, streamlined metal Arvin, was another instrument that could order a musical universe. There, at night, in darkness, volume turned down, a small orange light like a cigarette behind the plastic arc of printed station call numbers, I practiced a kind of audiomancy, turning the Bakelite dialer to any kind of music and "tuning in." The umbilical aerial wire at the back of the radio was part of my praxis. I'd move it like a dowsing rod to catch remotes and signals from stations out of the usual broadcast range. That was how I heard the Grand Ole Opry, urban blues, rhythm 'n' blues, big-band pickups from hotels with enormous names, as well as classical music and whatever jazz was out there. On weekends it was possible to hear klezmer music, Baptist gospel groups in churches of echo and random screams, the Metropolitan Opera, Toscanini and the NBC Symphony Orchestra, Cantonese opera, as well as mainstream adventure, comedy, variety, dramatic shows, soap operas, serials. Dialing into a chaos of electric waves and strands and particles of signals which today remind me of an updated version of a journey through hissing tiers of gilt medieval visions of hell: voices, shattered appearances and disappearances of music dissolving into other musics, voices abruptly vanishing or multiplying into glossolalia, shafts of fragmented phonemes, like being in the control booth of Earth Central—"Hello, Central, give me Doctor Jazz"—omnisciently scanning for sounds, human or otherwise, isolating a voice, a rapturous bar of music, shifting into chopped violence of code tapping out a furious telegraphy . . .

The precision of locating a music outside the net, pulling it into hearing range, wiggling the thin aerial, delicately moving the dial into place with the accumulated expertise of touch safecrackers know, an intensely focused procedure of virtuosic proportion. Pulling in sounds, music, voices, an electric spiritualist seeking contact with the Author. Ears tuned to decode a sound, place it into play: mid-bar dissonant chord of Stan Kenton, keening Hank Williams, insouciant signature guitar riff of T-Bone Walker, ever-mellow silk of Nat King Cole's trio, and by remembering, already re-assembling yet another telling of the myth of jazz.

What is "the myth of jazz"? Should it be confused with the history of jazz? As befitting myth, the music made a journey up a River, the Mississippi: imported African sacred/secular instrumental and vocal music that had disembarked in the exotic port of New Orleans, blended in that cosmopolitan city where European travelers and merchants infused Western martial and classical musics into the polyrhythmic African mix, transformed, recirculated into a propulsively dynamic form called *Jazz*. A circular process where enslaved (or oppressed) peoples subvert and transform the master's musics of definition (church, state) into one of defiance that, in turn, becomes a mystery to the master class who sets out to learn its secrets and, as with other property, own it, control its presence in "normative" culture. In turn, the music is reclaimed, re-subverted, re-syncopated, harmonized, like Bebop, and again the defiant intelligence is sapped of force and focus, diluted as soundtrack by the master class for film and ads. As the buried joker in the deck the ever-present dominance of slave music pervades all facets of American popular music.

The slave sings of the past and future of freedom.

The myth of jazz I unroll is pieced together from the flow of popular culture's lights: movies where Louis Armstrong sits on a cotton bale surrounded by a sudden impromptu band of black dock workers in a sweat-free moment singing and grinning the birth of the blues; Bing Crosby, benign paternal overseer of child-like darkies; Cab Calloway, lit from below, his face turned into African juju, the band casting long tribal shadows on white-washed Warner Brothers studio flats—the embodiment of streamlined Harlem sleaze that leisured slummers went uptown to ogle; movies where white horn players like Kirk Douglas, Jack Webb, Montgomery Clift lift their horns to reach for an inexpressible height of sound . . .

the trope (or tropic diorama) is that jazz is essentially a white discourse, a white mythology, a white form of control over its production, reproduction, history, and economics; a white reverie over blackness sustained and contained within the cultural plantation-system of late capitalism

a double-bind where black African music subverts European music into a soundtrack for a mainly white middle-class culture ever in quest for new or old musics to collect, colonize, legitimate in a flow of mass-cultural marketplace options of consumption

it is a tradition and history narrated by white voices; a tradition and history controlled by an immense and shrunken industry manufacturing tokens of culture and reality, like molecules, for the fragmented consumer

"Underlying all of these concerns, in a paraphrase of both Karl Marx and Herman Melville, is the question: How did white men in nineteenth-century America repress or 'mutilate' themselves, become 'less' than they 'were,' and construct a culture of 'self-renunciation' and 'alienation'? And how did this process of domination produce a rage so intense it overwhelmed even rationality itself?" asks Ronald T. Takaki.*

The compulsion (or curse) to dominate, to absorb "theirs" into "ours," to admire and envy qualities inaccessible or believed beyond embodying, to exaggerate and reduce difference, to "melt" into the ultimate containment of the melting pot, to freeze identities into one-dimensionality.

Rhapsodically nervous ideas about Nature and its dark interactions with equally anxious ideas of Death. The "progress" white culture makes from a bright green garden: a primitive, wild, child-like, spontaneous being becomes civilized (and civilizing), rational (and rationalizing), controlled (and controlling), a repressed (and repressing) entity dressed in ritual displays of class or trade, accouterments, emblems, armature, the withheld beholder, an upwardly mobile outsider who

---

*Ronald T. Takaki, *Iron Cages: Race and Culture in Nineteenth-Century America* (New York: Alfred A. Knopf, Inc., 1982), xvii.

collects Jazz, Eden breathing through coiled serpentine ear-horns.

the cannibal black, the devourer, the black plague, insatiable men and women free-ranging through (or buried within) the white jungle of psyche

a thirties Max Fleischer cartoon: Betty Boop pursued by the round black sun of Louis Armstrong—"I'm Gonna Get You, You Rascal, You"—chasing her from the cannibal kitchen stew-pot through a rippling jungle phantasm

if the black's a cannibal, the white becomes what's beheld; in the frenzy of what is blissfully dubbed postmodern is a trophy room of cannibalized cultures; to consume is to be consumed

black face, black form, white mythologers evoke on a first-name basis: "Wynton," "Bud," "Louis," "Ella," "Cecil," "Lester," bringing closer by trademark the imagined product; brands a bond of kinship or familial miniaturizing predicated on the ownership of a record (with a ghost text suggesting ownership of a people and their arts)

> "The black man's word is a sword," wrote Michel Cournot. "When he has thrust it into your wife, she has really felt something. It is a revelation. In the chasm that it has left, your little toy is lost. Pump away until the room is awash with your sweat, you might as well just be singing. This is *good-by* . . . Four Negroes with their penises exposed would fill a cathedral. They would be unable to leave the building until their erections had subsided; and in such close quarters that would not be a simple matter."*

When one reads this passage a dozen times and lets oneself go—that is, when one abandons oneself to the movement of its images—one is no longer aware of the Negro but only of a penis; the Negro is eclipsed. He is turned into a penis. He is a penis. It is easy to imagine what such descriptions can stimulate in a young girl in Lyon. Horror? Lust? Not indifference, in any case. Now, what *is* the truth? The average length of the penis among the black men of Africa, Dr. Pales says, rarely ex-

---

*Frantz Fanon, *Black Skin, White Masks*, Charles Lam Markmann, trans. (New York: Grove Press, Inc., 1967), 169–170. Quotation cited is from Michel Cournot, *Martinique.* (Paris: Gallimard, 1948), 13–14.

ceeds 120 millimeters (4.6244 inches). Testut, in his *Traite d'anatomie humaine*, offers the same figure for the European. But these are facts that persuade no one. The white man is convinced that the Negro is a beast; if it is not the length of his penis, then it is sexual potency that impresses him. Face to face with this man who is "different from himself," he needs to defend himself. In other words, to personify The Other. The Other will become the mainstay of his preoccupations and his desires.*

barriers and boundaries of the discourse (on the art, its subjects) is sustained by whiteness that cannot help reflect (and perpetuate) conditions of its own unresolved difficulty with blackness

—II—

The history of jazz, its canon, is as partial and malleable as that of any other art form

A history buried beneath the weight of its mythology: there's a consumer-simple über-myth cutting time into movements like Classic Jazz, Swing, Bebop, Free Jazz; each of these invented eras has a cast of significant and defining Heroes and Martyrs. It's a history reiterated by the recording industry with a subdivision allotted for the reinvention and/or resurrection of rediscovered (or re-foregrounded) players Frances Davis calls "outcats," those who fell beneath the first-wave steamroller of mythopoesis. There's an axial history and culture of recorded jazz that presents regional artists and groups, the so-called "territory bands," whose impact was localized, and whose rediscovery opens up a "thicker" history of jazz and the possibility that many players, arrangers, vocalists, bands might have been (or were) of equal originality and brilliance as those icons of the pantheon.

I and many friends collect jazz recordings, some of us more intensely and obsessively than others, and most of us have been doing so since the fifties. The collections are constellations, configurations, congeries: platters of varying widths, lengths, and weights, starting with solid 78 r.p.m. records, 7-inch, 10-inch, and 12-inch LPs, the 1949-spawned 45 r.p.m. disc, the EP; reel-to-reel prerecorded tapes and cassettes (I've yet to meet collectors of jazz on 8-track cassette, though I'm sure they exist); esoterica like 16-inch transcription discs, picture platters, session acetates, probably even wire-recordings (like the Dean Benedetti recordings of Charlie Parker solos), certainly CDs. Collections can be expanded to include any object relevant to the subject: magazines, books (biographies, autobiographies, critical studies, discographies, hagiographies, histories, jazz encyclopedias, yearbooks, annuals), concert programs, promotional booklets, flyers, posters, glossy photos, autographs, recent treats like R. Crumb's playing cards of jazz and blues artists, T-shirts with silk-screened jazz players, baseball caps, and sheet music. Eventually they include objects belonging to players, everything from horn-rimmed eyeglasses to instruments. (In our advanced bio-tech age, we can see fans bid for an organ from a dead icon to be used for transplant and, if surviving the procedure, to literally embody the imaginary beloved.)

The work of fans reflects the work musicians are engaged with in their professional lives, but the fans' work works outside the inner necessities of the jazz life. The fans' activities are either symbiotic or parasitic. They are deeply devoted to assumed and received mysteries, transmitting and reshaping these amongst themselves as a unifying lore.

(Have you ever read any "cyber-punk" stuff—like *Necromancer* by William Gibson or the anthology *Mirrorshades*? Science fiction, like many other genres, keeps expanding its discursive range and is still fun to contend with, providing pleasure and politics in familiar and de-familiarized narrative formulae. Maybe pop fiction genres are territories most free from scrutiny and therefore potentially most radical. Though I shouldn't be, I remain amazed by the massification of titles in any popular genre; an overwhelming deluge of excess whenever I enter a mainstream bookstore. I get the same feeling in record stores. Still resisting CDs, I've nevertheless gotten into the habit of clacking through CD stacks. CDs are the newest repository of the past. The majority of jazz CDs seem to be reissues. The jazz past is being re-written, re-packaged, re-formed through new CD compilations with added alternate takes and unissued cuts. There's a compulsion to legitimate key artists by issuing "complete" works in the same austere way DGG issues complete *werken* of Bach or Mozart. I suspect that since the reissuing of previously recycled material costs next to nothing for the record company/combines, they can afford the outlay for the often meticulous and scholarly booklets. This is the "classic"-fication of jazz, a monumentalized canon starting with Morton and leading up to Coltrane, a grand and irretrievable past that can be studied and interpreted like Classical music.)

Collectors collect after an epiphanic experience; it's a form of symbolic retrieval. What's left is shadow-play, echoes, residual elements, traces, as in a kaleidoscope, the fan (now collector) continues to rotate in hopes of getting the instant back the way it was when it first came through.

Not only archetypal "moldy figs" but now middle-aged rock 'n' rollers deeply within their collections of records, memorabilia, memory snapshots of concerts passed around in "thirtysomething" fast-cut overlapping conversation to remind each other where one is, where one was, and the darkening unrelenting progress from apparent joy to backward melancholia of memory turned into nostalgic grand opera and ultimately kitsch. As an adolescent in Bebop's present tense, it was soothing to draw lines, to put down middle-aged guys stuck in the rickey-tick wheel of classic jazz, trad jazz, Dixieland revivalists who seemed to be tumbling backward onto lush delusions of an impossible Currier & Ives past. As time and industry accelerated, their unmarred fictive daguerreotypes turned into papier-mâché silent-movie monumental statuary lining the Jazz Temple walkway in a fanciful De Mille New Orleans of the back lots.

The "square," "the moldy fig," cats stuck in a rut, caught in a groove, an eternal Nowheresville, fixed in exuberant cacophony of trad jazz bars where everybody was white, clean-cut, collegiate, violent and ecstatic, bellowing beery gusto into the din, snapping on beat, writhing against the grain, missing the point, maybe unaware, the next morning, of having been anywhere at all the night before.

In a thralldom, the Coffee Gallery bartender took us to his North Beach pad after the bar closed, waking his two infants and wiry wife, to play us his favorite Bix sides. In the present and past of his Revelation, turning us on and out, pass this tract on. Listen to this.

Rabid fans at Jazz At The Philharmonic concerts: thumbs-up, thumbs-down, mostly middle-class white males, engorged by endless drum solos by Norman Granz's platoon of tub-thumpers. Getting, going, native; becoming, being, swayed, persuaded, taken over, possessed by the primitive beat. Granz came on stage to quiet down the audience before Billie Holiday sang. Carnegie Hall in the early fifties.

———————

After World War ii, the A-Bomb, Auschwitz, the world as I imagined it was undone. It shattered apart like those imperfect kabbalistic vessels filled with an inrush of perfect light. I first heard Bebop in 1946. My parents sent me from Brooklyn to a summer camp in Maine where I was miserable and homesick. One afternoon while all the kids and counselors were swimming in Lake Raymond, I lay on my cot in the cabin staring at the planked ceiling. Suddenly Charlie Parker blasted out of the camp loudspeakers. The record was being played by the black kitchen workers. I don't know which record it was but the music made direct intense emotional sense to me. Its articularity exhilarated me. Its rhythms, harmonies, the speed of its urgency, expressed something I knew deeply but had no way of saying. I left the cabin and walked down to the mess hall where the kitchen workers were getting everything ready for supper. The music was as loud outside as it was inside the hall, ringing blatantly out to the empty campgrounds; its dissonances shook the cool birch tree woods, its complex unexpected drum riffs ricocheted down the back roads. It was an assault and an ascent. Nobody paid any attention to me when I walked into the hall. I listened to them play records over and over again until the campers and counselors returned. From then on, until summer was done, I'd go there during swim time and listen to the records, and to the fry cook playing bop-like riffs on the upright piano next to the kitchen doors. (And I loved swimming. It was the only sport, other than Ping-Pong, I excelled in; but I loved the music more and the black men who initiated me into it. Many of them were young veterans, including the fry cook pianist who could also play other styles on the impossible upright piano. I watched his hands, his long fingers, force coherency out of a seriously impaired instrument.)

The music moved differently than the dance-based jazz I heard at home. It made the mind dance; it was head music, complex and emotionally powerful. Each signature flatted fifth Dizzy Gillespie hit in seismic solos got me giddy. Parker and Monk re-assembled my relationship to music and jazz. Parker's breathtaking intelligence and articulateness, and Monk's complex reductions, contained recklessness, served as an approach to art I accepted without question.

When I got back home, my father played a 12-inch 78 r.p.m. record of "Salt Peanuts." He'd also bought "Oop Bop Sh'Bam." He was intrigued with the new music to the extent of taking me to the Royal Roost and, later, Birdland, to hear and see the music performed. Now myth machinery goes into high gear as I try to recall the "reality" of first hearing Charlie Parker play in a club. Most immediate and important: the volume of his sound, the unremitting power of it as voice for his overwhelming and riveting inventions. His sound put me into improvisation's core, its active and attentive center: an ineffable zone where intellect and intuition weave through the never-lost framework of a piece. His solos always seemed inevitable when released, when realized; all the adjectives poets build on only to realize at the end of a chain of words how incapable they are of describing music. Music can't be described; it can be played, heard, lived within, experienced, but remains immune to language.

Parker's velocity of ideas, references, quotes, rhythmic interplay, suspense, surge; a monologue in dialogic interplay; a person thinking out loud, tapping a huge archive, deeply enmeshed in the language of music, the music of action, action of thought, recall, recombining them in sonic curls and ribbons of music. How easy for me to abstract qualities present in the presence of the player and his music. Each moment heard is memory written. What's left? Something like Walter Benjamin's "aura," a tonal aura substitutes for the music long gone, a ghetto of ghosts made up of words.

———

like jazz, racism is a white construct, a white problem, a shifty fun-house mirror distorting bodies, distending, reducing, overwhelming the shapes of self into a liquid pretzel, a real Terminator powerless and unarmed and disarmed as body and music and idea move from mirror to undulating mirror

white world haunted by monsters imagined as horribly (horrifically) different; an unquestioned difference; an unreflected difference; a rejected monster, an Other buried in the violence of shadows, in the static fire of TV

revulsion, repulsion, leads to expulsion

terror the terrorists cloak their menace with, hooded difference unmasked by the imagination

———

Eternity is in love with the productions of time

signifying temporality, the passing (the passage) of time, remarked on and captured by the vocabulary of drums: what's coming, what's here, what's gone, what's past and present and future; unclocked, true to its own pulse and movement, traditional yet variable, in consort with (in concert with) other visible and invisible living forces, presences, and each a drum or spoken for by a drum, each implement and tool a name, a biography, a story, a force and purpose; symbol and actuality fused in a rhythm chain, sounding air-born words, sentences, shake the ground the song dances upon

Bebop renewed the spiritual dimension of the art and practice and constructed theories and theologies to explain the "spirit" of the art, how the event of improvisation was liturgic, a priestly sermon from the nightclub lectern of jazz. Its roots were in the mystery traditions of Africa, expanded in the diasporic displacement which scattered distinctive sacred activities of the enslaved without erasing the unfused sacred-secular meanings of music and song as a releasing and binding ceremony something happens, everyone agrees, though nobody knows exactly what it was other than it was "cool" or "beautiful"

yet it's through specifics, particulars, transcendence is made possible

recognizable and basic, familiar measures pulsing since creation; part of the process of beginning, of bringing into being

the rapture of discovery: the music changes the hearer's course

———

much jazz writing, record reviews, concert reviews, liner notes, can be forms of verbal kitsch, displaying both the virtues and impossibility of the kitsch vision—"Kitsch translates the stupidity of conventional ideas into the language of beauty and feeling," writes Milan Kundera

often judgment in its ornamentality turns easily into preposterous kitsch for the disbelieving wiseacre

kitsch in its optimism and tyranny shrinks large themes to small negotiable forms: knick knacks, bric-a-brac

kitsch re-describes popular mythologies in forms easily consumed; it flourishes on multiple plateaus of reverence; it makes sense and offers clues to belief

Bebop's chartreuse and burgundy cardigans, black felt berets, ink-black shades that shrunk the beyond into blue phantoms; neon circulatory systems keeping time against polyrhythmic bomb-dropping drummers like Max Roach; anti-fashion fashionability: rumpled blue-black gabardine suit, curled shirt collar, brass-chain shine hooked to leather axe strap; cigarette smoke, essential compositional element in black-and-white jazz photos and album covers, hovering over a hero; however they presented themselves, that was how the devotee imagined himself to be entering the world beyond the phonograph and photograph

the record player became the quintessential church of jazz, while records, liner notes, and magazines were encyclicals and theomorphic texts enabling the believer to create personal narrations around jazz and jazz life; jazz life was a black-and-white movie, angular, smoky noir with wailing sexy bluesy sax player drenched in a spotlight working his fate to the edge of a fall

— III —

There are two histories (and histories within histories within those two knowledges): one written by the consumer/fan/critic and the other lived by the player. Though often converging, their stories are never the same, their experiences are uniquely aspected and separate.

Two histories—the "traditionalist" one (as Neil Leonard dubs upholders of a cultural/aesthetic status quo) and that of present-tense advocates and converts to whatever's new and now. Each regards the other one-dimensionally and structures their narratives and critiques likewise. It's the familiar battle of bringers of light versus hoarders of darkness.

Whatever the polarities, it's a contested turf. By acknowledging jazz one assumes knowledge of it, authority to speak for or against its varied manifestations. This collection of writing demonstrates the ongoing (and ultimately irresolvable) struggle to own jazz in writing.

Marcuse writes: "The truth of art lies in this: that the world really is as it appears in the work of art."*

Two histories: the black and white in black-and-white in the gray exchange of contesting voices and shifting positions. From its perch each surveys what's immediately seeable. (History as perch or rung reflects the destabilized awareness of two major branches of history: that from above, that from below, and the difficult hope of an integral—and integrating—history detailing the interactions and influences shaping the dynamics of both histories.)

This collection is obviously polemical and presents work reflecting aspects of white culture's construction of jazz as property, either as fetish icon or demonic avenger. Jazz has been celebrated and damned for the same reasons: for possessing the body, for restoring a person

*Herbert Marcuse, *The Aesthetic Dimension: Toward a Critique of Marxist Aesthetics*, Herbert Marcuse and Erica Sherover, trans. (Boston: Beacon Press, 1978).

momentarily to a state of noble and innocent savagery, for inflaming sexual jungle fantasies, for being archaic, detrimental to modernity and progress, for being the absolute acme of all that's new and modern, for being America's only "authentic" art, for being a hypnagogic web sucking brains out of robotized consumers sedated by Mass Culture turning everyone into hopeless zombie cipher consumers, for being a model of pragmatic socialism: privileging both group and individual effort in a mutuality of intent and effort—jazz as emblematic of an improvisatory Metaphysic, jazz as religion, jazz as Devil-dealt spore, jazz as ecstasy, jazz as danger; jazz has jammed the circuits of renewed reformers; it has unknotted traditional bonds and liberated its followers; it's an insider's art practiced, initially, by outsiders; it is a convoluted loop spooled out of a racial matrix to affirm or deny racial romance and terror; jazz, like any art, is personal both in expression and reception and, therefore, allows for a diversity and constancy of approaches and responses. This collection assembles some of them, reiterating certain aspects while obviously rejecting others. As a polemic it celebrates difficulty; the texts, for the most part, veer clear of purely literary options of transcendence; if anything, the subtext of this collage describes the difficulty of *describing* jazz. Add to that a history of racism in the United States as a persistent formulating principle, conscious or not, informing a century of writing about jazz.

———

The name given to the twenties, the "Jazz Age," was a misnomer. While "jazz" was taken up as either challenge or novelty, real or authentic jazz was limited to an elite predatory audience of white hunters out to bag new primitive energy, to control it by interpreting it and to be transformed by it. Jazz as idea or crusade often splits into hymns of loss or pollution terrors. The body is "controlled," taken over, entered by an undeniable beat; cacophony shuts down rational process, short-circuits normative flight patterns. The slave music bags its hunters, turns them into pale-skinned savages in wild spasms juiced by galvanic bolts of electricity à la *Frankenstein*; the victim is hurled back into a primal state of being and, as such, repudiates the progress dynamo for the tom-tom of regress, and is, for the moment, out of control, no longer controlling destiny and nature; "out of control" yet controlled by thrombotic drums, spine-loosening wails, and horn-shrieks, the untying genital sounds of slurred squealing saxophones. For a moment the slave revolt wins. Loss of self, control, face, and the pollution wrought by "other," a pollination within, an incurable jungle parasite.

At its outset jazz adapts European formal band music concerns, loosening it up rhythmically, improvising more as an ensemble than an ensemble supporting an improvising soloist. In a compressed manner, jazz reflected new cultural notions of self and society, as seen in the nineteenth-century shift in Western music making from ensemble playing (participatory, social) to the virtuoso soloist. Jazz accelerates its "classical" tradition so that in less than half a century, it's moved from antiphonal to polytonal to atonal.

The rise of the virtuoso soloist reflects new notions of individualism and society in the aftershock of a trio of revolutions: French, American, and Industrial. It can be theoretically tied to the nineteenth-century formation of an audience passively consuming entertainments produced for them by a professional class (and often caste) of artists and artisans.

The "illegitimacy" of jazz fueled a cross-cultural allure and motivated a reform-minded white missionary desire to legitimate it, incorporate it into the menu of respectable Western classical concert music. The counter-argument advocated that jazz retain its distance from legitimacy and keep the music resistant in resilient autonomy. The struggle to define and own jazz was fought over such dichotomies. Claims of "seriousness" contended with claims of essential good-time social function to move the body, delight the spirit.

Beboppers challenged the socially and economically "acceptable," predominantly white swing-band movement in which jazz had become more permissible for white folks, letting them fox-trot and jitterbug to white bands led by clean-cut uniformed musicians. Bebop moved jazz out of the dancing body into the neuronal network of mind dancing. It demanded an audience that listened as intellectuals read texts; it asked the bopper to "dig" multileveled simultaneities of discourse. The post-war avantists advocated a repudiation of the Negro as entertainer cartoon replaying the white zookeepers' folklore of amiable black art-butlers serving up buffoonery and humiliation on master's silver trays. At the same time in New York, a revival of Dixieland and Chicago jazz, the rediscovery of elderly jazz players, and a young white middle-class college audience filling clubs in perhaps the imagined spirit of their forebears in the so-called Jazz Age, the Roaring Twenties. The revivalists were primarily white; the majority of Beboppers were black.

———

Varied and constant cultural options to dress, talk, gesture, pose, and be an imaginary icon out of an already synthetic and artificial past is another way one generation of consumers cannibalizes earlier ones in quest of continuity, tradition, and history. What's being devoured is almost always a comic-strip history. The consumer, used to being motivated by surfaces and images of surfaces, draws on postures, fashion, vocabulary, and gestures from movies, album covers, the turbid spawn of paperback originals, new and rerun TV shows, advertisements, to collage his/her impostorship.

Jazz is a music of appearances and disappearances. Its official histories are sustained through recorded performances that keep returning in repackaged formats with more expansive or reductive emphases and histories: projects like the Smithsonian Institution collection assembled by Martin Williams, or the earlier Riverside Records compilation assembled from their own recordings and from labels bought and absorbed into their company. In any kind of history-making there's the difficulty of working only with what's available; "what's available" often has to serve as cornerstone for a history monument. In the case of jazz, especially classic jazz, the cultural politics and technology of the emerging record industry determined what was to be its normative history. Jazz is a commercial history, at least the history we reconstruct from recordings.

there's an interlooping weave of meanings shuttling back and forth (into new configurations) around the fact that a professional musician's work is playing, is play; one's job, one's work, is to play for others in public spaces

one's work is public, one's play, one's inspired or routine message delivered before an unpredictable number of people who may (or may not) be listening to it or aware that for a series of moments the air is charged with high significance

the musician plays for pay as the consumer pays for play

Indo-European root: plek*: bend, fold; braid, twist, weave*

"Play is older than culture," writes J. M. Huizinga.* "Play . . . lies outside the reasonableness of practical life; has nothing to do with necessity or utility, duty or truth (which) is equally true of music . . . [M]usical forms are determined by values which transcend logical ideas, which even transcend our ideas of the visible and tangible. These musical values can only be understood in terms of the designations we use for them, specific names like rhythm and harmony which are equally applicable to play or poetry. Indeed, rhythm and harmony are factors of all three—poetry, music, and play—in an absolutely equal sense. But whereas in poetry the words themselves lift the poem, in part at least, out of pure play into spheres of ideation and judgment, music never leaves the play-sphere . . . All true ritual is sung, danced and played. We moderns have lost the sense for ritual and sacred play. Our civilization is worn with age and too sophisticated. But nothing helps us to regain that sense so much as musical sensibility. In feeling music we feel ritual."

> gig *n.* 1 A child's pacifier or any object, as a cloth square, spoon, or the like, used as a toy; any object to which a small child is attached and with which he likes to play; any object treated by a child as a fetish; a gigi or ju-ju . . . 2 [sometimes taboo] the rectum . . . 3 [taboo] The vagina . . . 4 A party, a good time; esp. an uninhibited party; occasionally, but not often, an amo-

---

*Johan Huizinga, *Homo Ludens: A Study of the Play Element in Culture* (Boston: The Beacon Press, 1955), 91.

rous session, necking party, or even a sexual orgy between a man and a woman. c.1915 . . . 5 A jam session; a jazz party or gathering; a party or gathering of jazz musicians or enthusiasts . . . 6 Specifically, an engagement or job for a jazz musician or musicians, esp. a one-night engagement . . . 7 Something, as a jazz arrangement, that is satisfying or seems perfect . . .*

— IV —

Trying to tag typologies, dialectical constructs, I came up with a few temporary players in a yet-to-be-written theoretical polemic. The nineteenth century found European knowledge bureaucracies fracturing into separate and distinctly anthropocentric categories: anthropology, sociology, psychology, philology, historiography. Great Britain exemplified the imperial reach and owned a major hunk of the planet, enforcing its civilizing mission upon all its subjects and their objects. Out of this industrializing revolution, ideas of the romantic and demonic were refigured and imprinted. The anthropologist stalked in the shadow of the Great White Hunter; the oneiromantic psychoanalyst unraveled a nervously civilized client back through myths of self to an Edenic primal self. The invented category of the "primitive," opposed to the "civilized," was associated, on the eve of the Modernist revolt and World War I, with new trends in avant-garde European art and poetry that discovered, if not ancestry, a kinship in African art as a precursor. Jazz was embraced with the same cultural mix of enthusiastic assumptions: Africa was in America expressing a fusion of tribal and European martial musics. Jazz enabled white moderns to live in the best of both imaginary worlds: the old and new, the savage and civilized. As in earlier saturnalias, it allowed a temporary release of socially rigid roles; it loosened the body, allowing it to become its dark Other. By establishing difference, division becomes socialized and mythopoeticized. A subject for endless blame and praise, difference becomes a boundary and barrier. Its culturally enforced apartness is both cause for discourse and cursed by discourse.

---

*Harold Wentworth and Stuart Berg Flexner, *Dictionary of American Slang* (New York: Thomas Y. Crowell Company, 1967).

———

How I read "reading" in *Reading Jazz* is worth exploring. First, I read "read" and "riddle" as integral; reading seeks to solve, explain, or decode meaning from something outside of self. The riddle conceals as much as one is willing to allow it to reveal. Reading both opens and closes; opens up new ways of addressing the familiar; illuminates, sheds light upon previously unseen forms. The closing happens when the unknown is known and named and the name becomes enough to describe the unknown.

Pillars of socially administered Knowledge corral civilians into a boundaried world of learning navigated by reiterating the Humanities litany: a liturgy of divine Names and Ideas beyond reproach, pure by-products of Genius operable in all the branch shrines of Civility, Status, and Power. The anthropocentric pantheon of "disciplines" (a word with older religious context and newer sexual aura) was hewn in the nineteenth century and remains firmly entrenched at the eve of the twenty-first century. *Fin de siècle* public discourse reflected a cleaved debate between bright enthusiasm and dark foreboding. For many the Machine Age would provide renewable utopias; for others the Machine was an omen, a signal to return to the pre-industrial past. In our present cycle of transit, there's a noticeable lack of utopian anticipation. If anything, most layers of cultural production reflect, if not dread, a lack of enthusiasm for the future. Personal, cultural, social doubt abounds, leading into the shrink-(w)rap of ideologies and theologies, or into paralytic self consciousness as short-shelf-life meanings encoded in appearances disappear. In the company-store culture of regulated abundance, acute layering of involuted and convoluted symbols emanating from consumer sacraments and the cathodic presence, the I and Eye struggle for domination: who owns whom. Irony, de-centeredness, disinterestedness, relativism, indeterminacy become active strategies to confront material culture, the "culture of abundance," as historian Warren Susman calls it.

The "capital" of jazz circulates from below up to a minority of entrepreneurs often one or two floors below a top-level elite with limited or no knowledge of the music that's usually an underfunded branch of their record division—a branch with even less sustainable prestige than their classical music division. Music is a sectioned pie chart linked to a congregation of other pie charts representing a dynastic conglomerate's interconnected ventures: magazine and newspaper publishing, radio and television stations, book and record stores, videos, movies, talent agencies, tie-in product franchising, and manufacture. This chart of interlinked enterprise is connected in the larger picture to unrelated international enterprises all narrowing down into fewer hands of ultimate corporate power. A managerial class, like problematic Gnostic angels, intercedes in all venues to administer first and last rites of merchandising. The Byzantine point I'm trying to make is that the culture industry's "support" of jazz also restricts its accessibility and economic stability. It creates and controls venues, production, distribution, enforces its own star systems, rewrites jazz history to suit its production schedules. Tied to the rewiring and attempted control of cultural codes, it activates the white professional (consumer) class to identify with a neutralized and conservative image of jazz as a professional possibility, a "career path" legitimated by colleges and universities.

———

Impasse. A one-note riff. No matter which version of jazz history one lives inside, pondering its ever ready messages, there's a lifetime of discs, discographies, biographies, analyses to pore over, over and over again, like the most erudite bibliophile, a homemade scholar of maze-like minutiae. Jazz for now is the past, a repertoire young musicians approach with the reverence of chamber musicians. The other jazz out there, an ersatz stew of mood music, soft rock, power rock, minimalism, often dominates the charts and the seasonal jazz festivals seeking to draw on a large and young pop music mentality. Odd, then, to be at the end of my history, not in a messianic, morbid, or Hegelian sense, but at the end of an unfolding art that appears to have folded back into itself and thus, as circle, is complete. Strange, too, to be talking with peers about what jazz was like but is not like anymore.

Taken out of its matrix, its aggressive, strident overt pleasure-palace point of origin, taken away from edges and margins of danger and disruption, of known unknowability, jazz has been (in both its black and white myths) overcome and transformed into an expression of white culture. Starting with Blues, and on to Dixieland, Swing, Boogie-Woogie, Bebop, explorers went into the jungle and returned with a cultural power they fused with media machinery that turned out a snow-blinding product safe enough for the anxious middle classes whose history in the United States is backed, fronted, and framed by the indelible invention and energy of the black slave culture.

———

Jazz has entered the elaborate inweaving maze of the archive; it's fixed in an upwardly mobile museum culture; a branch of nostalgia and amnesia.

The CD recycling of jazz: sessions repackaged with original covers and liner notes; the forties' cubist surreal album covers, the fifties' David Stone Martin ink-romances of jazz musicians or the Blue Note Herman Leonard photo covers framed in severe Dada type. Art assaults, like the music, get de-fanged, smoothed out, put into work as amuletic sizzle for ad-agency occultism. The discs continue the creation of a tradition, theology, and history of consuming. The short life span of mass-produced goods becomes elevated: material testimony to the battle with time's consuming powers. The reissued facsimile perpetuates a simulated immortality. Select records return again and again. A karmic wheel.

And always images, as if the image has to be there before the music can be heard. Black-and-white cigarette smoke weaving above snap-brim hats of musicians at a session; Italian-silk-suited Miles folded into a question mark; the re-fascination with Chet Baker's ruined beauty.

— v —

Assembled for maximum hector, this hyperbolic polemic blares its own side unquestioned by silenced partners. A white voice repeating a familiar explanatory voice-taking role; cultural ventriloquism many know as a form of repression. Repression conditions acceptance through the hammer of cultural tenderizing; it persists as long as what's "accepted" (therefore "acceptable") remains controlled by a dominant cultural bloc. Deeper issues involving late capital's darker nature hover in the wings like CIA operatives. This book emphasizes white descriptions of black music. It is a deliberate one-way street, a display of re-creation, making Adam in one's image only to re-exile him out into disorder.

Yet I insist that jazz (or any pop cult form) is highly resistant and durable. Jazz acts can not only be seen as reflecting institutional racism but as posing creatively resilient answers to the transcendence of racism. By offering inter-racial dialogue with a common cause, jazz practices what it preaches. Its art nightly demonstrates facets of cooperation, attention, regard, and play absent in most other workplaces. As both a private and public art, jazz declares options for moving beyond racial division. But, like other arts, it can also serve to reproduce them.

Racism (like trailing chains of other "isms") weighs upon and within American life, a deeply imprinted and inalienable truism hiding in the large shadows of blazingly huge myths of Equality and Freedom (and Culture). "Isms" organize by damage, form alliances around the pain of rejection and denial.

> It is a peculiar sensation, this double consciousness, this sense of always looking at one's self through the eyes of others, of measuring one's soul by the tape of a world that looks on in amused contempt and pity. One ever feels his twoness,—an American, a Negro; two warring ideals in one dark body, whose dogged strength alone keeps it from being torn asunder.*

> I am an invisible man. No, I am not a spook like those who haunted Edgar Allan Poe; nor am I one of your Hollywood-movie ectoplasms. I am a man of substance, of flesh and bone, fiber and liquids—and I might even be said to possess a mind. I am invisible, understand, simply because people refuse to see me. Like the bodiless heads you see sometimes in circus side-

---

*W. E. Burghardt DuBois, *Souls of Black Folk: Essays and Sketches* [1903] (Greenwich: Fawcett Publications, Inc., 1961).

shows, it is as though I have been surrounded by mirrors of hard, distorting glass. When they approach me they see only my surroundings, themselves, or figments of their imagination—indeed, everything and anything except me.*

The culture industry swerves to serve cultural eruptions, border them, blend them, pulp them into "product" like renewed market interest in "multiculturalism"—Otherness displayed in candybar-bright covers in culture stores. Complicity and difficulty resolved as a middle-class civic duty, a virtuous act of expiating tribal guilt by consuming the Other (the indirect Other, the illusion of the Other) in fiction, TV, movies, videos, records, magazines. The cover, not the Other; the Other covered up, buried beneath the hype of incandescent surfaces. But I'm back on invective's hamster-wheel instead of balancing my noise with caveats, true confessions.

> Lester [Young] took me into his dressing-room. He had a beer stein, one with a lid, filled with joints. "Eyes?" he asked. I lit one up. After a while I exhaled. "Bells?" he asked.**

The book of my unskinned self would be called Bells. The music's integral (it's world integrated), yet my eyes look out at a disordered disappearing world stuffed like exploding brains, squashed into easy-access images, finding jazz another fast-food consumer sign, and I become tragically despondent like any selfstyled lover perceiving the beloved dismembered before them.

But the jazz fan, however knowledgeable, is fundamentally a lover, while the old-style pop music . . . crystallized and preserved the relation of human beings in love ("They're playing our song"), jazz . . . is itself the love object for its devotees.

Cultural cannibalism is a repeating theme, how power works its ventriloquism through a sanctioned flow of faces, forms, and fetishes. Though the face may be multiracial and the music processed multicultural, what's being said, sung, and sold isn't. People without power

---

*Ralph Ellison, *The Invisible Man* (New York: Random House, 1952).
**E. J. Hobsbawm, "The Jazz Comeback," in *The New York Review of Books*, vol. 34, #2, February 12, 1987.

speak power's script. Subsumed into an environment of utopian ads, hand-in-hand, "we are the world" and the world's TV where whatever's culturally specific can be whited out, re-surfaced, re-created à la Michael Jackson's transmogrification into The Little Prince. In hideous melting-pot euphoria, Jackson becomes an actualized alien whose real power is Net Worth, not the unimaginable chaos his isolate self inhabits.

Love and vampirism, the irrational ecstatic mandate of total incorporation, becoming what one adores; literally, metaphysically, devour, consume, take within, and digest love until each beloved molecule, a sacrament, is within, nourishing and replenishing the body's stay on earth (as it is in heaven), amen. Fusionary shape-shifting, transmigrating, fluxing, can't get no satisfaction, no no no no, drawing love into destruction, memory's museum, all in the stop in the name of love.

The record producer tells me a great horn player told him at a session: I make better money, have bigger, more informed, appreciative audiences in Europe and Japan; my most lucrative gigs are outside the States. I should live in Japan since I spend so much time there making such good bread, but racism gets in the way. At least there it's up front, unsubtle, a matter of social fact and process. I can be their culture hero but I often can't eat in their restaurants.

"What is socially peripheral is often symbolically central, and if we ignore or minimize inversion and other forms of cultural negation, we often fail to understand the dynamics of symbolic processes generally," writes Barbara Babcock.*

Jazz took up cast-off instruments of European ritual and social affirmation (process and control, church and state) and turned them upside down, swinging martial music, syncopating liturgy, eroticizing repressed pop songs. The leveling unfettered topsy-turvy of carnival became the partytime norm of Harlem night clubs catering to whites; an image of escape and release, of cultural denial, that enthralled urban white middle/upper-class audiences. Mythic Jungle converted into

---

*Barbara Babcock, *The Reversible World: Symbolic Inversion in Art and Society*, (Ithaca: Cornell University Press, 1978).

mythic Garden where one witnessed the novelty of a choreographed unrepressed society, a free society embodied and undulating for slave masters. The market economy of packaging illusion as desire and desire as illusion spun a complex reversal offering white audiences a sense of participation without contamination; a redemptive fantasy, as if the slaves were putting on an extreme version of white blackness as an offering of forgiveness for the unthinkability of slavery.

"Putting on" is not "putting off" but is more aligned with "putting down." Nevertheless, this is a trio of acts weighted with social challenge. What's "down" is decidedly not what's "up." The music transgressed— trance graced—normalizing white mid-class culture; it took aim below the belt, down where the controlling fidgets of High Culture dreaded looking. It challenged the social graces of wedding-cake rigidity; its energy seduced bodies into moving free from the zoo culture of civility, mirroring an illusory sleek animal pacing back and forth within. The chains of slavery that brought the brass of jazz back-talk found an ever-anxious white managerial audience enslaved in bonds unbroken by finger snapping or foot tapping. For some the huge divide between cultural purpose and practice became intensely clear: the "other" mirrored the shadow of one's enslavement. It was the millennial double-shuffle where master is slave and slave is master.

"It was a golden age for jazz, and we knew it. What is more, the years between 1955 and 1961 were one of the rare periods when the old and the new coexisted in jazz and both prospered," writes historian Eric Hobsbawm.

When I was a preteen going to Birdland and Bop City to hear Bebop's immediate history through its founders and first generation disciples, it was also possible to hear major jazz artists of earlier styles in Manhattan: Art Tatum, Louis Armstrong, Duke Ellington, Sidney Bechet, Lester Young; to participate in the direct reception of jazz history from living ancients and fast-burning moderns. Now their digitally remastered electric ghosts echo out of CDs and, as befits tradition, through young conservatory players, the conservatives, conservators, of the music's redacted phases of alarm and becoming.

But I'm repeating, curdling in sumptuous (and diffident) nostalgia. Nostalgia is a revisionary act, emptying history of depth or texture, when having a manageable history is contingent on accumulation of time-trapped stuff. It's what people hold to, release into play, invent from, use for amusement and amazement, it's what and how people define their passage, their commonality and distinctiveness; a faith, a system of belief expressed in accumulated tokens and artifacts; a culture nourished by mythological narratives and seasonal events, by the passing of its gods and goddesses, by stacks of packaged time renewed in changing formats; it's a generality so resolutely particular to each adherent that often only myth and liturgy can serve as neutral rites of discourse. It's obviously the faith love invents to reassure its durability; a radical theology, a fusion of intensified sacred and secular yearnings and desires.

What is he (what am I) writing about? "What does he mean?"

What's he saying?

With off-synch entrepreneurial (and editorial) panache it's time to turn to the gathered texts: choirs and crowds of voices writing through and against time, describing and inventing jazz as writing, retelling the myth of their experience experiencing the myth of jazz, jazzing the riff of myths and meaning into endlessly distinct themes and variables herein assembled.

—DM [2-14-93]

Meanings, Origins

Like all cosmologies, the origin of jazz shares a variety of mysteries and facts. Tellings root its etymology in the sex act and in a mispronounced name. It is pleasure and identity; fusion and separation. Sourced somewhere in the Deep South, geographically associated with New Orleans, the Crescent City, the unnamed music was first transmitted from verdant soggy swamps like a primordial bog hulk whose body was montaged together from pieces of West Africa, the Caribbean, Europe, and points unknown. (Virgil Thomson suspects a Native American influx as well.) Like all mysteries, what it is and isn't is constantly contested, as well as whether or not it's an art "worthy" of high culture or merely a subterranean popular music of social outcasts, pariahs.

How speakers for ideological and controlling interests viewed jazz is also how they constructed (or created) their particular stories in contrast to other tribal tellings. Its dangers and the risks of its pleasures are underwritten from the start with sexual and racial contradiction. Whites want to become black; blacks want to live unnoticed in the palace of white culture. Middle-class urban whites dream of passage, of "passing" in the black jazz world; black musicians and composers want passage, passports to legitimacy from white culture brokers. Poor rural whites like Jimmie Rodgers and Bob Wills struggle within a degraded social/cultural margin, listen with recognition to blues and early jazz as powerful expressions of both suffering and resistance. George Lipsitz reiterates the working-class matrix of jazz and of most American popular music. White romance with otherness ranges from anthropologist Ashley Montagu to classical music critic R. W. S. Mendl, one of the first openly supportive defenders of the "seriousness" of jazz; Frankfurt School alumnus Adorno denounces jazz in complex cadences. A polyphony, a cacophony, of praise, legend, fantasy, demonology, testimony.

Another paradox of the creation of jazz in writing is that Europeans, especially French, British, and German, were first to fully receive jazz as art, as an aesthetic and expressive practice worthy of serious creative and intellectual engagement. America's initial difficulty with the music may have been due to vestigial nineteenth-century republican rigidities,

its anti-urbanism, anti-intellectualism; her conflicted desire to be free
of the Old Country yet still seeking parental approval, to be taken
seriously yet not overtaken, absorbed, re-owned by Europe. Jazz was
perceived as a supra-modern art, compatible with the cultural avant-
garde, easily "taken up" by vanguard poets, artists, composers, intellectuals of early European modernism. (In much the same way singular
eruptions in popular music—Frank Sinatra, Elvis Presley, the Beatles,
Bob Dylan, the Sex Pistols, Madonna—have been addressed and
incorporated by American vanguardists and new-wave academics from
the end of World War II.)

These entries show themes and variations of imagining, defining,
owning (and knowing) the genesis myth of jazz as word, practice,
symbol, and history. Hendrickson's entry, dictionary succinct, provides
thematic constancy: dancing slaves, refusing the African etymology,
opting instead for other orientalist possibilities exuding allure, drums,
desire, but, ultimately, as a standard bearer for sex. The sexual release
and realization invested by many whites in their relationship with jazz
as sexual utopia remains a secret and contradictory subtext, one
informing myth-dogmas of racism, antisemitism, sexism, homopho-
bism; it can be a revealing key in decoding much white writing on jazz.
As with any sexual construct, it's assembled by the imagination from
fragments turned into a seamless reconstruction of an already enslaved
image in the dreamer's control.

In the burgeoning consumer society, "difference" and "sameness"
sprouted new possibilities of value within the dream framework of
materialism, and bounced into play revisionary notions of "individuality" and "conformity." For the middling-class, "others" were negatively associated with toil, a heritage of slavery and serfdom, faceless
smudges, phantom forms from spawning grounds separated from the
main "respectable" population. "Others" were subjects of fear, contagion, pollution; in turn, because of the taboo nature of their mystery,
others were secretly desired as idealized sexual partners. They mirrored
the opposite image of the ways middle classes strived to see and be
themselves. "Others" were dirty, rude, sexually demonic, ignorant,
physically stronger, violent, abusive, overwhelmingly animal, and,

therefore, "uncivilized." Subhuman like those figurines in flowchart explaining basic Darwinism, paraphrased in newspaper and magazine cartoons describing Blacks, Jews, Irish, Italians as the brute missing links between apes and the fully-evolved white male breadwinner. Yet in compounds of otherness were found sites of middle-class transgression: music-halls, bawdy-houses, gambling and opium "dens," burlesque and vaudeville. Popular literature abounded with fictions and re-worked reportage on lower-class crimes and violent passions. The more lurid the divide between classes, the more middling and privileged men exerted their imaginal and physical presence into the "mysteries of the city," and middling and privileged women dreamed the divide by reading romances, highly charged moral tracts, and by stepping out into the malevolently inviting free-form flow of city street iconography to look and be looked at.

In subsequent "pulp" literature and paperback "originals" of the post-World War II era, sites of transgression were always geographically extreme from the respectable centers of the city, invariably in a domain of darkness far removed from sunshine living rooms of stable middle-class families. "Uptown" or "downtown," the night zone of bars, covert streets, grim rooms of hopheads and junkies, the enamel-red lips of Lilith-like hookers, closeted bars for gay men and lesbians played out dangerous forms of culture-building in paperbacked margins of poverty and nonconformity; narrow, labyrinthine streets of the "wrong side of town" with eroticized danger tapped out in telegraphic dialogue for the middle-class voyeur, the privileged player sinking into debauchery beneath his class and the deeper social thrill of exploiting the other, scandalizing the boundaries and wardens of one's class.

Jazz as an idea of freedom, an escape from the fixed grid of class expectations; jazz as a route of sensational tourism, going "native," allowing the inner savage escape into a world of dark strangers exuding carefree primitivism, a space to let one's "hair down," be uncivilized, revel in nightclub wonderlands of prelapsarian and essential being. The necessary other is an overwhelmed and irretrievable nature, an essence apparently lost by accepting civility's repressive power and gaining the detached ability to "harness" and "tame" Nature through industrial expansion and appetite. What one rejects can also be what one desires. To be the other, if only for moments, and finally (vampirically) withdraw their secret, their essence and difference, to merge with the other only to re-destroy it. To own it is to speak for it, to write its histories, determine its biographies; unable to be the other, to manage and control the circulation of otherness. To be insiders within a culture-producing dominion, an apparatus nourished by passive and active inventions of the other, the marginal, the "outsider." A material culture of music, style, language, experience, recirculated through vertical social systems nourishing young and old alike with constant transfusions from the bottom. A revivifying otherness is the base and infrastructure for/of American popular musics.

> Like Tramp scares in the late nineteenth century, or Red scares in the early twentieth, the contemporary Gang scare has become an imaginary class relationship, a terrain of pseudo-knowledge and fantasy projection, a talisman.*

Imagining otherness becomes a way of distancing oneself from it, shrouding the other in an unknowability. Its myth or justifying theory serves as barrier to specificity; it buries the subject by turning it into a token, an object, a cardboard lobby display of a black human figure. The privileged stalking, hunting, and imprisoning of bagged difference within the sameness of "otherness" created by the host culture's conflicted imagination. It's another kind of shopping.

—DM

*Mike Davis, "Los Angeles: Civil Liberties Between the Hammer and the Rock," *New Left Review*, #170, July/August 1988.

jazz, v HENCE N, LIKE JUKE (box), is orig(inally) an A(merican) Negro word: and both are traceable to W. Africa. Both, moreover refer ult(imately) to sexual activity and excitement; hence to excitant music. Among the Gullahs of SE U.S.A., *a juke house* is a brothel.

Eric Partridge, *Origins: A Short Etymological Dictionary of Modern English,* (New York: The Macmillan Company, 1958), 318.

ENOUGH MEN TO FORM A GOOD JAZZ GROUP are credited with lending their names to the word. One popular choice is a dancing slave on a plantation near New Orleans, in about 1825—*Jasper* reputedly was often stirred into a fast step by cries of "Come on, Jazz!"

Another is Mr. *Razz,* a band conductor in New Orleans in 1904. Charles, or *Chaz,* Washington, "an eminent ragtime drummer of Vicksburg, Mississippi circa 1895," is a third candidate. A variation on the first and last choices seems to be Charles Alexander, who, according to an early source, "down in Vicksburg around 1910, became world famous through the song asking everyone to 'come on and hear Alexander's Ragtime Band.' Alexander's first name was Charles, always abbreviated Chas. and pronounced Chazz; at the hot moment they called, 'Come on, Jazz!', whence the *jazz* music." Few scholars accept any of these etymologies, but no better theory has been offered. Attempts to trace the word *jazz* to an African word meaning hurry have failed, and it is doubtful that it derives from either the *chasse* dance step; the Arab *Jazib,* "one who allures"; the African *jaiza,* "the sound of distant drums"; or the Hindu *jazba,* "the ardent desire." To complicate matters further, *jazz* was first a verb for sexual intercourse, as it still is today in slang.

Robert Hendrickson, *The Encyclopedia of Word and Phrase Origins,* (London: The Macmillan Press Ltd., 1987) 286.

NOBODY KNOWS JUST HOW THAT NAME . . . got started. Some say it came from a spasm band player whose name was Jasper—Jas, for short. Some say the boy's name was Charles, but he wrote it abbreviated to Chas. Certainly some of the first bands to use the word spelled it with an "s" or a double "s"—"jas" or "jass." (People who could not read very well pronounced "Chas." as "chaz" or "jaz.") Others say that in New Orleans, in about 1900, there was a band called Razz's Band, and that somehow the name of this band got changed to Jazz Band. Others say the word "jazz" had an African origin. Anyhow, by the time Louis Armstrong got to Chicago, folks were calling all Dixieland bands jazz bands, and their new music was called jazz.

Langston Hughes, *Jazz.* Updated and expanded by Sanford Brown (New York: Franklin Watts, 1982) 33–34.

THOUGH THE ETYMOLOGY OF "JAZZ" is not clear, there is no reason to believe that the word springs from either French or African origins via American Negro dialect, in which it has sexual connotations. It begins to appear in print about 1914 (sometimes spelled "jass"), although the term was known in New Orleans as early as the 1880s. The *Literary Digest* in 1917 noted the spread of "a strange word, jazz, used mainly as an adjective descriptive of a band." Whatever its etymology, "jazz" described a kind of popular music that developed in lower-class Southern society (most visibly in New Orleans) out of French, Spanish, African, Caribbean, and American elements. The music drew from all the current popular forms: marches, quadrilles, waltzes, polkas, hymns; from the European heritage of formal music; from Afro-American work songs and gospel songs; from minstrel shows and popular ballads; and especially from blues and ragtime music. "Tiger Rag," for example, was adapted from a quadrille; "High Society" from a French band piece; "When The Saints Go Marching In" from a gospel hymn.

Russell Nye, *The Unembarrassed Muse: The Popular Arts in America,* (New York: The Dial Press, 1970), 331–332.

ANOTHER THEORY IS THAT THE WORD can be traced to a sign painter in Chicago who produced about 1910 a sign for the black musician Boisey James stating that 'Music will be furnished by Jas. Band.' James, a purveyor of hot music and particularly of the blues, became known as 'Old Jas,' and the music he played, 'Jas's Music.' Eventually the music was simply called jazz. It is unnecessary to report here all the many and varied theories that have been advanced over the years. James Europe denied, for example, having given an explanation that was attributed to him in the press—that the word jazz represented a corruption of 'razz,' the name of a Negro band active in New Orleans about 1905. It is noteworthy, however, that all of the theories suggest that the word is to be associated in one way or another with the folk mores of black men, either in the United States or Africa.

Eileen Southern, *The Music of Black Americans: A History*, (New York: W. W. Norton & Company, Inc., 1971) 374.

THERE WAS AND IS, HOWEVER, a difference between the vigor of real primitive music and that of jazz: for the music the negro sang in slavery and in urban exile was very different from that which he sang in his native village. Jazz is the music of a dispossessed race; and it was precisely because its vitality was uprooted, dislocated, that it made so potent an appeal to sophisticated, urbanized western man ...

For the materials of jazz were in part European. The rhythmic drive came from primitive sources, the roots of the melody, with its flat sevenths and false relations, from pentatonic and modal folk incantation: as did the rhythm and melody of Stravinsky's own early music. But the harmony and texture of jazz came from Europe: from the white military bands of the Civil War days, and from the Christian hymn. These in turn derived their material from nineteenth-century Italian opera and from the English oratorio (with German choral homophony behind that). Jazz showed Stravinsky how traditional European conventions—degraded perhaps to *cliché*—could be exploited in ways which divorced them from the idea of harmonic progression: and so liberated them from the European consciousness of Time.

Wilfred Mellers, *Man and His Music: The Story of Musical Experience in the West: Romanticism and the 20th Century*, (New York: Schocken Books, 1969) 201.

jazz n. 1 [taboo] Copulation; the vagina; sex; a woman considered solely as a sexual object. Original southern Negro use, probably since long before 1900— 2 Animation; enthusiasm; enthusiasm and a fast tempo or rhythm; frenzy. 3 The only original American music, traditionally known for its emotional appeal, rhythmic emphasis, and improvisation.

THIS IS THE MUSIC FIRST PLAYED by small Creole and Negro groups in and around New Orleans in the decades before 1900. Its rhythms were based in part on African songs, field chants used by slaves, work chants of railroad laborers and prisoners, and the Spanish and French music known to the Creoles of the region. It was first played on battered, secondhand instruments discarded by marching and military bands. Once inside the brothels of Storyville, the music became widely known to both local men and out-of-town travelers. Thus the music grew in appeal and the musicians, now professional, could devote full time to playing. The brothels competed with each other for the best musicians, thus encouraging new musical talent, compositions, and improvisations. Once the appeal of the music grew and the bands and musicians had gained some fame, various musicians and bands began to travel, playing throughout the Delta region and taking jobs on the riverboats that plied northward on the Mississippi as far as Minneapolis. With the ending of legalized prostitution in New Orleans during W.W. I, more musicians were forced out of the south. Some moved to St. Louis and other Mississippi river towns, but in the 1920's Chicago became the chief attraction for New Orleans musicians. There they played in beer halls, restaurants, and eventually in nightclubs. In Chicago, too, many young white musicians heard and imitated Negro players, and the first important school of white jazz emerged. From Chicago the interest in jazz quickly spread to other northern cities, especially to New York. With the attraction of radio, recordings, and more cities to play in, more and bigger bands were formed. With larger audiences, many of whom had no rapport with the lives or feelings of the early jazz musicians, jazz lost some of its early earthy quality. Styles changed, the small New Orleans group (now often called, though improperly, "Dixieland") gave way to the larger group playing written arrangements, and in the 1930's the style known as "swing" became predominant. Popular music, ballads, and dance tunes were incorporated in the jazz repertoire. Thus jazz has developed many styles and moods—the back alley or low-down dirty; the slurred gutbucket; the blaring tailgate; the smooth and mellow; the swinging. The latest developments, perhaps most appealing to the modern ear, are bop and cool jazz, or progressive jazz. In general, these new styles stem from Charlie Parker, the great alto saxophonist, who introduced advanced techniques, often requiring extraordinary instrumental skill and profound musical understanding.

Bop is known for its long, breathless series of notes, often in high registers and for quick changes in key and tempo; unusual rhythms, sometimes Spanish-American in origin, are used. Cool jazz originated in the West Coast c. 1950 and took much of its impetus from the work of modern classical composers. The music is known for its close, intricate harmonies, its improvisations based on chord extensions, complex phrasing, etc. The more advanced forms of cool jazz are called "far out" or "way out." Thus in only half a century jazz has evolved in many ways. With each change or addition, the backgrounds, personalities, and interests of the musicians have changed, too. The audience has grown. But all jazz is related in its American tradition and in certain fundamental approaches to rhythm and phrasing.

Harold Wentworth and Stuart Berg Flexner, *Dictionary of American Slang*, (New York: Thomas Y. Crowell Company, 1960) 286–287.

HISTORICALLY, AFRO-AMERICANS have treasured African retentions in speech, music, and art both as a means of preserving collective memory about a continent where they were free and as a way of shielding themselves against the hegemony of white racism. As long as Africa existed, as long as African forms contrasted with Euro-American forms, white racism was a particular and contingent American reality, not an inevitable or necessary feature of human existence. But music with retentions of African culture have long held enormous appeal for American whites as well. Pre-industrial values endured longer in Afro-American culture than among more privileged groups because slavery and racism prevented black assimilation. White workers, whose own ancestors had been farmers or peasants, made a painful break with the past as they journeyed from field to factory. Industrial culture demanded regular disciplined work, competition, thrift, individualism, and delayed gratification. Residual elements of opposition to industrial values had to be purged from most Euro-American workers, but Afro-Americans maintained a closer connection to the pre-industrial world. Thus working-class whites could find a consistent and eloquent critique of individualism and competition in Afro-American culture which also displayed a humane and human alternative to industrial values in music.

In historical practice, black music has emphasized community, creativity, and criticism. Constant repetition of familiar forms like call and response encourages a close relationship between artists and audiences in collaborative cultural creation. Music that explores the entire range of possible sounds open to voice and instruments stresses individual creation and emotion in contrast to the mechanical system of notation in Western music that demands replication of standardized "pure" notes. The rhythmic complexity of Afro-American music encourages listeners to think of time as a flexible human creation rather than as an immutable outside force.

The glorification of pleasure and play in song lyrics serves as implicit and sometimes explicit criticism of a society that places primary emphasis on the duty of labor. The sense of time conveyed within Afro-American music directly contradicts one of the main disciplining forces of industrial culture. Before the rise of the factory, people generally worked at their own pace for their own purposes, disciplined by necessity or desire, but not by the time clock. Industrial labor brought the clock and its incessant demands into the workplace and into the home; days became divided into units of working time and individuals lost control over the nature, purpose, and duration of their labor. Controlling workers accustomed to pre-industrial values was the primary focus of management for over one hundred years. Despite rewards of high wages and punishments including the threat of starvation, workers never wholeheartedly embraced time-work discipline, and their culture reflected that refusal. Instead of the regular beat that measured time by the clock, working-class musics embraced polyrhythms and playing off the beat as a way of realizing in culture the mastery over time denied workers in the workplace. [. . .]

Incorporating elements of Afro-American musics into their own cultures enabled white working-class musicians to taste in culture what they missed in life. Incorporating elements of Afro-American music into rock and roll enabled middle-class people to draw upon their own sedimented traditions and receive a working model of "the good life" at odds with the hegemonic norms of industrial society. At least in music, harmony with others could replace competition, work and art could be united in creative labor, and the repressions of the industrial workplace could be challenged by the uninhibited passions of love and play.

George Lipsitz, *Time Passages: Collective Memory and American Popular Culture*, (Minneapolis: University of Minnesota Press, 1990) 111–113.

1. BLACKS ARE PHYSICALLY, INTELLECTUALLY, and temperamentally different from whites. 2. Blacks are also inferior to whites in at least some of the fundamental qualities wherein the races differ, especially in intelligence and in the temperamental basis of enterprise or initiative. 3. Such differences and differentials are either permanent or subject to change only by a very slow process of development or evolution. 4. Because of these permanent or deep-seated differences, miscegenation, especially in the form of intermarriage, is to be discouraged (to put it as mildly as possible), because the crossing of such diverse types leads either to a short-lived and unprolific breed or to a type that even if permanent is inferior to the whites in those innate qualities giving Caucasian civilization its progressive and creative characteristics. 5. Racial prejudice or antipathy is a natural and inevitable white response to blacks when the latter are free from legalized subordination and aspiring to equal status. Its power is such that it will not in the foreseeable future permit blacks to attain full equality, unless one believes, like some abolitionists, in the impending triumph of a millenarian Christianity capable of obliterating all sense of human differences. 6. It follows from the above propositions that a biracial equalitarian (or "integrated") society is either completely impossible, now and forever, or can only be achieved in some remote and almost inconceivable future. For all practical purposes the destiny of blacks in America is either continued subordination—slavery or some form of caste discrimination—or their elimination as an element of the population.

George M. Fredrickson, *The Black Image in the White Mind: The Debate on Afro-American Character and Destiny, 1817–1914*, (New York: Harper & Row, 1971) 321.

NIGHT AFTER NIGHT, WE'D LIE on the corn-husk mattresses in our cells, listening to the blues drifting over from the Negro side of the block. I would be reading or just lying in my bunk, eyeballing the whitewashed ceiling, when somebody would start chanting a weary melody over and over until the whole block was drugg. The blues would hit some colored boy and out of a clear sky he'd begin to sing them:

> Oooooooohhhh, ain't gonna do it no mo-o.
> Oooooooohhhh, ain't gonna do it no mo-o.
> If I hadn't drunk so much whisky
> Wouldn't be layin' here on this hard flo'.

This would be to one of the other cats, and he'd yell, "Sing 'em, brother, sing 'em," trying to take some weight off himself. Then the first one, relieved of his burden because somebody has heard him, as though the Lord had heeded his prayer, answers back with a kind of playful resentment—he'd been admitting he had the blues but he's coming out of it now and can smile a little. So he comes back with, "You may make it, brother, but you'll never be the same." And now some third guy, who'd been listening to this half-sad, half-playful talking back and forth, would feel the same urge and chime in, "You might get better, poppa, but you'll never get well."

Those chants and rhythmic calls always struck a gong in me. The tonal inflections and the story they told, always blending together like the colors in an artist's picture, the way the syllables were always placed right, the changes in the words to fit the music—this all hit me like a millennium would hit a philosopher. These few simple riffs opened my eyes to the Negro's philosophy more than any fat sociology textbook ever could. They cheered me up right away and made me feel wonderful towards those guys. Many a time I was laid out there with the blues heavy on my chest, when somebody would begin to sing 'em and the weight would be lifted. Those were a people who really knew what to do about the blues.

The white man is a spoiled child, and when he gets the blues he goes neurotic. But the Negro never had anything before and never expects anything after, so when the blues get him he comes out smiling and without any evil feeling. "Oh, well," he says, "Lord, I'm satisfied. All I wants to do is to grow collard greens in my back yard and eat 'em." The white man can't feel that way, usually. When he's brought down he gets ugly, works himself up into a fighting mood and comes out nasty. He's got the idea that because he feels bad somebody's done him wrong, and he means to take it out on somebody. The colored man, like as not, can toss it off with a laugh and a mournful, but not too mournful, song about it. It's easy to say he's shiftless and happy-go-lucky and just doesn't give a damn. That's how a lot of white people explain away the quality in the Negro, but that's not the real story. The colored man doesn't often get sullen and tight-lipped and evil because his philosophy goes deeper and he thinks straight. Maybe he hasn't got all the hyped-up words and theories to explain how he thinks. That's all right. He knows. He tells about it in his music. You'll find the answer there, if you know what to look for.

In Pontiac I learned something important—that there aren't many people in the world with as much sensitivity and plain human respect for a guy as the Negroes. I'd be stepping along in the line, feeling low and lonesome, and all of a sudden one of the boys in the colored line, Yellow or King or maybe somebody I didn't even know, would call out, "Hey, boy, whatcha know," and smile, and I'd feel good all over. I never found many white men with that kind of right instinct and plain friendly feeling that hits you at the psychological moment like a tonic. The message you get from just a couple of ordinary words and the smile in a man's eyes—that's what saved me many a time from going to the shady side of the street in that jailhouse. I had plenty to thank those colored boys for. They not only taught me their fine music; they made me feel good.

Milton "Mezz" Mezzrow and Bernard Wolfe, *Really the Blues,* (New York: Random House, 1946) 13–15.

BUT FOLK ART IS NOT NAIVE IN ITS ELEMENTS, any more than are the babblings of the "purest" child. It is, more often, the naive mirroring and mimicry of ideas caught from above. The emotions of folk art are childish. Yet they are the result of unconsciously inherited ideas, imposed by ruling classes. Take, for instance, the folk arts of medieval Christian Europe, the spirituals of the American Negro slave. Did the folk invent the intricate theology and philosophy on which they rested? Rather, they vulgarized the products of intellectual minorities—Prophets, Plato, Plotinus and the Patrists: made it a pablum, at last, which later intellectuals could re-employ for the creating of more cultivated art. Another example: Russian folk music reveals traces of liturgical and synagogical music. Now, a new group of cultivated artists—Rimsky, Stravinsky, Ornstein—reforms this popularized pablum of older minorities into a fresh intellectualized music.

Or consider our jazz. Jazz is not so much a folk music—like the Negro spirituals—as a folk accent in music. It expresses well a mass response to our world of piston rods, cylinders and mechanized laws. The response is of the folk and is passive. The nature of our world itself is due to the work and temperament of minorities alien to the jazzmakers. Jazz expresses a personal maladjustment to this world, righted by sheer and shrewd compliance. And this, doubtless, is why the races at once most flexible and most maladjusted—the Negro and the Jew—give the best jazz masters. Since the rhythm of our age is not transfigured in jazz, as in truly creative art, but is assimilated, the elements of the age itself which we may disapprove will appear also in jazz. In other words, a folk art—being so largely an art of reaction and of assimilation—will contain the faults of the adult minorities that rule the folk, as well as the pristine virtues of the people.

And we have other folk arts. "The Rosary"—jazzless, European saccharine—is as truly a folk art as any of the Berlin or Gershwin ditties. Harold Bell Wright's books—messes of Victorian notions in decay—are also an American folk art. The New York "Daily News" is the daily art of a folk numbering several millions.

The adorers of folk art in its own divine right need but observe what they adore. That will be enough to cure them. Nor should they forget that in all culturally early epochs, dissatisfaction with folk art is one of the incentives for the production of great art.

Waldo Frank, *In the American Jungle (1925-1936)*, (New York: Farrar & Rinehart, Inc., 1937) 122–123.

[TED FOX] *Let's talk about how you got together.*

JERRY LEIBER: I was writing songs with a drummer, and going to Fairfax High School in Los Angeles. The drummer lost interest in writing songs and suggested I call Mike Stoller, whom he had worked with in a pickup dance band. I called Mike. He said he was not interested in writing songs. I said I thought it would be a good idea if we met anyway.

Mike, you were really into jazz and modern classical at that time, no?

STOLLER: I was a very big modern jazz fan really. At the time Jerry called me, 1950, I was very into Charlie Parker and Thelonious Monk and Dizzy. And through modern jazz I got interested in Stravinsky and Bartók. When I lived in New York—before I moved to California when I was sixteen—I used to hang out on 52nd Street.

Didn't you take piano lessons with James P. Johnson?

STOLLER: I did when I was ten or eleven. Four or five lessons. That was my earliest love, boogie-woogie and blues piano. But the thing that cemented our relationship was when Jerry showed me his lyrics and I saw that they were blues in structure. Most of them had a twelve-bar structure—a line, then ditto marks, then the rhyming line. So it wasn't difficult for me to relate to it and go back to my first love, which was Pine Top Smith and Meade Lux Lewis and Albert Ammons.

Jerry, were you more rhythm and blues oriented?

LEIBER: Boogie-woogie, rhythm and blues. I was working in a record shop on Fairfax Avenue after school. But actually I was exposed to boogie-woogie when I was a little kid in Baltimore. My mother had a grocery store just on the border of the black ghetto. She had many black customers.

It seems like an almost fateful encounter. You were both so heavily into black culture.

STOLLER: We were, but my background was a bit different. I went to an interracial summer camp, which was very unusual in those days. Starting in 1940, I went there every summer for eight years. I heard the older black kids playing the upright piano in the barn. A couple of them played very good boogie-woogie. I tried to emulate what I'd heard.

When you first started, were there songwriters you tried to emulate or whom you admired?

LEIBER: I was trying to imitate certain styles—sounds that I heard on records. Some of the writers I was imitating, I found out later were actually the performers.

You were both totally into the black scene in L.A. at that time. You had black girlfriends, and would go to the black clubs.

LEIBER: Oh yeah. We lived a kind of black existence. I'd say eighty percent of our lives were lived that way. It's an interesting thing. I some-

times look back on it and I think, why did I do that? I think that somehow or other I was alienated from my own culture and searching for
something else. My father died when I was five. My mother was a refu-
gee from Poland. I don't know what fragments of tradition there were
left in my family, but they were so slight, there was little to go on.

Did you feel the same way, too, Mike?

STOLLER: No, not exactly. My family life was very warm, very emotionally comfortable. My mother and father were very supportive. My
mother in particular was very supportive of me, and later of Jerry as
well. But I must have felt somewhat alienated from my white peers. I
felt there was something more special about not only the music I heard,
that came from black people, but the black people themselves who
made the music. I belonged to a social club in Harlem when I was about
thirteen or fourteen.

LEIBER: The black neighborhood was groovy, and I was accepted
there right away. Part of it was my mother's doing. Her store was the
only store within ten blocks of the ghetto that extended credit to black
families. So I was a welcome person in the black neighborhood.

*This translated itself immediately and automatically into the stuff you were writ-
ing, didn't it? Your songs became authentic black songs of the period.*

LEIBER: Leroi Jones, writing about us in the sixties, said that we were
the only authentic black voices in pop music. [Laughs.] He changed
his tune a few years later when he became [Amiri] Baraka. We were
flattered. Actually I think we wanted to be black. Being black was being
great. The best musicians in the world were black. The greatest athletes
in the world were black, and black people had a better time. As far as
we were concerned the worlds that we came from were drab in com-
parison.

Ted Fox, *In the Groove: The People Behind the Music,* (New York: St . Martin's Press,
1985) 192–194.

To UNCERTAIN NATURES, WILD SOUND and meaningless noise have an
exciting, almost intoxicating effect, like crude colors and strong perfume, the sight of flesh or the sadistic pleasure in blood. To such as
these, the jass is a delight. A dance to the unstable bray of the sackbut
is a sensual delight more intense and quite different from the languor

of a Viennese waltz or the refined sentiment and respectful emotion of the eighteenth century minuet.

Times-Picayune (New Orleans) June 17, 1917.

JAZZ IS NOT NECESSARILY THE GATEWAY TO HELL. It may be the portal to life eternal. For jazz is a protest against machine methods, against the monotony of life. Professional reformers and evangelists and the timid folk to whom everything new is of the devil can see nothing ahead but destruction for those who prefer syncopated time to the long meter doxology as though the tempo of the long meter doxology were the tune of heaven or had been inspired by God.

Jazz is an attempt at individual expression. No two people jazz dance alike. Others may smile and even sneer at the way the young factory girl and her boy friend fling themselves into the anarchy of individual jazz expression—but it is their dance, and they are finding freedom, liberty, release in it. They need it to get away from the awful humdrum and monotony which are starving their souls.

Jazz is a surfacy thing. It does not give expression to the real life and longings of the individual. It is merely the "outward sign of an inward grace." To look at a room full of people dancing to the weird tunes of a saxophone orchestra may arouse very serious questions as to their sense or even their sanity. But if we knew these people more intimately we would discover that for the most part they are just normal human beings who are trying to let go of the unnatural restraints of life.

It must be admitted there are grave dangers in this experience, but the same thing may be said of highly emotional religious processes. Religion often stirs emotions which sweep men and women into a maelstrom. Meanwhile the wise and prudent need to exercise patience and understanding. They should not forget that each new generation must settle its own problems. It *will* not accept the verdict of the past, nor can the experience of its forebears vicariously become those of the present generation. Each of us must work out his own salvation and live his own life and learn in the living.

Reverend Charles Stelzle [1925].

THE COMEDY OF COMMERCE is a comedy of display. It is a denial of the industrial gloom by a boast of brightness. And yet its materials and its very rhythms are conditioned tragically by the tragic world it aims to deny. It is only a disguise; often frenetic, often wistful, never more than momentarily successful. Nowhere is this more plain than in the music of the comedy of commerce—Jazz. I do not desire to discuss the music roots of jazz: whether they lead you back to the Barbary Coast of San Francisco or to the Argentine or to the Congo. The product we have naturalized is the song of our reaction from the dull throb of the machine. Jazz syncopates the lathe-lunge, jazz shatters the piston-thrust, jazz shreds the hum of wheels, jazz is the spark and sudden lift centrifugal to their incessant pulse. Jazz is a moment's gaiety, after which the spirit droops, cheated and unnurtured. This song is not an escape from the Machine to limpid depths of the soul. It is the Machine itself! It is the music of a revolt that fails. Its voice is the mimicry of our industrial havoc.

Waldo Frank, *In the American Jungle (1925–1936)*, (New York: Farrar & Rinehart, Inc., 1937) 118–119.

IN THE FIRST PLACE, it is said that this music is sensual. What is meant by that expression as applied to a piece of music? Primarily the word means (according to the admirable dictionary which I possess) "pertaining to or affecting the senses, as distinguished from the mind or soul." Undoubtedly jazz appeals through one's sense of hearing as all music does; it must, however, be apprehended by the mind, otherwise we could neither enjoy it nor even criticize it. The second interpretation of the word "sensual" is "carnal," which is the same as fleshly. This does not seem to carry us much further. Music is not made up of flesh and blood and bones and sinews, and so I pass on to the third definition of the term, which is "not spiritual or holy." This, at any rate, is something which can be intelligibly be said of jazz, because clearly not all music is religious in quality. It happens, however, to be somewhat inappropriate to modern syncopated dance music; for not merely is the latter, as we have seen, to a considerable extent derived from negro spiritual songs which were directly expressive of the religious fervor of their creator and strike even the white man as possessing a devotional quality, but in a certain degree the ragtime melodies to which we dance nowadays reflect that very characteristic which has come down to them from the sacred songs of the negroes. This is only manifested occasionally, but the plaintive kind of pathos which obtrudes itself from time to time in these dance tunes is undoubtedly inherited from the wistful longing of an enslaved and exiled people who found their solace, amid their oppression and yearning for their African homes, in a soothing, unquestioning devotion to the Christian faith. Quite apart from this, however, and even if it were to be assumed that there were no vestige of a sacred lament in modern syncopated dance music, that would hardly be a reflection upon the latter. For in this respect it would be in no worse plight than most of the instrumental, vocal, and operatic masterpieces of the world!

Probably, however, what is meant by describing jazz music as sensual is that it is voluptuous in quality, or that it expresses musically the lustful passions of men and women. This charge, if well-founded, might help to explain the repulsion which some people feel for this music, but even so we should have to bear in mind that jazz would by no means be alone in this field. If the expression of carnal passions in music be objectionable, we must, in all fairness, condemn on the same ground such things as the Flower Maiden's chorus from *Parsifal* and the Venusberg music from *Tannhauser*, or some of the more luscious parts of Strauss' *Don Juan*.

But now, is jazz music sensual at all? Does the ordinary unprejudiced listener discover it to be expressive of sexual desire? I venture to reply in the negative. There may be isolated instances of syncopated dance tunes which seek to convey the emotion of love, not usually in a very profound sense; but if we are really honest with ourselves can we discover a strong element of sex in it? Bear in mind, too, that if there is anything in this particular line of criticism the sex feeling must be excessive. There is nothing wrong in sex *per se*, and nothing wrong in expressing it musically. If we thought there were, then we ought to forbid the performance of all Schubert's and Schumann's and Brahms' and Wolf's love songs, of *The Lass of Richmond Hill*, of the slow movement of Beethoven's *Fourth Symphony*, of Mozart's *Voi che Sapete*, and a few hundred more of the world's acknowledged masterpieces. But if we find the unrestrained excess of sexual desire or gratification, or some kind of sexual perversion, portrayed in terms of music, then we may reasonably object to it. We may say that this goes too far, that there must be some artistic limit to the frank portrayal of human impulses; that an emotion which has broken its bounds becomes a crude and ugly thing, and is therefore beyond the province of art which should always be aiming at beauty and proportion.

Surely we cannot fairly say this of jazz. Personally I find the element of sex present in a far weaker degree in this music than I do in many waltzes. Numbers of the waltz tunes which have been popular during the last thirty years have been literally steeped in sexual desire of the most voluptuous kind imaginable. A great deal of their popularity must, if we are quite honest with ourselves, be traced to this source. But jazz! Frankly, I rub my eyes at the strange notion that it is markedly sensual. I find in it an abundance—sometimes a superabundance—of vigor; a rhythmic verve so exhilarating that one can hardly keep one's feet still; a good deal of musical humor, due not so much to melodic touches or harmonic peculiarities as to the bizarre effects which a jazz band can produce; occasional twinges of pathos; and in far too many instances a string of trite musical commonplaces and a big streak of vulgarity in the worst sense of the term. But the last epithet which I should apply to this music is sensual, and I believe that most people—music-lovers or others—who asked themselves whether they really considered jazz music to be markedly voluptuous would reply in the negative.

R. W. S. Mendl, *The Appeal of Jazz*, (London: Philip Alan & Co. Ltd., 1927) 60–65.

THERE IS NO ACCOUNTING FOR JAZZ SINGERS, that is to say, singers who suffer from the dangerous delusion that they are jazz singers. I am not talking about people like Louis Armstrong and Jack Teagarden, whose methods of vocal expression are so clearly extensions of their instrumental personalities, but of that curious group of non-playing singers, most of them women, who at most stages in the development of the music, have clung with such tenacity to the myth of their own jazz relevance as to occasionally convince other people. However, it remains sad but true that the number of non-playing singers sincerely respected by practicing musicians remains so small as to be very nearly non-existent. The sincerity of these singers is of course unimpeachable, but then so was Genghis Khan's, and they remain a band of brave but deluded pilgrims marching resolutely in the wrong direction.

The reasons for this are obvious enough. The art of making jazz consists in creating melodic patterns based on a given harmonic foundation. It is an elusive and highly demanding art, extremely difficult to perform with any degree of subtlety, and the only known way of mastering even its rudiments is to spend ten or twenty years of instrumental practice, learning by trial and error how to play a game whose rules can never really be formulated. It is noticeable that this process is exclusively a musical one, and that lyrics play no part in it. In any case, if there are to be lyrics, whose must they be? Not those of the original lyricist, because once improvisation takes place, all the note pitches and note values to which the words were matched, are jettisoned and new pitches and values, those of the improvised melody, take their place. The utter impossibility of the situation becomes apparent the moment one tries to wed the words of a song to the improvised solo based on its harmonies, for instance the words of 'Body and Soul' with the new melodic line created by Coleman Hawkins in his monumental recording of that song. There is a further drawback, which is that while the improvised findings of the great jazz musicians are free of the responsibility to make explicit statements, the lyrics of many of their favorite vehicles are often trite to the brink of imbecility.

These are shocking handicaps, and over the years various attempts have been made to overcome them. Some singers have been so dense that the banality of the lyrics has never occurred to them, others so egocentric as to believe that the banality could be relieved by the amazing beauty of their voices. Still others have dropped the lyrics altogether and concentrated on making vocal noises which they hope with touching optimism will be constructed as approximations of instrumental effects. One or two singers have even attempted to compose their own lyrics to existing fragments of improvisations, although they have usually been undone by the fact that there are in an improvised solo so many notes, and even the most clearly enunciated lyric tends to disappear in a blur of syllabic frenzy.

The truth of it is that there is no such thing as a jazz singer, which raises the awkward problem of people like Bessie Smith and Billie Holiday, whose jazz credentials are irrefutable. Their advent can only be described as fortuitous, a bonus for which our expectations must always have been nil. These two remarkable ladies represent two quite different lyric, though not jazz, traditions; Bessie Smith the uncompromising realism of the Blues, Billie Holiday the soft-centered escape from that realism so cunningly devised by Tin Pan Alley. In a sense, therefore, Billie Holiday's achievement is the greater of the two, for while Bessie Smith interpreted the poetry of the Blues, Billie contrived somehow to solidify that soft center of the Moon-June syndrome, creating what poetry she could from a convention which had little regard for it.

Most of the jazz musicians I came to know well spoke to me at some time or another about which particular fragment of recorded jazz first impelled them to try making their own jazz, the first piece of music to offer them the categorical imperative of doing the thing for themselves. In some cases these primal sources might scandalize the purists. Indifferent big bands and inept small ones; three-chord tricksters from New Orleans and semi-commercial warblers who were not only devoid of jazz talent but didn't care. Of course it would all have been much more proper if every apprentice jazz musician had taken up his craft at the instigation of some respectable figure like Armstrong or Ellington or Parker, but the truth is that any old second-rater will do so long as he succeeds, however accidentally, in lighting the fire of ambition.

Billie Holiday was not the first great jazz musician whose work I enjoyed, but she was the first whose work brought home to me the injustice of neglect, and whose career taught me the simple truth that to be magnificently accomplished at something is no guarantee that people will ever realize it. A few girl singers I came across in my own career really did think that Billie Holiday was a man, but as they knew only the name and not the voice, that is hardly surprising. When I think of the vocalist who night after night sang

> You go to my head
> and you linger like a hunting refrain

Then I remember the boy who ended 'Laura' with 'but she's only a fool,' and after being told that the correct ending was 'but she's only a dream,' compromised with 'but she's only a drool'; when I think of the girl who amended the phrase 'Creole babies with flashing eyes' to 'three old ladies with flashing eyes,' was told of her error and then managed 'Creole baby with flashing eyes' and being told that it was plural, ended up with 'Plural babies with flashing eyes.' When I remember incidents such as these, I am amazed, not that there should have been so few competent jazz singers, but that there should have been any at all.

Benny Green, *Drums in My Ears*, (London: Davis-Poynter Limited, 1973) 132–134.

JAZZ IS THIRTY-TWO YEARS OLD. Thirty-two years, plus radio and records, is a much more important time period than before, as far as the dissemination of art and its possible influence is concerned; but just because jazz has spread and fermented more rapidly than so-called serious music doesn't mean that in this brief time period as many great jazz musicians would have emerged as did great bearded musicians over the past three hundred years. But the critic's simple soul needs to discover genius; that's why fat old Hughes Panassie makes a fool of himself ten times a year by declaring ten times a year, "Whatshisname is incontrovertibly the greatest." Let me make one thing clear: Whatshisname's different every time. As far as jazz criticism's concerned (and elsewhere too, but don't let's interfere . . .), genius is common coin. We're ankle-deep in genius. It's blowing on every corner of the scenery. And every instant you read stuff like "Louis Armstrong is jazz incarnate" which makes you hit the ceiling. Don't be so bloody impatient! In a hundred years you'll have today's geniuses. I'll get together with you then . . . we'll figure it out. How could you not be influenced by reading the same idiocies in ten different jazz journals? You're forgiven, you know, because I'm going to let you in on something: they all copy each other . . .

Fortunately, jazz is music. And music's got a characteristic, pretty neglected these days, but in which, as far as we're concerned, dwells its essential charm—it's listened to. So after digesting the eleventh-hour enthusiasts' asserted effusions, there remain the albums and the records inside and the phonograph needle. And as the needle descends into the groove, the geniuses evaporate. Little remains of them. Everything goes back to normal: you forget about the eras, the "ruptures with the past." You discover the perfect continuity of everything that's been done in jazz up until now, and consequently you know that everything's okay, that things are still in the formative stages, and that if it is convenient and amusing to make up chapters and subdivisions, the only possible classification remaining is alphabetical order.

Jazz is barely beginning. Do you want proof that it's still in gestation? Look at the little episode that's occasioned the spilling of so much critical ink since Liberation: the case of be-bop. What a ruckus after the first Dizzy Gillespie and Charlie Parker records were heard in France: a lot of shouting about the total repudiation of the past, the profound modifications of the very basis of jazz, i.e., the recurring rhythmic structure, the exaggerated distortion of the themes, messing around with harmony, chords, thirteenths, seventy-fifths, and so on and so forth. People get together, listen cursorily, and then immediately tear each other apart. The same critics who readily admit that once, little old jazz nibbled on big pieces of repertory of Brives-la-gaillarde-type choral societies, howled with fear when they saw Gillespie add a bongo player to his band. Imagine! A Cuban who wasn't from New Orleans! (This is a deliberate pleonasm to show how stupid they were.)

It was all quite humorous. The one time that poor old jazz recovered one of its original African influences, the pens started flying, a schism was born in the midst of the Hot Clubs, critics confronted each other in the arena, and jazz continued to get along fine. "Bop is still-born," shouted one. "Long live bop," retorted another. And both saw their causes triumph. "Bop," as something topical for journalistic copy, doesn't sell any more. And in reality, it fit quite nicely into its chronological slot. . . . Innumerable are those who have undergone the influence of these records—original but in no way revolutionary—that have been released since 1940 or so by the folks at Minton's: Gillespie, Parker, Monk, and their disciples. It is possible to put together with the greatest of ease the links in the chain that binds a traditionalist like Sidney Bechet, sensitive to sentimental popular tunes, to a "far-out" musician like Parker whose favorite musician, according to him, is Hindemith—which should, all talk of influence aside, suffice to make it clear that these two gentlemen don't at all play in the same way.

The critics all have narrow ears. Were they larger, these guys would see that, to our unmitigated pleasure, we are swimming in a delicious chaos. It all comes and goes and moves and comes together without saying so and everybody goes his merry way in his own private darkness.

"Hey, you lousy bum, how do you know what is or isn't jazz?"

This is a problem that embarrasses the critics enormously. The Americans get around it smoothly. Admittedly, they're lucky enough to have a popular music that, like jazz, is in four-four time. They put everything in the same bag and call it "American popular music," mixing up dishtowels and napkins. (I called this "smooth," but looking at it more closely, it's pretty damn stupid.) As for us bearded ole You-roe-peens, we waltz along to accordion music, right? So the people, in its infinite wisdom, baptizes everything in 4/4 time as jazz. It's even worse than in America. We need criteria, criteria, damn it all! In France, lots of sleep's been lost over this problem, and like Fermat's theorem, it's double-edged. It's even spread abroad: jazz music has been endowed with a mysterious and subtle characteristic, swing. Various definitions of this beautiful word have been proposed. A lot of incessant carping has been mouthed about this fabulous swing, specific to black music, which whites, at the price of certain miracles, would succeed in occasionally obtaining—with a little bit of divine grace—in extremely limited circumstances. For sure, it'd be real convenient to dispose of a con-un-drum like this. It'd make everything more simple and we'd know where we were going. But there you are, we don't know where we're going and that just goes to prove the critics' bankruptcy, because some recognize swing where others see only an overheated performance, and the humor of certain languorous furnishings of Lunceford's, saturated with swing for some, eludes others who only see in it unadulterated fluff. The truth, I believe, is simpler and more deceptive, like 75% of all naked women: just as a classical musician has to be steeped in the right tradition to play a page of Bach properly, so also will a jazz musician be unable to play good and true jazz unless he respects his own tradition. And that tradition is black—and American black—and therein lies the difficulty; a somewhat secretive minority—as, indeed, are all downtrodden minorities—will not surrender its mysteries to the first passer-by. A long initiation must be undergone. And whatever comes quite naturally to the young black man who lives "in the thick of it" will be assimilated by the white man with difficulty and over a long stretch of time, because the latter will have to divest himself not just of three-quarter time but of his own tradition.

Here, I think, is the explanation of that famous problem of swing: because in addition, the black tradition in question is not yet fixed and enriches itself, every hour of the day, on new elements, like those Cuban elements we were talking about. Just go ahead and try to assimilate an art which changes daily! Isn't the best illustration in support of this thesis the recent so-called "revival" of the New Orleans style, the revival (due to those unimaginative young people around the world) of the themes and interpretations of King Oliver, Johnny Dodds, and Jimmy Noone—in short, of all the great specialists of the Twenties? Almost all the great veterans are dead and recordings fix them in the styles of the past; little else is needed for these good little white people—with such stable benchmarks and models at their disposal—to give a highly convincing and reasonably satisfying approximation of the atmosphere of 1920-1930 waxings. But at the very moment when musicians and critics manage to get to know an aspect of jazz, the latter sprouts new wings, flies a little further away, and everything has to start from scratch. Following the movement requires a supple and expansive ear, because jazz's teeming qualities reflect those of the fifteen million Blacks who, bullied and terrorized, carved themselves, by dint of the tears and labor, a place in the Benighted States.

Jazz criticism is suffering from a serious illness: the public's short attention span. In reality, everything's happening as if the only time the white man was really sensitive to jazz was during his adolescent years. He gets carried away, listens to the first smooth talker to cross his path, displays opinions that are all the more trenchant for his being new to the biz, and suddenly it's all over, he gets married and no longer has either the time or the opportunity. Moreover, jazz no longer interests him because it's not a sentimental music. Besides, it's difficult to hear good jazz; it's not exactly dashing through the streets, and when the radio grinds you down all year round with the same old piaffish tales, you end up giving in. Jazz requires passion, and where we come from, you aren't young for long.

Jazz criticism has also barely progressed (to the extent criticism can progress). It limits itself to very little. A lot of going in circles, reprinting the same basics, stumbling around, dissecting long-dead waxings, and hollering at each other. It doesn't go any further; it's the kind of "Mister Whatshisname thinks that Mister Whatshisname is a better musician than Mister Whatshisname, does he? Well, Mr. Whatshisname is a jerk because in reality Mister Whatshisname is the greatest" thing. That sums it all up. There are other lunatics; the ones who *say,* "jazz is this and nothing else and anyone who says that jazz is that are morons because I'm telling you that jazz is this." That's how Mezzrow in particular puts it. The papacy has its attractions.

Finally, there are those who are waiting. Who aren't in a hurry to crown or classify. Who mock the permitted values, rejoice at the unexpected element that overturns their system, write a paper about jazz because it's fun, and are interested in it because, above all, it's music. These folks put records on their turntables and play them. They quickly come to notice that jazz records hold their own next to Albinoni, Berg, or Ravel. They cheerfully read the articles about their favorite sport because it amuses them to hear somebody talk—even in a completely idiotic way (or especially because of that)—about something they care for.

I'd like to have people like you for my readers. It's nice to see people laugh—even at your expense.

Boris Vian, "50 Years of Jazz," Christopher Winks, trans., from *La Parisienne* #2, February 1953.

ONLY AMERICANS CAN PLAY JAZZ. One has but to hear an English band attempting to play it to know the reason why. Essentially jazz is a free-swinging natural expression of feeling, of emotion. That is why it lends itself so well to improvisation. Americans are very good at that. The English are not. Louis Armstrong once put it in a hemidemisemiquaver. Asked to define jazz, he replied, "If you have to ask what it is, you'll never know."

Jazz, as the whole world knows, is an exclusively American invention and one of America's more considerable contributions to the jollity of nations.

Pop music is an expression of America's cultural diversity, unified. Rock 'n' roll in its contemporary form may be new, but it is so only in the sense that it represents an evolutionary form of a quite old style of music and dance. Pop music is music in evolution. It goes all the way back to the music of our pioneer ancestors. One can still hear the bagpipes, the fiddle, the Irish jig, the Elizabethan melodic elements, and the melancholy of the Jewish folk song in much of the popular music of our day.

Deep in the roots of this multiple American tradition the great river of American popular music has flowed into musically replenishing and refreshing waters. The Scotch-Irish tradition of the Ozarks and Appalachians, with the fiddle, banjo, and mandolin playing in bluegrass or country style; the Negro spirituals and Negro church music entering into the gospel and blues feeling of so much of jazz; and the folk music of southeastern European Jews—all have contributed to the popular music and especially to the development of jazz.

No one knows quite where or when, but it is generally agreed that jazz originated around the turn of the century, maybe in New Orleans and maybe in New York and maybe in the coming together of the early jazz makers somewhere along the road between—the product originally of American Negroes and subsequently of American Jews, by no means exclusively, but certainly in a major way. The Negroes and the Jews brought something of the African and Jewish feeling and style for musical expression to bear on the already uniquely styled American music and proceeded to make it swing. W. C. Handy and Irving Berlin, the one a Negro and the other a Jew, were among the earliest creators of jazz, whoever may finally claim to be its actual parents. Following them by far the larger contributors to the making of jazz in America were Negroes and Jews: Jelly Roll Morton, Fats Waller, Louis Armstrong, Art Tatum, Duke Ellington, George Gershwin, Jerome Kern, Benny Goodman.

All the many non-Negro, non-Jewish jazz composers, instrumentalists, and singers of distinction were influenced by the style of the creators of jazz and helped establish it as the thoroughly American medium it is.

Perhaps there somewhere exists a non-American band that can play jazz. It is possible. Experience, however, tells me that if such a band does exist, then it must rank among the rarest things on this earth. Foreign bands seldom manage the rhythm or the beat, and almost invariably they are lacking in that quality which Louis Armstrong undoubtedly had in mind when he said, "If you have to ask what it is, you'll never know." That quality is oomph. You either is or you ain't, and that's the long and short of it.

Some people believe that English plumbing is to be reckoned among the four wonders of the world. They are wrong. Let them listen to what an English band imagines it is doing when it attempts to play jazz. Such a caterwauling was never heard anywhere else on this earth. The poor things haven't the slightest notion of what the music is supposed to do, and so they are unable to get with it. This difference in the ability to produce and play jazz is anthropologically very interesting. It is not that the English lack the necessary musical genes that so disables them, but rather, we may suspect, it is their cultural conditioning. The English have not enjoyed an environment, such as Americans have, with a polycultural population of immigrants drawn from almost every country in the world. Nor have the English until the last dozen years or so enjoyed a sizable Negro population. The Jewish population has always been relatively small. The relative homogeneity of English cultural pressures has constituted the chief impediment to the development of any original musical contribution in England—with one exception that we shall soon note. The cultural crosscurrents that would spark the kind of creativity that produced jazz in America were virtually entirely wanting in England.

A widespread myth is that Negroes are born more musical than whites. If that were really so, then given the opportunities for musical development, Negroes raised in any musical environment should exhibit superior musical abilities to whites. Anyone who has observed Negroes' musical performances in England, especially in English nightclubs where the best Negro talent is to be found, will know that Negroes raised in England are as unable to sing and play jazz, let alone compose it, as are the English. It is something to experience. Neither Negroes, nor Jews, nor Englishmen in England produce jazz for the simple reason that the necessary chemical alchemy it takes to synthesize jazz is incapable of occurring in the uncongenial climate of England.

It is, of course, possible to claim that Negroes, like Jews, possess the genes for musical ability but that the English environment simply fails to afford opportunities for their development. This is evidently the case, but it throws no light on the question of the superior musical abilities that Negroes and Jews are supposed to possess. The English in Elizabethan times were the most musical people in Europe. Whatever happened to the "superior" musical genes of the English in the centuries following? Did they suffer a molecular or a cultural eclipse? The answer is surely clear. Whatever the cause, England has for the last three centuries failed to provide a favorable climate for the development of musical talent. America during the last hundred years and more very clearly has. The combination of Negro, Jewish, and other ethnically derived talents gave us jazz and its developing offshoots. The interaction of these with other American influences produced the American musical.

Jazz and the American musical have reached their highest development in America as a result of the unique interaction of so many ethnic elements, a unique intermingling of many musical traditions.

American pop music has now spread all over the world, and the appearance of such phenomena as the Beatles in England is largely due to that influence and possibly to the influx of a large number of Negroes. The Beatles' principal contribution seems to have been long hair—a fashion which has now spread all over the heads of young men over a large part of the globe. But who can really rationalize the charm and appeal of the Beatles?

Ashley Montagu, *The American Way of Life*, (New York: G. P. Putnam's Sons, 1967) 179–183.

THE QUESTION HAS BEEN ASKED: "Is jazz an art?" and the answer usually given even by its most enthusiastic supporters is that it has not yet attained the level of art but that it may well do so in time to come.

For once, the strong partisan of jazz has understated his case unnecessarily. Whether we have a high or a low opinion of jazz, it is a form of music; and as music is an art, it follows that jazz is an art form. To deny that, is merely to be guilty of a terminological inexactitude.

This, however, does not in the least imply that it is artistic. For this epithet means that object to which it is applied is good art. To describe something as an art is not in itself a term of praise any more than to call it an industry is really to utter a reproach against it. It has been said that jazz making is an industry; so it may be, but that does not prevent it from being also an art. Its creators or producers hope to, and frequently do, make money out of it; but the same might be said of such great artists as Handel, Richard Strauss, Kreisler, and Casals.

Clearly jazz, in spite of certain interesting or attractive features, has great limitations. What are we to make of it—this strange, excitable visitor from another continent? How does it fit into our scheme of things? What is its place in the world of music?

. . . Although its origins may be of comparative antiquity it is in itself essentially a modern baby. No doubt the speed with which it has grown up, the pace at which it has careened from town to town among the white peoples of the world, and the immense grip which it has acquired upon the instincts and fancies of millions of people, compensate for its youth to some extent. Nevertheless, it has not had time to become a tradition, and unless or until that happens it can hardly be expected to be treated by eminent musicians with the respect which is accorded to other forms of folk music. It is hardly to be wondered at that they should regard it rather as a precocious young upstart. Moreover, no composers of real eminence have yet been produced by the United States of America, and thus jazz has not had the advantage of influencing great musicians in the country which gave it birth, as the folk music of other nations has been able to do.

There are, however, reasons for thinking that the jazz idiom might well be taken up by some notable composers in the future. Although America has not produced any great musical geniuses in the past, there is always a possibility that she may do so hereafter; her musical traditions have still to be created to a large extent; if composers of real distinction arise in the United states it is reasonable to believe that they might direct their attention to native material—not only in the form of the original nigger folk songs, but in that of the characteristic folk music of the twentieth century. A truly national American composer could hardly ignore so widespread and potent a force emanating from his own country.

But even in the absence of a musical genius in the States, jazz has become so much the people's music in other countries of the world that it would hardly be surprising if in days to come the eminent composers of those nations should utilize it for their own purposes.

Jazz is the product of a restless age: an age in which the fever of war is only now beginning to abate its fury; when men and women, after their efforts in the great struggle, are still too much disturbed to be content with a tranquil existence; when freaks and stunts and sensations are the order—or disorder—of the day; when painters delight in portraying that which is not, and sculptors in twisting the human limbs into strange, fantastic shapes; when America is turning out her merchandise in an unprecedented speed and motor cars are racing along the roads; when aeroplanes are beating successive records and ladies are in so great a hurry that they wear short skirts which enable them to move faster and cut off their hair to save a few precious moments of the day; when the extremes of Bolshevism and Fascismo are pursuing their own ways simultaneously, and the whole world is rushing helter-skelter in unknown directions.

Amid this seething, bubbling turmoil, jazz hurried along its course, riding exultantly on the eddying stream. Nevertheless, the end of civilization is not yet, and jazz will either be trained and turned to artistic uses or else vanish utterly from our midst as a living force. But even if it disappears altogether it will not have existed in vain. For its record will remain as an interesting human document—the spirit of the age written in the music of the people.

R. W. S. Mendl, *The Appeal of Jazz*, (London: Philip Allan & Co., Ltd., 1927) 162–163, 167, 169–170, 186–187.

THERE IS A STORY, writes the *New Orleans Item* man, that as far back as twenty years (1895) a blind newsboy known to his particular gang as "Stale Bread," felt the creep of the "blues" coming on him and translated them on a fiddle acquired from a minstrel show passing through town.

With his moaning, soothing melodies he was soon threatening to corner the trade, playing as he sold his papers. Then one by one other denizens of the street, picking up the strain and whatever instruments they could lay their hands on, joined him until there were five, christened by their leader as "Stale Bread's Spasm Band." But theirs was the music of the street and the underworld and years passed before it penetrated into the homes, the clubs and restaurants of the fashionable.

Allowing a bit for the reporter's imagination, that is probably as correct and truthful as any of those great folk legends about which wars have been waged or upon which creeds have been founded. And it is picturesque. New Orleans could do much worse than to start a fund for the erection of a monument to Stale Bread, father of the jazz band.

Before finding this account I had already been told a story in which a blind Negro was connected with the origination of jazz, though it seems hardly likely that this one and Stale Bread were identical. According to this second version the blind Negro's instrument was the trombone, whereas Stale Bread is described as beginning on a "fiddle acquired from a minstrel show passing through town." Of course Stale Bread might very well have mastered the trombone later on, but—well, read the story and decide for yourself.

Along in 1912 and 1913 Geoffrey O'Hara, the song writer, who told me this when I asked him what he knew about the origin of jazz, was an accompanist and "song-plugger" in the professional department of one of the leading New York publishers of popular music. This was before O'Hara had written his own big song hits and become known as a lecturer and entertainer all through the land. His work brought him into contact with most of the vaudeville singers and instrumentalists of that time, who came into the professional department looking for new material whenever they were in New York between tours around the various variety circuits. From some of them O'Hara heard about the new kind of music down in New Orleans. They all told the same story, that in a certain New Orleans cafe much frequented by vaudevillians, there was a negro orchestra of four pieces, the playing of which was very eccentric and specially notable for one thing, the musical antics of a blind trombonist, who did all sorts of impromptu embroidery with his instrument, particularly in the way of glissandos; also, that if you asked the trombonist what he was playing, he would reply, "oh, I dunno—jest jazz."

Henry O. Osgood, So This Is Jazz [1926] (New York: Da Capo Press, 1978) 36–37.

The Jazz Age

racing the origin of the "Jazz Age," locating an exact historic moment for its birth, determining how long "it" lived, sinks the questing soul into myth's deep-dish multicolored Jello mountain. F. Scott Fitzgerald is often assigned paternity for the age's name; the popular press and magazines of the twenties, along with booming and burgeoning movie and recording industries, reinforced the synthetic periodization. There's a big divide between the actual jazz being developed and the commercial jazz-inflected novelty and dance bands busily whiting out scandal and revolt for middle-class consumption. As Neil Leonard shows, the twenties marks a watershed in the consolidation of mass culture, fought over by clusters of entrepreneurial interest groups. As the technology of telegraph and railroad opened new spaces, congealing economic power for a celebrated few, the technologies of recording, motion pictures, and radio began colonizing inner space.

Jazz in the twenties infiltrated and animated public discourse, fueled as much by European input as by conflicting tides of repression and idealism, by postwar aftershocks and anxiety over suddenly inadequate social institutions. "The war to end all wars" helped inaugurate modernist de-centering; for many, the unholding center's force propelled them into a disruptive ever-changing (ever-new) Now; the replaceable became a surety and stability became ever replaceable. For many this disruption was emancipatory, underwriting the expressive arts of modernity; for others, traditionalists, anti-modernists, it was a newfangled version of bubbling-over fundamentalist hell. The press and magazine culture expressed both exhilaration and hysterical rejection, as did the book and film cultures. The body became a symbol of all that was either right or wrong with the Jazz Age: the image of the new woman, the Flapper, challenged the Victorian ideal of the Perfect Woman. Where the ideal Victorian middle-class woman was shrouded in colorless and sexless drapery, fit inside constructs of corsets, layered wrapping, hobbled high-button shoes, the Flapper projected an undomesticated look celebrating sexual abandon and androgyny. Where the Victorian's body was unimaginable beneath the fortresses of her garb, the Flapper's thin and shape-hugging dress announced the body as an emblem of youth and sexuality on display and dancing to the accompaniment of "jazz." Lewis Erenberg describes the night life of urban night clubs and dance halls, social spaces for dance and other leisure activities. A counterculture challenged earlier codes of public behavior and display. Ironically, the Flappers of the Jazz Age moved to ersatz jazz; the authentic jazz remained unknown to them. "Jazz" became a word describing style and attitude, newness, ultramodernity. In the middle-class culture arguing about the immorality of hooch-swigging, shimmying middle-class youth, jazz was colonialized as a word used as a negative moral epithet.

—DM

AT THE CORNER of One hundred and thirty-seventh Street, surrounded by a numerous group of spectators, many of whom clapped their hands rhythmically, a crowd of urchins executed the Charleston. Apparently without intent, Anatole joined these pleasure-seekers. His eyes, however, quickly shifted from the dancers and stole around the ring of onlookers, in hasty but accurate inspection. Suddenly he found that for which he had been searching.

She was a golden-brown and her skin was clear, as soft as velvet. As pretty a piece, he reflected, as he had seen around these parts for some time, and he had not happened to see her before. Her slender body was encased in coral silk, the skirt sufficiently short to expose her trim legs in golden brown stockings. A turquoise-blue cloche all but covered her straight black shingled hair. Her soft brown eyes seemed to be begging. Withdrawing his own gaze almost immediately, so swift had been his satisfactory appraisal, he was nevertheless aware that she was contriving, without appearing to do so, without, indeed, appearing to look at him at all, to edge nearer to him. Never once, while she carried out her design, did her hands refrain from the rhythmic clapping which accompanied the juvenile dancers. When at last, she stood by his side, so close that he might touch her, she continued to pretend that she was only interested in the intricate steps of the Charleston. Anatole, outwardly, gave no sign whatever that he was aware of her presence.

After they had played this game of mutual duplicity for some time, she, losing patience or acquiring courage, accosted him.

Hello, 'Toly.

He turned, without a smile, and stared at her.

Ah doan seem to recerlic' dat I got duh honour o' yo' acquaintance.

You ain', Mr. 'Toly, an' dat's a fac'. Mah name's Ruby.

He did not encourage her to proceed.

Ruby Silver, she completed.

He remained silent. Presently, in an offhand way, he began to clap his hands. A particularly agile lad of six was executing some pretty capers. Hey! Hey! Do that thing!

Everybody knows who you is, Mr. 'Toly, *everybody!* Her voice implored his attention.

The Creeper continued to clap.

Ah been jes' nacherly crazy to meet you.

The Creeper was stern. What fo'? he shot out.

You knows, Mr. 'Toly. I guess you knows.

He drew her a little apart from the ring.

How much you go?

Oh, Ah been full o' prosperity dis evenin'. Ah met an ofay wanted to change his luck. He gimmer a tenner.

The Creeper appeared to be taking the matter under consideration. Ah met me a gal las' night dat offer me fifteen, he countered. Nevertheless, it could be seen that he was weakening.

Ah got anudder five in mah lef' stockin', and Ah'll show you lovin' such as you never seen.

The Creeper became more affable. Ah do seem to remember yo' face, Miss Silver, he averred. Will you do me duh favour to cling to mah arm.

As they strolled, their bodies touching, down a dark sidestreet, his hand freely exploring her flesh, soft and warm under the thin covering of coral silk.

Wanna dance? he demanded.

Luvvit, she replied.

She stooped to fumble in her stockings, first the right, then the left. Presently she handed him two bills which he stuffed into his waistcoat pocket without the formality of examination.

Winter Palace? she inquired.

A nasty shadow flitted across Anatole's face.

Naw, he retorted. Too many ofays an' jig-chasers.

Bowie Wilcox's is dicty.

Too many monks.

Atlantic City Joe's?

Too many pink-chasers an' bulldikers.

Where den?

Duh Black Venus.

A few moments later they were swallowed by an entrance on Lenox Avenue, flanked by two revolving green lights. Arm in arm, they descended the stairs to the basement. As they walked down the long hallway which led to the dance-floor, the sensual blare of jazz, slow, wailing jazz, stroked their ears. At the door three waiters in evening clothes greeted the Creeper with enthusiasm.

Why, dat's sartainly Mr. 'Toly.

Good evenin'.

Gwine sit at mah table?

Mine?

Mine, Mr. 'Toly?

Expanding his chest, Anatole gazed down the length of the hall. Couples were dancing in such close proximity that their bodies melted together as they swayed and rocked to the tormented howling of the brass, the barbaric beating of the drum. Across each woman's back, clasped tight against her shoulder blades, the black hands of her partner were flattened. Blues, smokes, dinges, charcoals, chocolate browns, shines, and jigs.

Let's hoof, Ruby urged.

Let's set down, Anatole commanded. Passing his straw hat to the hat-check girl, he followed a waiter to an empty table, pushing Ruby ahead of him.

Hello, 'Toly! A friend greeted him from an adjoining table.

Hello, Licey.

A pint, the Creeper ordered.

The waiter Charlestoned down the floor to the intoxicating rhythms, twirling his tray on palm held high overhead.

Put ashes in sweet papa's bed so as he can' slip out, moaned Licey in the Creeper's ear. Ah knows a lady what'll be singin' Wonder whah mah easy rider's gone!

Bottle et.

Licey chuckled. Hush mah mouf ef Ah doan!

The waiter came back, like a cat, shuffling ingeniously from one side of the room to the other, in and out of the throngs of dancers. Charleston! Charleston! Do that thing! Oh boy!

On his tray were two glasses, two splits of ginger ale, and a bowl of cracked ice. From his hip-pocket he extracted a bottle containing a transparent liquid. He poured out the ginger ale. Anatole poured out the gin.

Tea for two! he toasted his companion, almost jovially.

She gulped her glassful in one swallow, and then giggled, 'Toly, you's mah sho' 'nough daddy an' Ah sho' does love you wid all mah h'aht.

Everybody loves mah baby, tooted the cornet.

But mah baby doan love nobody but *me*, Ruby chimed in.

She tentatively touched the Creeper's arm. As he did not appear to object to this attention, she stroked it tenderly.

Jes' once 'roun', she pleaded.

He humoured her. Embracing her closely, he rocked her slowly around the hall. Their heels shuffled along the floor.

Their knees clicked amorously. On all sides of the swaying couples, bodies in grotesque costumes rocked, black bodies, brown bodies, high yellows, a kaleidoscope of colour transfigured by the amber searchlight. Scarves of bottle green, cerise, amethyst, vermilion, lemon. The drummer in complete abandon tossed his sticks in the air while he shook his head like a wild animal. The saxophone player drew a dilapidated derby over the bowl of his instrument, smothering the din. The banjos planked deleriously. The band snored and snorted and whistled and laughed like a hyena. The music reminded the Creeper of the days when he worked as a bootblack in a Memphis barber-shop. Hugged closely together, the bodies rocked and swayed, rocked and swayed. Sometimes a rolling-eyed couple, caught in the whirlpool of aching sound, would scarcely move from one spot. Then the floor-manager would cry, Git off dat dime!

Unexpectedly it was over. The saxophone player substituted the stub of a black cigar for the tube of his instrument. As if they had been released from some subtle enchantment, the dancing couples broke apart, dazed, and lumbered towards their tables. Now that music was lacking their bodies had lost the secret of the magic rhythm. Normal illumination. A new mood. Laughter and chatter. A woman shrieked hysterically. The Creeper drew the bottle from his hip-pocket and poured out two more drinks.

Again Ruby drained her portion at one gulp. This time she had repudiated the ginger ale. Again she caressed her companion's arm. Again she sought his eyes, his great brown eyes, like a doe's.

Ah sho' will show you some lovin', daddy, she promised.

The Creeper grunted his approval.

Does you know what Ah calls dis? she continued rapturously.

Calls what?

Dis place, where Ah met you—Harlem. Ah calls et, specherly to-night, Ah calls et Nigger Heaven! I jes' nacherly think dis heah is Nigger Heaven!

On the floor a scrawny yellow girl in pink silk, embroidered with bronze sequins in floral designs, began to sing:

> Mah daddy rocks me with one steady roll;
> Dere ain' no slippin' when once he takes hol' . . .

The Creeper sipped his gin meditatively.

Carl Van Vechten, *Nigger Heaven*, (New York: Alfred A. Knopf, 1926) 1–5.

WHY DO PEOPLE GO TO SUCH PLACES? It is hard to make out. To lose themselves in the color and gayety? I could discern no more gayety than is usual in a Bible class, and the standard color scheme is far more exhilarating to bulls than to human beings. To be soothed and carried away by the music? There is no music, but only idiotic beating of tom-toms, with occasionally a few measures of a banal tune. To seek grace and exercise in the dance? There is no grace in such stupid wriggling, and no exercise in doing it over a few square yards of floor. To dally with amour? But surely the place for amour is not under 5,000 candle-power of red, yellow, green and blue lights, with strangers ricocheting from the cabooses of the high contracting parties, and catapulting them hither and yon.

The music interested me most, for one often hears, even from good musicians, that jazz is not to be sniffed at—that there is really something in it. But what, precisely? I can find nothing in what is currently offered. Its melodies all run to a pattern, and that pattern is crude and childish. Its rhythms are almost as bad; what is amusing in them is as old as Johann Sebastian Bach, and what is new is simply an elephantine hop, skip and jump. Nor is there anything charming in jazz harmony, once it has been heard a couple of times. The discords, three times out of four, seem to be due to ignorance far more than to craft, and the modulations, in the main, are simply those of a church organist far gone in liquor.

As for the instrumentation, it appears to be based frankly on the theory that unpleasant sounds are somehow more pleasant, at least to certain ears, than pleasant ones. That theory is sound, and it has many corollaries; indeed, the love of ugliness is quite as widespread, and hence quite as human, as the love of beauty. But it still remains a scientific fact that a thin and obvious tune, played badly on an imperfect reed instrument, is hideous, and no metaphysics, however artful, can ever reduce that fact to fancy. And it is likewise a fact that a single fiddle, if it be pitted against three or four saxophones, a trumpet, a bull-fiddle, and a battery of drums, gives a very bad account of itself, and can make little more actual music than a pig under a fence.

My guess is that jazz remains popular not because of any virtue (even to anthropoid ears) in its melodies, harmonies and instrumentation, nor even to any novelty in its rhythm, but simply to its monotonous beat. No matter what syncopations may be attempted in the upper parts, the drums and bass-fiddle bang along like metronomes, and that is the thing that apparently soothes and delights the customers. It is music reduced to its baldest elementals, and hence music that they can follow. It might be made just as well by a machine, and some day, I suppose, the experiment of so making it will be tried.

The dancing that goes with this noise is, if anything, even worse. It is the complete negation of graceful and charming motion. In its primeval form I used to watch it in the Negro dives of Hawk Street thirty-five years ago. There would be a dance-floor packed to the walls, and on it the colored brethren and their ladies, policed by Round Sergeant Charles M. Cole and his storm troopers, would stamp and wriggle, each sticking to a space of a few square feet. In those days the proud Aryan pursued the waltz and two-step, and ballroom dancing had sweeping linear patterns, and went to tripping and amusing tunes. But now the patterns are gone, and dancing everywhere degenerates to what it was in Hawk Street—a puerile writhing on a narrow spot.

It is a feeble and silly art at best, and so its decay need not be lamented. It comes naturally to the young, whose excess of energy demands violent motion, but when it is practiced by the mature it can never escape a kind of biological impropriety, verging upon the indecent. The real damage that the new mode has done is to music, the cleanest and noblest of all the arts. There is in the repertory a vast amount of dance music, and in it are some of the loveliest tunes ever written. But now they are forgotten as if they had never been, and people heave and pant to rubbish fit only for tin whistles.

That we owe the change to Prohibition is certainly arguable. By putting all social intercourse in America on an alcoholic basis, it forced people to dance when they were not quite themselves, and in consequence they had to avoid the complications of the waltz and its congeners, and to seek safety in more primitive measures. The simple beat of the tomtom was the safest of all, so it came in. Simultaneously, ears and brains were dulled, and it became painful to follow the complicated and exciting tunes of Johann Strauss, so the crude banalities of jazz were substituted. Thus we have music purged of everything that makes it music, and dancing reduced to a ducklike wobbling, requiring hardly more skill than spitting at a mark.

This is not my hypothesis: I have heard it from authorities worth attending to. They seem to agree that the gradual deboozification of the country, following upon Repeal, will eventually restore decent music to the ballroom and with it a more seemly kind of dancing. As I have noted, the people that I saw in that night club the other evening all seemed to be soberer than was common in Anti-Saloon League days. I should add that most of them looked a bit sad, and that many even looked a bit shamefaced. They had little applause for the music, and were plainly not having anything properly describable as a high old time. In the main, they were old enough to have the pattern of the waltz packed in their knapsacks. What if the professor had choked his horrible saxophone and burst into "Wiener Blue"? My guess is that a wave of genuine joy would have rolled over that dismal hall.

H. L. Mencken, from *The Baltimore Evening Sun*, September 3, 1934.

NOWHERE IS THE FAILURE OF THE NEGRO to exploit his gifts more obvious than in the use he has made of the jazz orchestra; for although nearly every negro jazz band is better than nearly every white band, no negro named has yet come up to the level of the best white ones, and the leader of the best of all, by a little joke, is called Whiteman. The negro's instinctive feeling for colourful instruments in the band is marked; he was probably the one to see what could be done with the equivocal voice of the saxophone—a reed in brass, partaking of the qualities of two choirs in the orchestra at once. He saw that it could imitate the voice, and in the person of Miss Florence Mills saw that the voice could equally imitate the saxophone. The shakes, trills, vibratos, smears, and slides are natural to him, although they produce tones outside the scale, because he has never been tutored into a feeling for perfect tones, as white men have; and he uses these with a great joy in the surprise they give, in the way they adorn or destroy a melody; he is given also to letting instruments follow their own bent, because he has a faultless sense of rhythm and he always comes out right in the end. But this is only the beginning of the jazz band—for its perfection we go afield.

We go farther than Ted Lewis, whom Mr. Walter Haviland calls a genius. M. Darius Milhaud has told me that the jazz band at the Hotel Brunswick in Boston is one of the best he heard in America, and stranger things have happened. The best of the negro bands (although he is dead, I make exception for the superb 369th Hell-fighters Infantry Band as it was conducted by the lamented Jim Europe) are probably in the neighborhood of 140th Street and Lenox Avenue in New York and in the negro district of Chicago. Many hotels and night clubs in New York have good jazz bands; I limit myself to three which are representative, and, by their frequent appearances in vaudeville, are familiar. Ted Lewis is one of the three; Vincent Lopez and Paul Whiteman are the others. There is a popular band led by Barney Bernie (as I recall the name, perhaps incorrectly) which is an imitation Ted Lewis, and not a good one. Lewis must be prepared for imitators, for he does with notorious success something that had as well not be done at all. He is totally, but brilliantly, wrong in the use of his materials, for he is doing what he cannot do—*i.e.,* trying to make a negro jazz orchestra. It is a good band; like Europe's, it omits strings; it is quite the noisiest of the orchestras, as that of Lopez is the quietest, and Lewis uses its (and his) talents for the perpetration of a series of musical travesties, jokes and puns, and games. I quote a eulogy by Mr. Haviland:

> For instance, there is his travesty of the marriage ceremony. To the jazzed tune of the good old classic "Wedding March" Lewis puts a snowy, flower-decked bridal veil on the sleek, pomaded head of the trombone player. He puts it on crooked, with a scornful flip of his slender, malicious hands. Then he leads forward the hardest-looking saxophone player, and pretends to marry "Ham" and "Eggs"—and incidentally draws the correct conclusion as to marriage as it exists in America to-day. Perfect satire in less than three minutes.

Well, this is extraordinarily tedious and would be hissed off the stage if it were not for the actual skill Lewis has in effecting amusing orchestra combinations. His own violence, his exaggeration of the temperamental conductor, his nasal voice and lean figure in excessively odd black clothes, his pontificating over the orchestra, his announcement that he is going to murder music—all indicate a lack of appreciation of the medium. He may be a good vaudeville stunt, but he is not a great jazz leader. Again Mr. Haviland:

> It is not music. It has the form of music, but he has filled it with energy instead of spirituality. What is the difference? You'll understand if you hear his jazz band. It interprets the American life of to-day; its hard surface, its scorn of tradition, its repudiation of form, its astonishing sophistication—and most important, its mechanical, rather than spiritual civilization.

Jim Europe seemed to have a constructive intelligence and, had he lived, I am sure he would have been an even greater conductor than Whiteman. To-day I know of no second to Whiteman in the complete exploitation of jazz. It is a real perfection of the instrument, a mechanically perfect organization which pays for its perfection by losing much of the element of surprise; little is left to hazard and there are no acci-

dents. Whiteman has been clever enough to preserve the sense of impromptu and his principal band—that of the Palais Royal in New
York—is so much under control (his and its own) that it can make
the slightest variation count for more than all the running away from
the beat which is common *chez* Lewis. Like Karl Muck and Jim Europe,
Whiteman is a bit of a *kapellmeister;* his beat is regular or entirely absent;
he never plays the music with his hand, or designs the contours of a
melody, or otherwise *acts.* I know that people miss these things; I would
miss them gladly a thousand times for what Whiteman gives in return.
I mean that a sudden bellow or a groan or an improvised cluck is all
very well; but the real surprise is constructive, the real thrill is in such
a moment as the middle of Whiteman's performance of *A Stairway to
Paradise* when a genuine Blues occurs. That is real intelligence and the
rest—is nowhere. The sleek, dull, rather portly figure stands before the
orchestra, sidewise, almost somnolent, and listens. A look of the eye,
a twitch of the knee, are his semaphoric signals. Occasionally he picks
up a violin and plays a few bars; but the work has been done before
and he is there only to know that the results are perfect. And all the
time the band is producing music with fervour and accuracy, hard and
sensitive at once. All the free, the instinctive, the wild in negro jazz
which could be integrated into his music, he has kept; he has added to
it, has worked his material, until it runs sweetly in his dynamo, without
grinding or scraping. It becomes the machine which conceals machinery. He has arrived at one high point of jazz—the highest until new
material in the music is provided for him.

[This] essay is provoked by that of the best and bitterest attack
launched against the ragtime age—Clive Bell's *Plus de Jazz.* (In *Since
Cezanne.*) "No more jazz," said Mr. Bell in 1921, and, "Jazz is dying."
Recalling that Mr. Bell is at some pains to disassociate from the movement the greatest of living painters, Picasso; that he concedes to it a
great composer, Stravinsky, and T. S. Eliot, whom he calls "about the
best of our living poets," James Joyce whom he woefully underesti-
mates, Virginia Woolf, Cendrars, Picabia, Cocteau, and the musicians
of *les six,*—remembering the degree of discrimination and justice which
these concessions require, I quote some of the more bitter things about

jazz because it would be shirking not to indicate where the answer may lie:

> Appropriately it (the jazz movement) took its name from music—the art that is always behind the times . . . Impudence is its essence—impudence in quite natural and legitimate revolt against nobility and beauty: impudence which finds its technical equivalent in syncopation: impudence which rags . . . After impudence comes the determination to surprise:
>
> You shall not be gradually moved to the depths, you shall be given such a start as to make you jigger all over . . .
>
> . . . Its fears and dislikes—for instance, its horror of the noble and the beautiful are childish; and so is its way of expressing them. Not by irony and sarcasm, but by jeers and grimaces, does Jazz mark its antipathies. Irony and wit are for grownups. Jazz dislikes them as much as it dislikes nobility and beauty. They are the products of the cultivated intellect and Jazz cannot do away with intellect or culture . . . Nobility, beauty, and intellectual subtlety are alike ruled out . . .
>
> . . . And, of course, it was delightful for those who sat drinking their cocktails and listening to nigger bands, to be told that, besides being the jolliest people on earth, they were the most sensitive and critically gifted. They were the possessors of natural, uncorrupted taste Their instinct might be trusted: so, no more classical concerts and music lessons . . .
>
> The encouragement given to fatuous ignorance to swell with admiration of its own incompetence is perhaps what has turned most violently so many intelligent and sensitive people against Jazz. They see that it encourages thousands of the stupid and vulgar to fancy that they can understand art, and hundreds of the conceited to imagine that they can create it . . .
>
> Even to understand art a man must make a great intellectual effort. One thing is not as good as another; so artists and amateurs must learn to choose. No easy matter, that: discrimination of this sort being something altogether different from telling a Manhattan from a Martini. To select an artist or dis-

criminate as a critic are needed feeling and intellect and—most distressing of all—study. However, unless I mistake, the effort will be made. The age of easy acceptance of the first thing that comes is closing. Thought rather than spirits is required, quality rather than colour, knowledge rather than irreticence, intellect rather than singularity, wit rather than romps, precision rather than surprise, dignity rather than impudence, and lucidity above all things: *plus de Jazz.*

It is not so written, but it sounds like "Above all things, no more jazz!" A critic who would have hated jazz as bitterly as Mr. Bell does, wrote once, alluding to a painter of the second rank:

> But, besides those great men, there is a certain number of artists who have a distinct faculty of their own, by which they convey to use a peculiar quality of pleasure which we cannot get elsewhere; and these, too, have their place in general culture, and must be interpreted to it by those who have felt their charm strongly, and are often the objects of a special diligence and a consideration wholly affectionate, just because there is not about them the stress of a great name and authority. [Walter Pater.]

—and besides the great arts there is a certain number of lesser arts which have also a pleasure to give; and if we savour it strongly and honestly we shall lose none of our delight in the others. But if we fear and hate *them*, how shall we go into the Presence?

Gilbert Seldes, *The Seven Lively Arts,* (New York: Sagamore Press, 1957) 100–109.

Negro Dancer

Exile solarium pulsate! percuss!
Puppet
of skeletal escapade
wired with tropical liana
shaking your lumbar
molding of mahogany

on the orchestral crash.
The optic, the ivory
candor
of ape and angel
opens your face.
The ancestral smoulder
of jungle ritual
excites the satin limb
to excel in
posturing
these aboriginal innocencies
of an overwrought Eros
The cosmic spasm aquiver
in the glare of a theatre.

[c. 1930s]

Mina Loy, *The Last Lunar Baedeker*, Roger L. Conover, ed., (Highlands, NC: The Jargon Society, 1982) 216.

IN HER SONG NOTHING MELTS, YIELDS OR SEDUCES. Her voice is harsh and coarse, undeterred by everything she knows about touring in tents, street fights and casual sex. She isn't trying to please anyone. The habit of submission, of letting yourself be used, comes too easily to women. In Bessie's voice is a full-hearted rejection of any such foolishness. The strength to do so comes from the big voice itself, with the growl and rasp of a jazz trumpet in it.

Her phrasing is unhurried and subtle. She knows exactly where to place an extra syllable, where to stress a word. And always, under the sadness, lie a sense of freedom and the triumph of her own courageous spirit.

On long-haul drives across country it is Bessie's voice I hear in my ears as I make up my own songs to her music. Her lonely voice opposes a stubborn pride to the ordinary justice of men.

And bawdy lyrics, delivered with gaiety, are as much part of her message as the stoicism of the blues. They don't flatter men, for all their desperate insistence on a share of the male "jelly roll." On the contrary, the playfulness is the counterpart of men's most arrogant interest in women. The heroines of her lyrics are Amazonian and Junoesque, indefatigably sexual; her voice and Louis' trumpet exchange brazen and derisive comment.

'Once I lived the life of a millionaire.' So begins the song most closely linked to Bessie's name. Bessie never was a millionaire, but for the six years or so in which she made large sums of money she lived exactly as she would have done if she had been. She never saved or invested or acquired much property. The things she enjoyed buying were for immediate consumption, or gifts. She loved spending money on jewelry or clothes for herself or her husband, or even giving her dollars away, to her family, old friends down on their luck or strangers. And when she went out drinking, she liked to give a drink to everyone in the bar.

She had no interest in making a home in any of the flats or houses she rented as her main base. She could have afforded to buy any furniture she wanted, but she was satisfied with comfortable sofas and chairs. Home wasn't the place in which she felt most herself.

Her single most extravagant acquisition was characteristically on the move with her and her show: a custom-built, brightly painted railroad car made for her by the Southern Iron and Equipment Company in Atlanta. It was large enough to carry her whole show on their travels. Seventy-eight feet long and built on two storeys, it was altogether magnificently appointed: but it was functional, not a folly, because there were many small towns which had no hotel in which to house her troupe. They could live on the train instead, since there was a kitchen and a bathroom, hot and cold water, and plenty of room for everyone to relax or have parties. The train was her brother Clarence's idea, but it altogether fitted Bessie's idea of luxury, which was to be unrooted and Empress of her own domain.

Bessie played in theatres from Memphis to Chicago and New York, and wherever she went her voice declared her determination to live as fully as possible.

> I'm a young woman and ain't done running aroun'.
> Some people call me hobo, some people call me bum,
> Nobody knows my name, nobody knows what I've done.

I'm as good as anyone in your town.
I ain't a high yellow, I'm a deep yellow brown.
I ain't gonna marry, ain't gonna settle down,
I'm gonna drink good moonshine, and run these browns
    down.

Bessie's size impressed her audience, because she learnt to use it. When she first went to Frank Walker's studio in Columbia in 1924, she was awkwardly 'tall, fat and scared to death,' but she could already dominate a stage. Her bulk became a massive fact there, overwhelming her listeners with a sense of her majesty even as they recognized their own pain in her voice. On stage she was 'a *big* woman, with that beautiful bronze color and stern features, stately, just like a queen,' as Zutty Singleton remembers her (quoted in Hentoff and Shapiro's *Hear Me Talkin' to Ya*).

If I try to conjure up Bessie's presence, in wig and feathers, ready to go on stage, she rises before me, a large-framed woman, with a quick temper, used to resorting to violence when crossed. She was strong enough to fell a man; and she didn't always wait to be attacked before using her fists.

I don't want to be prissy about this physical fury, which came out of her early days on Chattanooga streets, and was part of black ghetto life. Her use of her fists was akin to the obscenity of her ordinary speech; and she never allowed success to modify her behavior in any way. But if I had met Bessie, cruising round her streets, I might not have recognized her great spirit, and she might have disliked my white skin, long face and skinny figure. I should like to have told her that her voice has given me courage. Perhaps she would have understood. I'm not her only unlikely admirer, not even the unlikeliest. Perhaps I could explain that nearly half a century after her death we still take fire when we listen to her.

Elaine Feinstein, *Bessie Smith: Empress of the Blues*, (New York: Viking Penguin, 1985) 11–15.

While commercial dilutions dominated the music output of the phonograph, the radio, and the movies, real jazz remained on the fringes of the business. Jazz men seldom played on the radio or in film, and made relatively few recordings. Yet despite their comparatively small number, jazz records affected the growth of jazz significantly.

At first, most of the jazz diffused mechanically was on so-called race records, which were directed to Negroes. All of the King Oliver, Bessie Smith, early Duke Ellington, and Louis Armstrong, and even some of the Bix Beiderbecke disks came out as race records. Far from considering their contents to be art music, issuing companies regarded them as popular music and advertised them as "red hot," "guaranteed to put you in that dancing mood," or as "the latest hot stuff to tickle your toes." Race records were cheap to make. They required from one to ten musicians, who frequently earned no more than five dollars a side, ten dollars for the leader. Often the performers composed their own material inexpensively in the recording studio, and if there were any royalties, they were small. And race records were easy to market as they were cheap to make. They required no expensive, nationwide promotion or distribution since they could be sold readily in Negro areas.

Even though race and the few other real jazz records were but a trickle in the enormous tide of disks that came from the recording industry, they immeasurably speeded the acceptance of jazz. The phonograph, the first device to preserve the music of improvising bands, permitted a single performance to be heard simultaneously and repeatedly at different places throughout the country. The first few sides made by the Original Dixieland Band, selling as they did in the millions, did more to facilitate the acceptance of jazz than hundreds of jazz bands playing "live" could have done. Furthermore, records served as devices of self-instruction. In 1916, when the Victor Talking Machine Company approached Freddie Keppard and his Original Creole Band with a recording offer, he is reported to have said to his musicians, "Nothin' doin', boys. We won't put our stuff on records for everybody to steal." A few months later the recorded music of the Original Dixieland Jazz Band provided a model for aspiring jazz men everywhere to imitate. In such widely separated places as Boston, Chicago, and Spokane young musicians copied or learned to accompany their favorite performers on records.

The experience of cornetist Jimmy McPartland and his high school friends illustrates how young jazz men learned from records. One day in a local soda parlor they found a record of the New Orleans Rhythm Kings. "Boy, when we heard that—I'll tell you we went out of our minds," McPartland recalls. "Everybody flipped. It was wonderful." They replayed the record during the course of several days and "we decided we would get a band and play like these guys." In one way or another they obtained instruments and tried to accompany the record. "What we used to do was put the record on . . . play a few bars, and then all get our notes. We'd have to tune our instruments up to the record machine, to the pitch, and go ahead with a few notes. Then stop! A few more bars of the record, each guy would pick out his notes and boom! We would go on and play it . . . It was a funny way to learn, but in three or four weeks we could finally play one tune all the way through." Records permitted aspiring jazz men to learn music without bothering with the formalism, discipline, technique, and expense of traditional training.

Mechanical reproducing devices hastened the acceptance of jazz not only by familiarizing both listeners and musicians with non-traditional characteristics of the new music but also by helping to bring it into closer alignment with traditional values.

The widespread diffusion of canned music had an all-important part in bringing to a head traditional opposition to "jazz." Live performances of jazz before lower-class audiences in unsavory locations had caused traditionalists concern enough but when reproducing devices brought the music with astonishing frequency to the ears of the general public, traditionalists became alarmed. It was one thing to know about "jazz" played in brothels and other disreputable places patronized by supposedly disreputable people, yet it was quite another thing to hear sound tracks and records bring it to middle- and upper-class places of amusement and to find radios and phonographs blaring it into "respectable" homes. Sound-reproducing devices translated traditionalists' concern about "jazz" into demands to suppress it. One of the most powerful suppressive measures was the pressure on the music business to purify or eradicate "jazz."

The popular music industry has long sought to produce the lowest common denominator in its material: that music which will please as many and offend as few potential customers as possible. After 1917 the industry ignored complaints about "jazz" as long as they did not threaten profits. By the late twenties, however, creators and distributors of popular music had grown sensitive to traditionalist criticism about jazz, and many of them became concerned to clean it up for both business and ethical reasons.

As early as 1921 a group of Tin Pan Alley publishers organized the Music Publishers' Protective Association to censor popular songs. Citing the increasing use of mechanical, sound-reproducing devices, the chairman of the Executive Board, E. C. Mills, explained: "The publishers do not want to be sponsors of indecent material. These songs go into the homes of the country . . ."

Nor were the radio, film, and eventually the phonograph industries deaf to traditionalist objections about "jazz." Radio broadcasters were particularly sensitive to any complaints. In 1925 Carl Dreher wrote: "They are in a constant stew about 'adverse publicity.' A few letters from irate listeners give them the horrors. They run their stations for advertising or good will, and as soon as any one looked at them cross-eyed their knees shake. When in doubt, they wield the blue pencil, and any one who tries to please the whole world is in doubt most of the time." Two years later the federal government began to encourage broadcasters' squeamishness about questionable material. In 1927 Congress passed the Radio Act creating a commission to allocate wave lengths, license stations, and generally oversee broadcasting. Section 26 of the Act declared that the commission had no powers of censorship, but added that "no person within the jurisdiction of the United States shall utter any obscene, indecent or profane language by means of radio communication."

Growing centralization of the entertainment business had an important role in bringing jazz closer to traditional values. As technical improvements permitted increased commercial exploitation of sound-producing devices, show business became, more than ever, big business. By the twenties Wall Street had invested heavily in commercial entertainment and at the end of the decade radio and film were among the nation's leading industries. While the process of centralization may be said to have begun before World War I, not until the twenties and thirties did the entertainment business fall under the control of a handful of corporations. In 1926 N. B. C. marked the beginning of network broadcasting by linking 19 stations. In 1937 it had 138. The Columbia Broadcasting System, which had started in 1927 with 16 stations, was sending its programs to 110 in 1938. As radio became centralized, it swallowed up the leading phonograph companies. In January, 1929, the Victor Talking Machine Company merged with R. C. A. (Radio Corporation of America). Nine years later C. B. S. bought the American Record Company, whose catalogue included Columbia, Okeh, Vocalion, Brunswick, and some minor labels. The arrival of the talking picture brought about further concentration. R. C. A. took over the Keith-Albee-Orpheum vaudeville circuit and the Pathé film company, and formed R. K. O. (Radio-Keith-Orpheum). Warner Brothers merged with the Stanley Corporation of America and First National Pictures.

To satisfy their unending need for songs, film companies purchased the leading New York music-publishing firms or created their own musical affiliates. Warner Brothers bought the Tin Pan Alley house of Harms, Witmark, Remick, and that of DeSylva, Brown, and Henderson. R. K. O. controlled the firms of Leo Feist and Carl Fischer. Robbins became a subsidiary of Metro-Goldwyn-Mayer. Paramount owned the Famous Music Company and Twentieth-Century Fox incorporated the Red Star Publishing Company.

This process of centralization gave a progressively smaller number of executives more and more control over the choice of material to be distributed. Owning or controlling affiliates in almost every phase of the entertainment business, the men in charge sought above all a standardized product which they could sell through every medium to as many people in as many places as possible. To be fully exploitable, music now had to be suitable not only for dance halls, the stage, and phonograph records (all of which could cater to minority tastes) but also for radio and films, which reached the general, nationwide audience.

Although collectively improvised jazz of Louis Armstrong's Hot Five
or the blues sung by Bessie Smith sounded less strange than they had
a few years earlier, they still had less market appeal for the general audience. Furthermore, the suggestive lyrics, which shocked traditionalists,
met with the disapproval of the Radio Commission and the Hays office.
The words of "It's Tight Like That" by "George Tom" and "Tampa
Red" offer a good example.

> Now the girl I love is long and slim,
> When she gets it it's too bad, Jim.
> It's tight like that, beedle um bum,
> It's tight like that, beedle um bum,
> Hear me talkin' to you, it's tight like that.

Record companies continued to sell such material to the Negro
audience, but they knew that lyrics like these and the music associated
with them could never be sold for use on radio or in films. Thus, centralization of the entertainment business helped to prevent the spread
of collectively improvised jazz and certain blues.

Neil Leonard, *Jazz and the White Americans: The Acceptance of a New Art Form*, (Chicago:
University of Chicago Press, 1962) 95–99, 102–104.

IT WAS DURING THIS VISIT TO LONDON (1920) that I first began to take
an interest in jazz. Billy Arnold and his band, straight from New York,
were playing in a Hammersmith dance hall, where the system of taxi-
girls and taxi-boys had been introduced. A dozen young men in evening
dress and girls in blue dresses with lace collars sat around in a box, and
for sixpence any timid young man or neurotic old maid could have one
of them to dance with. For the same fee they could have another dance
with the same or any other partner.

In his *Coq et L'arlequin* Cocteau had described the jazz accompaniment to the number by Gaby Deslys at the Casino de Paris in 1918 as
a "cataclysm in sound." In the course of frequent visits to Hammersmith, where I sat close to the musicians, I tried to analyze and assimilate what I heard. What a long way we had traveled from the gypsies
who before the war used to pour their insipid, mawkish strains intimately into one's ears, or the singers whose glides, in the most dubious

taste, were upborne by the wobbling notes of the cimbalon, or the crudity of our bals-musette, with the unsubtle forthrightness of cornet, accordion, and clarinet! The new music was extremely subtle in its use of timbre; the saxophone breaking in, squeezing out the juice of dreams, or the trumpet, dramatic or languorous by turns, the clarinet, frequently played in its upper register, the lyrical use of the trombone, glancing with its slide over quarter-tones in crescendos of volume and pitch, thus intensifying the feeling; and the whole, so various yet not disparate, held together by the piano and subtly punctuated by the complex rhythms of the percussion, a kind of inner beat, the vital pulse of the rhythmic life of the music. The constant use of syncopation in the melody was of such contrapuntal freedom that it gave the impression of unregulated improvisation, whereas in actual fact it was elaborately rehearsed daily, down to the last detail. I had the idea of using these timbres and rhythms in a work of chamber music, but first I had to penetrate more deeply into the arcana of this new musical form, whose technique still baffled me. The musicians who had already made use of jazz had confined themselves to what were more or less interpretations of dance music. Satie in the *Rag-Time de Paquebot* of *Parade* and Auric in the fox-trot *Adieu New York* had made use of an ordinary symphony orchestra, and Stravinsky had written his *Ragtime* for eleven solo instruments, including a cimbalon.

. . . In Boston, Dr. Davidson introduced me to some of his friends, who at once decided to offer me a party. This was right in the middle of Prohibition, and the tiniest authentic drink cost a small fortune. Whiskey was served in teacups, which were filled underneath the table. Dr. Davidson had chosen the Hotel Brunswick for the party, because it had an excellent jazz orchestra and he knew I would like to hear it. When I arrived in New York, I had told the newspapermen interviewing me that European music was considerably influenced by American music. "But whose music?" they asked me; "Macdowell's or Carpenter's?" "Neither the one nor the other," I answered, "I mean jazz." They were filled with consternation, for at that time most American musicians had not realized the importance of jazz as an art form and relegated it to the dance hall. The headlines given to my interviews prove the astonishment caused by my statements: "Milhaud admires jazz" or "Jazz dictates the future of European music." Of course, my opinions won me the sympathy of Negro music-lovers, who flocked to my concerts. The chairman of the Negro musicians' union even wrote me a touching letter of thanks. Little suspecting what complications this would cause, I immediately invited him to lunch: no restaurant would serve us, but at last Germaine Schmitz solved this delicate problem by asking the manager of the Hotel Lafayette to receive us. I was also called upon by Harry Burleigh, the famous arranger of Negro spirituals, who played me the Negro folk tunes and hymns, which interested me keenly, for I wished to take advantage of my stay to find out all I could about Negro music. The jazz orchestra of the Hotel Brunswick was conducted by a young violinist called Reissmann, who got from his instrumentalists an extreme refinement of pianissimo tones, murmured notes, and glancing chords, whisperings from the muted brass, and barely formulated moans from the saxophone, which had a highly individual flavor. The regular rhythm was conveyed by the muffled beat of the percussion, and above it he spun the frail filigree of sound from the other instruments, to which the high notes of the violin lent an added poignancy. It made a great contrast to Paul Whiteman's lively orchestra, which I had heard a few days before in New York and which had the precision of an elegant, well-oiled machine, a sort of Rolls-Royce of dance music, but whose atmosphere remained entirely of this world.

I owe to Yvonne George my introduction to the pure tradition of New Orleans jazz. In the course of a little reception that followed a lecture I gave at the Alliance Française, she came up to me and said: "You look bored, come and have dinner with me, and afterwards I'll take you to Harlem when I've done my number." She lived in the Hotel Lafayette. In the next room to hers Isadora Duncan and her Russian poet Essenin used to quarrel and chase one another right out on the fire escape. Yvonne introduced me to Marcel Duchamp, an old friend of Satie and Picabia, whose paintings were closely associated with the beginnings of cubism and had played a dominant part in its development. After dinner I heard Yvonne George give her number. She was on Broadway, singing French songs of an intensely realistic character in a style that was both plain and charged with desperate feeling.

Harlem had not yet been discovered by the snobs and aesthetes: we were the only white folks there. The music I heard was absolutely different from anything I had ever heard before and was a revelation to me. Against the beat of the drums the melodic lines crisscrossed in a breathless pattern of broken and twisted rhythms. A Negress whose grating voice seemed to come from the depths of the centuries sang in front of the various tables. With despairing pathos and dramatic feeling she sang over and over again, to the point of exhaustion, the same refrain, to which the constantly changing melodic pattern of the orchestra wove a kaleidoscopic background. This authentic music had its roots in the darkest corners of the Negro soul, the vestigial traces of Africa, no doubt. Its effect on me was so overwhelming that I could not tear myself away. From then on I frequented other Negro theatres and dance halls. In some of their shows the singers were accompanied by a flute, a clarinet, two trumpets, a trombone, a complicated percussion section played by one man, a piano, and a string quintet. I was living in the French House of Columbia University, enjoying the hospitality of Mlle Blanche Prenez; the Schmitzes were my close neighbors. As I never missed the slightest opportunity of visiting Harlem, I persuaded my friends to accompany me, as well as Casella and Mengelberg, who were in New York at the time.

When I went back to France, I never wearied of playing over and over, on a little portable phonograph shaped like a camera, Black Swan records I had purchased in a little shop in Harlem. More than ever I was resolved to use jazz for a chamber work.

Darius Milhaud, *Notes Without Music: An Autobiography*, (New York: Alfred A. Knopf, 1953) 118–119, 135–137.

BLACK SHADOW. Black silence. Not *violet* silence, interspersed with *violet shadows*.

YOUTHFULNESS. Nothing is so enervating as to lie and soak for a long time in a warm bath. Enough of music in which one lies and soaks.

Enough of clouds, waves, aquariums, water-sprites, and nocturnal scents; what we need is a music of the earth, everyday music.

Enough of hammocks, garlands and gondolas; I want someone to build me music I can live in, like a house.

A friend tells me that, after New York, Paris Houses seem as if you could take them in your hands. "Your Paris," he added, "is beautiful because she is built to fit men." Our music must also be built to fit men.

Music is not all the time a gondola, or a racehorse, or a tightrope. It is sometimes a chair as well.

A Holy Family is not necessarily a holy family; it may also consist of a pipe, a pint of beer, a pack of cards and a pouch of tobacco.

In the midst of the perturbations of French taste and exoticism, the cafe-concert remains intact in spite of Anglo-American influence. It preserves a certain tradition which, however crapulous, is none the less racial. It is here, no doubt, that a young musician might pick up the lost thread.

THE CAFE-CONCERT IS OFTEN PURE; THE THEATRE IS ALWAYS CORRUPT.

The music-hall, the circus, and the American Negro bands, all these things fertilize an artist just as life does. To turn to one's own account the emotions aroused by this sort of entertainment is not to derive art from art. These entertainments are not art. They stimulate in the same way as machinery, animals, natural scenery, or danger.

This life-force which is expressed on the music-hall stage makes, at first sight, all our audacities appear old-fashioned. This is because the art is slow and circumspect in its blindest revolutions. There, there are no scruples; you jump upstairs.

A LIGHT STEP PRODUCED BY HEAVY FEEDING. Much fun has been made of an aphorism of mine quoted in an article in the *Mercure de France*: "An artist must swallow a locomotive and bring up a pipe." I meant by this that neither painter nor musician should make use of the spectacle afforded by machinery in order to render their art mechanical, but should make use of the measured exaltation aroused in them by that spectacle in order to express other things of a more reliable kind.

Machinery and American buildings resemble Greek art in so far as their utility endows them with an aridity and a grandeur devoid of any superfluity.

But they are not. The function of art consists in seizing the spirit of the age and extracting from the contemplation of this practical aridity an antidote to the beauty of the Useless, which encourages superfluity.

We must soon hope for an orchestra where there will be no caressing strings. Only a rich choir of wood, brass and percussion.

The public, accustomed to redundancy, disregards works that are terse.

To the musical public terseness signifies emptiness, and stuffing prodigality.

The longer an artistic expression is destined to last, the fuller and denser it will be, compact like an egg, and the more it will facilitate surface-trickery.

The public does not like dangerous profundities; it prefers surfaces. That is why, when an artistic expression appears to it to be suspect, it leans toward a belief in trickery.

THE PUBLIC ONLY TAKES UP YESTERDAY AS A STICK TO BEAT TODAY.

The indolence of the public: its armchair and its stomach. The public is ready to take up no matter what new game so long as you don't change it, when once it has learned the rules. Hatred of the creator is hatred of *him who alters the rules of the game.*

PUBLICS. Those who defend today by making use of yesterday, and who anticipate tomorrow (1 per cent).

Those who defend today by destroying yesterday, and who will deny tomorrow (4 per cent).

Those who deny today in order to defend yesterday (which is their today) (10 per cent).

Those who imagine that today is a mistake, and make an appointment for the day after tomorrow (12 per cent).

Those of the day-before-yesterday who defend yesterday in order to prove that today exceeds legitimate bounds (20 per cent).

Those who have not yet learnt that art is continuous and believe that art stopped yesterday in order to go on again, perhaps, tomorrow (60 per cent).

Those who are equally oblivious of the day-before-yesterday, yesterday, and today (100 per cent).

NEGROES. It is only by distributing lots of bric-a-brac and by much imitation of the phonograph that you will succeed in taming the Negroes and making yourself understood.

Then substitute gradually your own voice for the phonograph and raw metal for the trinkets.

Too many miracles are expected of us; I consider myself very fortunate if I have been able to make a blind man hear.

WE HAVE IN OUR KEEPING AN ANGEL WHOM WE ARE CONTINUALLY SHOCKING. WE MUST BE THIS ANGEL'S GUARDIAN.

Jean Cocteau, *Cocteau's World: An Anthology of Writings*, Margaret Crosland, ed. (New York: Dodd, Mead & Co., 1972) 311–313, 315–316, 319.

THE BROADWAY COMPROMISE between restraint and rebellion is perhaps best epitomized by the history of jazz. Although a number of bands have laid claim to being the original jazz band, the Original Dixieland Jazz Band (ODJB) introduced New Orleans-style brass band music to New Yorkers when they played in Reisenweber's in late 1916 and early 1917. Sophie Tucker, at the same spot, also at one time billed herself as the Queen of Jazz and Her Five Kings of Syncopation. The Original Jazz Band, composed of five young men, many of them second-generation Italians, picked up their music from the brass bands—black and white—in the New Orleans area prior to World War I. Their music differed from ragtime in its greater syncopation and its large component of improvisation. Untutored musically, the band members rarely wrote down their scores, unlike ragtime. They also broke open the semi-formal quality of ragtime by making their instruments duplicate animal sounds, such as a horse whinnying or a tiger growling. Being brassier in sound than early bands, the ODJB forced patrons to experience a wild, anarchic music, which seemed to be without structure.

After the ODJB demonstrated the power and the draw of the new music, a number of other black and white bands, composed largely of young men, began working northern dance halls and cafes. No one was sure what jazz was or even how to spell it, but the music meant that the dancing would become more energetic, with even more room for body movement and personal expression. Dancers did faster fox-trots, the less inhibited ones could shimmy, and the band played them on, the music being a perfect companion to the dances.

With its roots in black culture, jazz relied heavily on personal expressivism, outside of formalism, expressed through improvisation. It also offered white musicians and audiences an outlet from their own particular cultures. In his investigation of jazz in the twenties (*Jazz and the White Americans*), Neil Leonard suggests that Benny Goodman, Mezz Mezzrow, Hoagy Carmichael, and Bix Beiderbecke were attracted to jazz because it offered a standard of music and life different from the gentility of midwestern values. As Hoagy Carmichael quoted one black musician, "You may not make much money, but you won't get hostile with yourself." The music itself gave vent to one's experience of life. The underlying appeal of the legendary Bix Beiderbecke, a cult figure in life and death, lay in his living the jazz life, searching for the purity that came out of his cornet. According to contemporaries, Beiderbecke cared little for surroundings, food, or clothes, drank a good bit, and died young from the fast but happy life. For many musicians, the authentic jazz life was an experiential life outside the conventions of white America.

It is perhaps no wonder that in the twenties these hot jazz players were for the most part outsiders. Most people in the early twenties did not listen to real jazz. Instead they might have heard "nut" jazz, played by Ted Lewis, the clarinetist-comedian who began making his way in the Broadway cabarets from 1919 on. Nut-jazz men picked up the anarchic animal sounds and unusual instrumentation but gloried in the comic effects rather than in the music.

While the nut-jazz men discounted the potential of jazz and emphasized the happy-go-lucky nature of the music, commercial and refined jazz players defused the potential of jazz in other ways. Paul Whiteman, perhaps the best-known band leader of the 1920s, was the son of the conductor of the Denver Symphony Orchestra. Abandoning classical music early, he went into the dance music field, becoming a major attraction in his own right. Perhaps it is no accident that white musicians of the twenties achieved star prominence, moving out from supporting roles of the dancers, a role played by the black bandsmen such as James R. Europe in the 1910s. Whiteman made his first appearance in New York in 1921 at the Palais Royale on Broadway. He became a star by doing for jazz what the Castles had done for black dances. Black music could not be absorbed in unadulterated form; reformers, church leaders, and parents in the early twenties were up in arms about the new music. Whiteman perceived that he could make jazz respectable by uplifting it and demonstrating its classical, harmonic qualities. Starting out as a commercial bandleader, playing smooth music that downplayed improvisation and raucousness, by 1924 he gave concerts at Aeolian Hall, in which George Gershwin performed his "Rhapsody in Blue." While using jazz shadings, Whiteman relied essentially on written scores and European harmonics. The result was harmonious rather than anarchic, and the public made him a star. In a culture that had learned to see love as the justification for sex, popular white dance bands played romantic, smooth, or athletic music, with the passionate and wild side downplayed.

The styles that whites worked out in the Broadway cafes along the lines of romantic love, the private fun home, and personal experiences were not the only important elements of the 1920s. In the early 1920s, the split between the public world and the private personal world permitted the exploration of greater impulse and passion. Prosperous youths and adults explored the more adventurous implications of the cabarets of the 1910s, turning to Greenwich Village for drinks. The Village, an authentic bohemian and Italian ethnic community in the 1910s, had increasingly become a tourist area and nightlife zone for uptown whites since 1917. The cafés offered secrecy to young and old of college and noncollege background. The area had other potent associations. As a bohemian section, the Village became a playground where uptowners could indulge in wilder forms of sensuality. The Village's overtones of free sexuality attracted uptowners and out-of-towners, for in the Village they could see people apparently uninterested in success, caring little about money, desiring only to live the good life without responsibilities. Beyond that, the Village, then as now, had the reputation for homosexuality, and conventional whites could see lesbians and homosexuals on the streets.

Lewis A. Erenberg, *Steppin' Out: New York Nightlife and the Transformation of American Culture, 1890–1930*, (Chicago: University of Chicago Press, 1981) 250–253.

THE BOOK NOOK WAS A LITTLE HOUSE ORIGINALLY. It was situated hard by the campus on Indiana Avenue and it really was a book store. Gradually it had grown and been added to until it seated a hundred or so coke-guzzling, book-laden, high-spirited students. There new tunes were heard and praised; lengthy discussions were started and never quite finished. There the first steps of the toddle were taken and fitted to our new rhythm. Dates were made and hopes were born. Jordan's band continued playing for the local dances and sometimes they could be prevailed upon to stay over and play for a Sunday afternoon session in the Book Nook. *"Shake it and break it, and hang it on the wall"* —that was the Sunday ritual.

Let me take you gently by the hand and lead you into the Book Nook on a normal afternoon. That little guy, over there, flogging the piano—that could be me. The one with the long nose and exerted purple face. And the large freckled youth with the saxophone, the one making those long blue notes, that's Batty De Marcus. The high-cheekboned unshaved youth perched yonder in a booth, that is Moenkhaus, composing a poem, perhaps, for we hear his weird coyote-howl laugh even above our efforts.

A few couples are seated in booths at the far side and Pete Costas, the proprietor, is punctuating his English with Greek epithets because Klondike Tucker, the Negro chef, has balled up an order.

Wad Allen is curved into a seat across from Monk, and the thing he toys with, stroking sensuously, is a piece of lemon meringue pie—though blueberry will serve in a pinch.

Those round yellow objects arising as the twilight creeps softly upon the scene? Why, those are grapefruit rinds hurled at me because my music has grown too sedate.

I dodge the grapefruit rinds and stop. Monk is going to read his creation. There is a moment of quiet. Quiet fraught with expectancy. Nerves too tight. Minds keyed to vistas beyond the horizons of so-called rational thought.

Monk reads:

> Blooters, thou knowest no Heaven
> Blooters, thou knowest only us
> Bugs, men, whores and fowls—
> They are the Children of Heaven.

There are wild yells. Wad Allen shrieks his appreciation. I hear in my ear a voice. The voice of a non-Bent Eagle. It is a plaintive voice, timid with query.

"What does it mean?"

I turn and smile pityingly. This poor guy doesn't know what those immortal lines convey.

"It means just what it says," I hear Wad Allen say. "Just *exactly* what it says."

That's normal.

It's also normal for the Book Nook to be nearly deserted and for Moenkhaus and Wad Allen and myself, and Harry Hostetter too, to be there. We talk of things we are puzzled about. We confess bewilderment and doubts and fears and we never laugh at each other. We wonder where we are going.

"I'm going to be a lawyer," I say firmly. "Jazz is okay, but—"

Harry interrupts. "Thanksgiving comes but once a dozen," he says, looking at Monk. "But what we call jazz comes but once."

"It originated in the South," Wad says. "Buddy Bolden blew hot jazz for the Creole dances. They get most of the credit for it."

"Jazz" meant "play it faster." Buddy put a hat over the bell of his horn to get fuzzy effects and Freddie Keppard, another Creole, brought his band to the Columbia Theatre in New York about 1911 and showed 'em how to use a mute. They liked their music more in keeping with their climate though—slow and raspy.

"I hear they put Buddy in an asylum," I say and I hope with all my heart that they didn't take his horn away from him. "Law is the best."

"Buddy Bolden, the Original Creole Band, and the Original Dixieland Band were preceded by at least two people I've heard of," Harry says. "One was blind Tom Harney. He was sort of a prodigy on the piano, around Lexington and Louisville . . . That was back in the eighties and early nineties . . . he was feeble-minded too. He played his real hot licks as an introduction to his concert. He was great, but he wasn't original except when he played it wrong—but, oh, so right—as an attention rouser."

"So what?" Monk says lazily. "Hogwash isn't any too bright, and he plays them all wrong. As a matter of fact," he admits modestly, "I am perhaps the greatest piano player who ever fell off the Matterhorn."

I like jazz . . . kinda like law too . . . like people . . .

"I'm wondering what Buddy Bolden had in his brain when he blew the introduction to what is now *Tiger Rag*," I say.

Monk yawns. "Who cares? I'm going to die any day now."

And he did die. Just a year before Bix, also strangely, the same year Buddy Bolden, now an old man, finally went to the place where nobody's crazy.

They got Buddy, but they never got us. A lot of people listened to us and were dubious and we knew it. But they never *proved* we were nuts.

Hoagy Carmichael, *The Stardust Road* [1946], (Bloomington, IN: Indiana University Press, 1983) 35–38.

I GOT A LITTLE RESPITE through looking out the window, but not for long. The vociferations of the company would have awakened the dead. The glasses of alcoholic drugs traveled from hand to hand. The colored waiters in turquoise-blue jackets raced round laden with things to eat. Every ten minutes the shouting gentleman leaped up like a jack-in-the-box, and told us how the people of New Jersey or of Connecticut had voted. The diners freed their jaws with a swallow and threw out a salvo of noise in honor of Smith and Hoover. Then they called for music.

The music suddenly burst forth from a corner. It was the falsest, shrillest, the most explosive of jazz—that breathless uproar which for many years now has staggered to the same syncopation, that shrieks through its nose, weeps, grinds its teeth, and caterwauls throughout the world. Jazz is a triumph of barbaric folly that has received praise, interpretation, and technical commentary from those educated musicians who, more than anything else, fear to be regarded as not in the least degree "modern," and thus vex their clientele, and who bow down to jazz as the painters of 1910 bowed down to cubism, for fear, as the phrase is, of missing the bus, and as the novelists of today bow down to the prevalent taste and introduce into all of their stories a "pair" of homosexuals and "three-of-a-kind" drug addicts.

Saxophone, drums, inebriated violin, cooing piccolo—jazz has sounded its call, and, I beg you to believe, not in vain. There was commotion in the company. The old women rose first of all, with an ardor and an eagerness that you would not dare to expect from such venerable hips, such swollen ankles, and such sagging bosoms. O jazz, stimulant supreme! by what miracle have you driven back the hour of sunset, and raised all these ghosts?

These respectable ladies with their white hair—O moving moment! Do tell us all about it, Grandmamma!—began to stomp round in the open space among the tables. A long time afterwards the young women rose nonchalantly. They ventured to take a few disdainful steps in the crowd of dancers (. . .) while the jazz lost all decency and restraint and spat joyously in the face of music.

"They are having a good time," said the benign Dr. Brooker, lifting his eyebrows. "They are right to amuse themselves in the evening; they work so hard all day."

(. . .) The woman whom I indicated with a slight nod wore on her fingers some of those diamonds which Americans call "rocks" on account of their insolent size. And those prodigious jewels were bound to her wrists with solid clinking gold chains. Her gown was gold and her slippers were gold. Of gold, too—red and green gold—was her old, a hundred times retinted hair. And behind all that jeweler's shop, I seemed to see a hundred thousand squealing pigs whose throats were being cut by a Negro all over blood.

It was not the pigs that were screaming; it was the enthusiastic dancers . . .

The jazz went roaring on. The rose-tinted alcohol poured down the throats. The Negro waiters in their dark blue jackets slipped among the dancers with strained faces, staring eyes, and drops of sweat on their nostrils.

Georges Duhamel, *America the Menace: Scenes from the Life of the Future*, Charles Miner Thompson, trans. (London: George Allen & Unwin, Ltd., 1931) 121–122, 124–125, 126.

BY JAZZ, OF COURSE, I MEAN THE WHOLE MOVEMENT roughly designated as such, and not merely that section of it known as Afro-American, or more familiarly as 'Harlem.' The Negro once enjoyed a monopoly of jazz, just as England once enjoyed a monopoly of the industrial revolution, but for the Negroes to imagine that all jazz is their native province is as if an Englishman were to imagine that all locomotives were built by his compatriots. Even the Harlem section of jazz is by no means so African as it might be supposed.

There is a double yet opposed conspiracy to persuade one that modern dance music represents a purely negroid tradition. On the one hand, we have the crusty old colonels, the choleric judges and beer-sodden columnists who imagine they represent the European tradition murmuring 'swamp stuff,' 'jungle rhythms,' 'Negro decadence' whenever they hear the innocent and anodyne strains of the average English jazz band, hugely enjoying their position of Cassandra prophesying the downfall of the white woman. On the other hand, we have the well-meaning but rather sentimental propagandists of the Negro race, only too eager to point out that the Negroes are the only begetters of a movement that has admittedly swept all over the world and that provides an exotic influence far exceeding the localized exoticism of Cocteau and his followers. The only flaw in both these arguments is that most jazz is written and performed by cosmopolitan Jews. Were this fact sufficiently realized, it would hardly abate the fury of the colonels and the columnists, for from their point of view the Jew is just as much the enemy of the British and Holy Roman Empire as the Negro; but it might slightly curb the hysterical enthusiasm of the poor-white Negro propagandists whose sentimental effusions must be so embarrassing to the intelligent Negro himself. The particular type of white inferiority complex responsible for this propaganda has been so ruthlessly dealt with by Wyndham Lewis in his *Paleface* that one can add little to his conclusions except to point out that in music also the same game of intellectual 'pat-a-cake' is taking place.

The European's enthusiasm for so-called Negro music is in equal ratio to the Negro's appropriation of European devices, and the more the European tries to imagine himself 'down on the Delta' the more the Negro tries to imagine himself in an aristocratic salon. In this connection, it is amusing to recall the situation that arose recently when a well-known Negro dance arranger was called in to produce a ballet for a highbrow company trained in the classical tradition. While all the Europeans flung aside their carefully won training to indulge in an orgy of pseudo-Charlestons the Negro himself was moved to tears, not by his own work but by the classic elegance of *Lac de Cygnes*.

If anyone doubts the essential element of European sophistication in jazz, it is a simple matter for him to compare a typical piece of jazz music, such as Duke Ellington's *Swampy River*, first with a lyric piece by Grieg and then with a record of native African music. It must be clear to the most prejudiced listener that apart from a few rhythmical peculiarities the Ellington piece has far more in common with the music of Grieg. I am not denying for a moment the racial characteristics implicit in these rhythmical peculiarities—I am only pointing out that Ellington, like all Negro composers, has to use the European harmonic framework. Ellington's works are no more examples of African folk song than James Weldon Johnson's poems are examples of the Dahomey dialect; they both represent the application of the Negro temperament to an alien tradition and an acquired language. (Paul Morand tells us that African natives, far from reacting favorably to jazz records, find records of Russian folk songs more exciting and sympathetic.)

The emotional appeal of jazz depends not only on its rhythms which, though childishly simple compared with those of African folk music, may legitimately be accounted African in origin, but also on its harmonic color, which cannot conceivably be traced back to Africa for the simple reason that harmony as we understand it does not exist in primitive African music. Hornbostel in his admirable handbook on African music records only one example of pure harmonic writing in the whole history of his discoveries, and that consisted of two chords at the end of a satirical song about the local missionary, the intention of which was obviously to parody the lugubrious effect of his harmonium.

The lack of any innate harmonic sense in the Negro can be realized by listening to the bands in the poorer bals nègres in Paris, where the orchestra consists of unsophisticated Negroes who have been brought up in the French colonies and not subjected to the influence of the succulently harmonized Anglo-Saxon religious music. Here we can find no hint of the typical 'blue' harmony of the Negro New York composers. The same rhythmic and improvisatory sense is there, but applied to the rudimentary harmonies of the French musical song.

The superiority of American jazz lies in the fact that the Negroes there are in touch not so much with specifically barbaric elements as with sophisticated elements. Negro talent being on the whole more executive than creative, and modern Negro music being essentially an applied art, jazz is naturally largely dependent for its progress on the progress of the sophisticated material used as a basis for its rhythmic virtuosity. The sudden post-war efflorescence of jazz was due largely to the adoption as raw material of the harmonic richness and orchestral subtlety of the Debussy-Delius period of highbrow music. Orchestral color, of course, is not a thing that can really be appreciated in itself; it is largely dependent for its color on the underlying harmonies. The harmonic background drawn from the impressionist school opened up a new world of sound to the jazz composer, and although the more grotesque orchestral timbres, the brute complaints of the saxophone, the vicious spurts from the muted brass, may seem to belie the rich sentimentality of their background, they are only thorns protecting a fleshy cactus—a sauce piquante poured over a nice juicy steak.

Jazz, or to be pedantically accurate, 'ragtime,' from having a purely functional value—a mere accompaniment to the tapping of toe and heel, the quick linking of bodies and the slow unburdening of minds—has suddenly achieved the status of a 'school,' a potent influence that can meet the highbrow composer on his own terms. Though popularly regarded as being a barbaric art, it is to its sophistication that jazz owes its real force. It is the first dance music to bridge the gap between highbrow and lowbrow successfully . . .

. . . In point of fact, jazz has long ago lost the simple gaiety and sadness of the charming savages to whom it owes its birth, and is now for the most part a reflection of the jagged nerves, sex repressions, inferiority complexes and general dreariness of the modern scene. The nostalgia of the Negro who wants to go home has given place to the infinitely more weary cosmopolitan Jew who has no home to go to. The Negro associations of jazz, the weary traveler, the comforting old mammy, the red-hot baby, have become a formula of expression only, as empty and convenient as the harlequin and columbine of the nineteenth century. The pierrot with burnt-cork face symbolizes not the England of yesterday but the Jewry of today.

The importance of the Jewish element in jazz cannot be too

strongly emphasized, and the fact that at least ninety per cent of jazz tunes are written by Jews undoubtedly goes far to account for the curious sagging quality—so typical of Jewish art—the almost masochistic melancholy of the average foxtrot. This masochistic element is becoming more and more a part of general consciousness, but it has its stronghold in the Jewish temperament . . .

There is an obvious link between the exiled and persecuted Jews and the exiled and persecuted Negroes, which the Jews, with their admirable capacity for drinking the beer of those who have knocked down the skittles, have not been slow to turn to their advantage. But although the Jews have stolen the Negroes' thunder, although Al Jolson's nauseating blubbering masquerades as savage lamenting, although Tin Pan Alley has become a commercialized Wailing Wall, the only jazz music of technical importance is the small section of it that is genuinely negroid. The 'hot' Negro records still have a genuine and not merely galvanic energy, while the blues have a certain austerity that places them far above the sweet nothings of George Gershwin.

An artist like Louis Armstrong, who is one of the most remarkable virtuosi of the present day, enthralls us at a first hearing, but after a few records one realizes that all his improvisations are based on the same restricted circle of ideas, and in the end there is no music which more quickly provokes a state of exasperation and ennui. The best records of Duke Ellington, on the other hand, can be listened to again and again because they are not just decorations of a familiar shape but a new arrangement of shapes. Ellington, in fact, is a real composer, the first jazz composer of distinction, and the first Negro composer of distinction. His works—apart from a few minor details—are not left to the caprice or ear of the instrumentalist; they are scored and written out, and though, in the course of time, variants may creep in—Ellington's works in this respect are as difficult to codify as those of Liszt—the first American records of his music may be taken definitively, like a full score, and are the only jazz records worthy studying for their form as well as their texture. Ellington himself being an executant of the second rank has probably not been tempted to interrupt the continuity of his texture with bravura passages for the piano, and although his instrumentalists are of the finest quality their solos are rarely demonstrations of virtuosity for its own sake.

The real interest of Ellington's records lies not so much in their color, brilliant though it may be, as in the amazingly skillful proportions in which the color is used. I do not only mean skillful as compared with other jazz composers, but as compared with so-called highbrow composers. I know of nothing in Ravel so dexterous in treatment as the varied solos in the middle of the ebullient *Hot and Bothered* and nothing in Stravinsky more dynamic than the final section. The combination of themes at this moment is one of the most ingenious pieces of writing in modern music. It is not a question, either, of setting two rhythmic patterns working against each other in the mathematical Aaron Copland manner—it is genuine melodic and rhythmic counterpoint which, to us an old-fashioned phrase, 'fits' perfectly.

Ellington's best works are written in what may be called ten-inch record form, and he is perhaps the only composer to raise this insignificant disc to the dignity of a definite genre. Into this three and a half minutes he compresses the utmost, but beyond its limits he is inclined to fumble. The double-sided ten-inch *Creole Rhapsody* is an exception, but the twelve-inch expansion of the same piece is nothing more than a potpourri without any of the nervous tension of the original version. Ellington has shown no sign of expanding his formal conceptions, and perhaps it is as well, for his works might then lose their peculiar concentrated savor. He is definitely a petite maitre, but that, after all, is considerably more than many people thought either jazz or the colored race would ever produce. He has crystallized the popular music of our time and set up a standard by which we may judge not only other jazz composers but also those highbrow composers, whether American or European, who indulge in what is roughly known as 'symphonic jazz.'

Constant Lambert, "The Spirit of Jazz," [1934] from *Music Ho! A Study of Music in Decline* (London: The Hogarth Press, 1985) 177–188.

IN THE DEEP STILLNESS RESOUNDS THE DRY KNOCKING of an idiotic hammer. One, two, three, ten, twenty strokes, and after them, like a mud ball splashing into clear water, a wild whistle screeches; and then there are rumblings, wails and howls like the smarting of a metal pig, the shriek of a donkey, or the amorous croaking of a monstrous frog. This insulting chaos of insanity pulses to a throbbing rhythm. Listening for a few minutes to these wails, one involuntarily imagines an orchestra of sexually driven madmen conducted by a man-stallion brandishing a huge genital member.

The monstrous bass belches out English words; a wild horn wails piercingly, calling to mind the cries of a raving camel; a drum pounds monotonously; a nasty little pipe tears at one's ears; a saxophone emits its quacking nasal sound. Fleshy hips sway, and thousands of heavy feet tread and shuffle. The music of the degenerate ends finally with a deafening thud, as though a case of pottery had been flung down to earth from the skies.

Maxim Gorky, "O muzyke tolstykh," in *Pravda*.

THE PLANTATION CLUB ANTICIPATED THE RISE OF HARLEM as a nightlife zone for whites. Just as whites had looked to the Village as a place to experience real life while keeping it at a distance, they did the same in Harlem, but with more dedication, especially after the Village became too touristy and lost its exotic attraction. New York had long had black and tans, but police, citizenry, and reformers considered them dangerous. In the Tenderloin, blacks and whites often intermingled, but this produced violence in 1900 and again in 1910 as whites attacked blacks, especially black performers. By the late 1910s and 1920s, however, blacks were living in their own segregated zone, too far away to be dangerous yet close enough to be exciting. A number of Tenderloin places, tiring of police harassment, began moving to Harlem in the mid-1910s. By 1925 whites began making the trek north in large numbers, partly for the wide opportunities for alcohol and partly because of the aura of exotic release surrounding the area and blacks. *Shuffle Along* (the musical) in 1921–1922 publicized black entertainment, the Plantation made it acceptable in the intimate space of a cabaret, and Carl Van Vechten's novel, *Nigger Heaven*, opened up Harlem itself to white eyes. While attempting to analyze the black community and its various social groups, Van Vechten was fascinated with the expressivism of the Negro, and the sexuality of the cabarets played a large part in the book's success.

The true Negro conformed to a white vision: he represented joy in life unfettered by civilization.

To meet the influx of people, a number of nightclubs opened their doors on 133rd to 135th Streets between and on Lexington and Seventh avenues, and those already in existence began to accept white patronage. The Cotton Club, Connie's Inn, and Ed Smalls's Paradise were the most famous, but the area was also home to innumerable small clubs, many of which did not open until the late hours after others had closed. Most of the big clubs were white owned, and they appealed to a white vision of Harlem life. Blacks made up the entertainment core, but the creative and business talent was usually white. While many of the big clubs presented revues that were merely extensions of Broadway ideas, whites had the image that black men and women, unlike themselves, really enjoyed performing. More than this, they were not performers in the conventional sense; this was the real thing. Black entertainers were perceived as natural, uncivilized, uninhibited performers, naturally smiling, because they had what whites lacked: joy in life. Guidebooks advised visitors to go to Harlem late, after the unadventurous whites downtown had gone to bed. The lateness of the hour added to the sense that one was venturing to the heart of darkness, the city of night where all things forbidden during the day were available in those few hours stolen from conventional life. In hard-working New York, Harlem was the Montmartre of America, its dramatic counterpoint. The numerous descriptions of driving up to Harlem, through the park by cab, made it seem as if one journeyed out from civilization, to the heart of impulses. Whites could find anything they wanted in Harlem, a city that never slept. Out for an evening, thus, whites created an entire fantasy land out of Harlem. From the mid-1920s to the early 1930s, Harlem represented the apotheosis of slumming.

The "real life" of Harlem was the creation of white fantasies. It is commonplace to assert that black entertainment serves white needs; this is particularly true where Negroes are perceived as natural entertainers, comics, and buffoons for whites. In the 1920s, the image of the Negro entertainer underwent a subtle shift at the same time that white culture's perception of what was respectable for themselves also changed. In minstrelsy, whites had played blacks on stage. It was only in the 1880s and 1890s that blacks began playing out the stereotypes of the happy-go-lucky Sambo or Jim Dandy that whites had already established in the form. By then minstrelsy itself was too tied to an ascetic and rural mode—the plantation—to mirror new urban values fully. Moreover, black composers and performers at the turn of the century were moving the form of black musicals slightly out of the old formal definitions of what roles blacks could play. . . . By the mid-1920s, black culture was still perceived in the older sensual terms, but now the emphasis was on the positive nature of that sensuality. In the Harlem clubs black men and women were portrayed as primitive dancing fools, whose sensuality civilized whites could not hope to match. The only soul left had to be black.

Harlem clubs catered to these white fantasies of a natural race. Duke Ellington's band played "Jungle Music," the waiters at Ed Smalls's charlestoned in the aisles as they served food, and the women in the revues were "tall, tan, and terrific." Dancers like Earl "Snakehips" Tucker and Bill "Bojangles" Robinson danced in a happy and sensual way with their feet doing all the work, uncontrolled by the mind. The women, too, appealed to white tastes, for the revues presented light-skinned women who could appeal to white concepts of beauty, but had a touch of darker exoticism and hence animality. In all the clubs, white visitors felt they were experiencing real life, hotter music, hotter dancing, life lived at its quickest.

The Cotton Club, Connie's Inn, and several others were also segregated. Blacks performed; the audiences were largely white. Ed Smalls was warned by local police that he would be ill advised to permit mixing of blacks and whites in his club. Moreover, white visitors tended to crowd out the blacks, making it uncomfortable for them. Consequently while Harlem clubs broke from the minstrel form by presenting sex as desirable, Negro women as beautiful, and blacks in general as capable of love, they also retained the underlying element of minstrelsy. Blacks wore masks and served whites. The setting in the big clubs rendered the experience safe because whites did not have to mix with blacks on equal footing; instead blacks played the role they always did, the servants of and performers for the more powerful race. The fact that blacks were denied admittance to Broadway clubs unless they worked there reinforces the inequality of the Harlem experience. While whites had the power in the situation to define the relationship, blacks had little control over the exchange. Whites, however, felt they could relax with the blacks precisely because the latter were their social inferiors. They were less civilized, yet they were also of a lesser racial stock, and need not be taken seriously as a model of how to live one's life in the daytime world of reality. Whites thus enjoyed a safe Montmartre in Harlem, one that gave them the chance to act black and feel primitive personally without having to change their downtown, public lives.

Lewis A. Erenberg, *Steppin' Out: New York Nightlife and the Transformation of American Culture, 1890–1930*, (Chicago: University of Chicago Press, 1984) 254–257.

CHRISTMAS EVE IN NEW CASTLE, with the little maimed tree, was somewhat different from the night I went up to Chicago to see Bix. It's the summer of 1923. We took two quarts of bathtub gin, a package of muggles, and headed for the black-and-tan joint where King Oliver's band was playing.

The King featured two trumpets, piano, a bass fiddle and a clarinet. As I sat down to light my first muggle, Bix gave the sign to a big black fellow, playing second trumpet for Oliver, and he slashed into *Bugle Call Rag.*

I dropped my cigarette and gulped my drink. Bix was on his feet, his eyes popping. For taking the first chorus was that second trumpet, Louis Armstrong. Louis was taking it fast. Bob Gillette slid off his chair and under the table. He was excitable that way.

"Why," I moaned, "why isn't everybody in the world here to hear that?" I meant it. Something as unutterably stirring as that deserved to be heard by the world.

Then the muggles took effect and my body got light. Every note Louis hit was perfection. I ran to the piano and took the place of Louis's wife. They swung into *Royal Garden Blues.* I had never heard that tune before, but somehow I knew every note. I couldn't miss. I was floating in a strange deep-blue whirlpool of jazz.

It wasn't marijuana. The muggles and gin were, in a way, stage props. It was the music. The music took me and had me and it made me right.

Louis Armstrong was Bix Beiderbecke's idol, and when we went out the next night to crash an S.A.E. dance where Bix was playing with the Wolverines, I learned that Bix was no imitation of Armstrong. The Wolverines sounded better to me than the New Orleans Rhythm Kings. Theirs was a stronger rhythm and the licks that Jimmy Hartwell, George Johnson and Bix played were precise and beautiful.

Bix's breaks were not as wild as Armstrong's, but they were hot and he selected each note with musical care. He showed me that jazz could be musical and beautiful as well as hot. He showed me that tempo doesn't mean fast. His music affected me in a different way. Can't tell you how—like licorice, you have to eat some.

Those incongruous times. Not long before the Wolverines could race our heartbeats, a member of the Utah state legislature introduced a bill providing a fine and imprisonment for those who wore, on the streets, "skirts higher than three inches above the ankle."

While we were doodling and weaving our own mystic pattern across crowded dance floors, audiences sat spellbound and quiet beneath the shadows on a screen. Marguerite Clark could bring a lump to your throat with the magic of her make-believe. The youngsters were calling them the "shifties." Elsie Ferguson and the Talmadge girls lived excitingly and bravely in the world of the cinema.

There was a "Red" under every bed, in those days, and the membership in the Ku-Klux Klan was rising by the hundreds of thousands. Rising highest in Indiana. Home of the brave and the land of the free. Right in the middle—remember that flagpole in Bloomington?

All over the country people were wildly playing mah-jong. And a good many of us were listening, with all our hearts, to the steady pulsation of jazz. And then, the sudden change. People became restless. The music took on a down beat and illicit liquor flowed. Dances were "rat-races," women were "monkeys," and Dad was called "governor."

Hoagy Carmichael [1946], *The Stardust Road*, (Bloomington, IN: Indiana University Press, 1983) 53–55.

. . . I INTEND TO SKETCH, MUSICALLY, from the beginning of American history, the development of our emotional resources which have led us to the characteristic American music of today; the most of which, by the way, is not jazz. My object in giving such a concert is with the hope that eventually our music will become a stepping stone which will be helpful in giving the coming generations a much deeper appreciation of better music.

The experiment is to be purely educational. I intend to point out, with the assistance of my orchestra, the tremendous strides which have been made in popular music from the day of the discordant jazz, which sprang into existence about ten years ago from nowhere in particular, to the really melodious music of to-day, which—for no good reason— is still called jazz. Most people who ridicule the present so-called jazz and who refuse to condone it or listen to it seriously are quarreling with the name jazz and not with what it represents. Neither our protest nor the combined protest of all musicians will change the name. Jazz it is, and jazz it will remain . . .

If we are successful in breaking down only a small portion of the antagonism toward jazz, which is so prevalent among lovers of opera, oratorio and symphony, we will feel amply repaid for our efforts, and so will our associates. If, in addition, we encourage creative musical talent in but one person, we shall be happy.

Paul Whiteman, press release for 1924 concert, in *So This is Jazz* [1926], by Henry O. Osgood, [1926], (New York: Da Capo Press, 1978) 144–145.

NEW YORK CITY IS A CITY OF EPHEMERALITIES, and nowhere are things more ephemeral than along the Rialto, which occupies Broadway and Seventh Avenue from Forty-Second Street eight or ten blocks north, with Times Square for its heart, and of late years has added to itself by throwing out tentacles through the Forties, east almost to Sixth Avenue and west to Eighth Avenue and even beyond. There is a certain flower, the night-blooming cereus, of dainty and modest mien, that folds its beauties away from the public gaze by day and only blooms when hidden by the kindly dusk. It would take a severe stretch of the imagination to liken the Rialto to the night-blooming cereus. The Rialto is not dainty and modest of mien. It makes no attempt to hide its beauties by day. As a matter of fact, it has practically no beauties to hide; it resembles the flower in being at its best only after dark. Dark, in this instance, is a word of comparative meaning. The Rialto is never dark. It is not even dusky until well into the wee, small hours. Nowhere in this world is so much electrical illumination concentrated upon so small an area.

At this precise moment of writing this (. . .)—and one has to be particular about this sort of thing in speaking about the Rialto, whose ephemeral character has already been noticed—four structures dominate Times Square. On the west, the Hotel Astor, the only quiet, comfortable bit of architecture along the whole way; on the east, the new Loew Theater with its tier on tier of office floors above the stage; on the south, the *Times* Flatiron Building squeezed into the little triangle between Broadway, Seventh and Forty-Second; and at the north another flatiron only two meek stories high but plodding along doggedly in its quiet way, earning enough to pay for taxes and upkeep until some one comes along, as some one will before long, covers the land on which it stands with golden eagles, tears it down and shoots a new skyscraper aloft.

To speak of the present building in any way as "dominating"Times Square would be incorrect were it not for the electric clock on its blunt south end, which tells the world just how late for the theater subway jams and traffic tangles have made it. The temporary eclipse of that clock a year or so ago roused more indignation than a dozen crime waves.

At this precise moment the gentleman from Kankakee viewing the night sights of New York with his wife, sees, stretched along the second story of this modest flatiron on the Broadway side (duplicated, also, on Seventh Avenue), an electric sign of rather agreeable design and color, "PALAIS D'OR." It was not always thus, for the sign is older than the Palais d'Or itself. In other days it read "Palais Royal." An economical new management, renaming the place, was obliged to purchase only a "D" and an apostrophe, though it must have wrung the managerial soul to throw away "YAL."

The Palais d'Or describes itself on supplementary signs as that peculiar hybrid, a "Chinese-American Restaurant," but in Palais Royal days it was quite something else, with an entire omission of the Chinese department. Round about its spacious, gracious dance floor were tables at which sat guests more interested, as a rule, in bottles than in birds, and at the south end there stood a raised dais with lengthy pink drapes.

Pyramided against this refined background, Paul Whiteman and his orchestra gathered nightly to dispense nerve-tickling, toe-inciting music that did its share to make Americans what they are—the best dancers in the world. No wonder, either, for Americans alone invented and developed jazz, the best dance music in the world.

The time cannot be far off now that the Palais d'Or and all the little shops on whose shoulders it rests will go the way of all buildings in busy parts of New York; and when some tall new structure takes its place, it is to be hoped that the New York Historical Society will not overlook the opportunity to erect a significant tablet. It should be bolted on one of the marble slabs that separate the elevators from one another in the new building—the most conspicuous spot, you will concede when you stop to think of it, in any home of business, where waiting for the elevator is invariably the favorite indoor sport—and this is the inscription it should bear:

Site of the
P A L A I S   R O Y A L
where
P A U L   W H I T E M A N
First Conceived the Idea of Making
An Honest Woman
out of
J A Z Z

Yes. Standing there night after night, fiddle in hand, leading his band through the simplicities of fox trot after fox trot, and supplying himself an occasional E string obbligato, the Whiteman soul began to yearn for something better. With him to yearn is to act. Though the Bible distinctly assures us that no one can add even an inch to his physical stature by taking thought, this is fortunately not true of spiritual nature.

Here is a date to remember—February 12, 1924. On that date Whiteman gave the first jazz concert ever given.

[T]he idea germinated in the Whiteman brain one evening right in the middle of a particularly blue Blues and that, once there, it grew and grew until, able to contain it comfortably no longer, the redoubtable leader relieved himself and startled New York with the announcement that the Palais Royal orchestra was to invade Aeolian Hall. Thus, by the simple process of taking thought, Whiteman added to his stature.

It *was* startling, this announcement—for New Yorkers. The Palais Royal orchestra to give a concert in Aeolian Hall! It was much as though the Pope had announced he would step across the City of Rome and read Mass at the American Church in the Via Nazionale. And when, after the Aeolian Hall concert, Whiteman proceeded to invade Carnegie Hall—well! To appreciate what a step that was you have to be a New Yorker. The moan of the saxophone, the plunk of the banjo were to intrude on premises sacred since their construction to staid symphony orchestras, staider oratorio and choral societies, Heifetz, John McCormack, the Beethoven Association, Burton Holmes' Travelogues, Ignace Paderewski and numerous other forms and luminaries of Art!

New York, true to form, soon recovered from its astonishment and, still truer to form, made up its mind to be present by hook or crook, begging, buying or stealing tickets by any means, fair or foul.

[L]et me recall my premier hearing of that remarkable work that first enabled jazz to stick its head outside the cabaret door, the Gershwin "Rhapsody in Blue." What is more stale and unprofitable than a dance hall in daytime,—decorations planned for artificial light, drab and dull beyond relief; the long window drapes hanging limp in dejection; the tables and chairs standing about in the crazy and illegitimate relations to one another into which a careless departing crowd pushed them the night before; and over the whole scene a tawdry shabbiness that positively depressed the sensitive soul? Yet it was amid just such surroundings at the old Palais Royal that the "Rhapsody" was rehearsed. Paul Whiteman and his men, having left at two A.M., were back again before noon for this extra work, and they were in it heart and soul. For the most part in shirt sleeves, they gathered in one corner of the big room, sitting on the gilded chairs usually occupied by the regular patrons. Scattered about in, upon and among the confusion of furniture were curious persons who had heard of this new work and were anxious to know what it was; musicians—Victor Herbert, who had written a new suite of serenades for the first program; writers—Carl Van Vechten and Gilbert Seldes, discoverers of this new "lively art"; and large unclassified elements, Rialtoites and musical comedy friends of Gershwin. From outside, through the lurchy, half-drawn drapes, leaked in a cold, pallid light from the uncomfortable February day.

Gershwin took his place at the piano; the rotund Whiteman, in shirt sleeves and one of his snappiest vests, climbed up on a little stand. They were off. And after the first five minutes it was easy enough to gauge the value of a work that made one forget all those depressing, unaesthetic surroundings.

Those who entered Aeolian hall on the afternoon of February twelfth —and enough persons did enter to occupy every seat and as much standing room as the fire department allows to be filled—found the usual ugliness and austere severity of the stage concealed behind an elaborate erection of colorful Japanese screens, with additional color supplied by skillfully disposed stage lights. The orchestra was arranged in a rough semicircle on a platform of three steps. Its composition was as follows: eight violins, banjo, two trumpets, two trombones, two pianos, two tubas, two French horns, three saxophones, drums.

These details are introduced as a matter of historical record, since this, remember, was the very first step toward the elevation of jazz to something more than the accompaniment for dancing. It was the first concert of its kind ever given anywhere.

Henry O. Osgood, *So This Is Jazz* [1926], (New York: Da Capo Press, 1978) 129– 132, 133–134, 135–136.

WE HAVE ALL BEEN TAUGHT TO BELIEVE that "music soothes the savage beast," but we have never stopped to consider that an entirely different type of music might invoke savage instincts.

Never in the history of our land have there been such immoral conditions, and in surveys made by many organizations, the blame is laid on jazz and its evil influence on the young. Never before have such outrageous dances been permitted in private as well as public ballrooms, and never has there been such a strange combination of tone and rhythm as that produced by the dance orchestras of to-day.

If this music is in any way responsible for the immoral acts which can be traced to these dances, then it is high time that the question be raised: "Can music ever be an influence for evil?"

To-day, the first great rebellion against jazz music and such dances as the "toddle" and the "shimmy" comes from the dancing masters themselves. The National Dancing Masters' Association, at their last session, adopted this rule: "Don't permit vulgar cheap jazz music to be played. Such music almost forces dancers to use jerky half steps, and invites immoral variations, for, after all, what is dancing but an interpretation of music?"

Many people classify under the title of "jazz" all music in syncopated rhythm, whether it be the ragtime of the American Negro or the csardas of the Slavic people. Yet there is a vast difference between syncopation and jazz.

The Encyclopaedia Britannica sums up syncopation as "the rhythmic method of tying two beats of the same note into one tone in such a way as to displace the accent." This curious rhythmic accent on the short beat is found in its most highly developed and intense forms among the folk of Slavic countries. It was also the natural expression of the American Negroes, used by them as the accompaniment for their bizarre dances and cakewalks. Negro ragtime, it must be frankly acknowledged, is one of the most important and distinctively characteristic expressions to be found in our native music. Many of the greatest compositions by American composers have been influenced by ragtime. Like all other phases of syncopation, ragtime quickens the pulse, it excites, it stimulates; but it does not destroy.

Jazz is neither a definite form nor a type of rhythm; it is rather a *method* employed by the interpreter. Familiar hymn tunes can be jazzed until their original melodies are hardly recognizable. Jazz does for harmony what the accented syncopation of ragtime does for rhythm. In ragtime the rhythm is thrown out of joint, as it were, thus distorting the melody; in jazz exactly the same thing is done to the harmony. The melodic line is disjointed and disconnected by the accenting of the partial instead of the simple tone, and the same effect is produced on the melody and harmony which is noticed in syncopated rhythm. The combination of syncopation and the use of these inharmonic partial tones produces a strange, weird effect, which has been designated "jazz."

The jazz orchestra uses only those instruments which can produce partial, inharmonic tones more readily than simple tones—such as the saxophone, the clarinet and the trombone, which share honors with the percussion instruments that accent syncopated rhythm. The combination of the syncopated rhythm, accentuated by the constant use of the partial tones sounding off-pitch, has put syncopation too off-key. Thus the three simple elements of music—rhythm, melody and harmony—have been put out of tune with each other.

Jazz originally was the accompaniment of the voodoo dancer, stimulating the half-crazed barbarian to the vilest deeds. The weird chant, accompanied by the syncopated rhythm, also has been employed by other barbaric people to stimulate brutality and sensuality.

The human organism responds to musical vibrations. What instincts then are aroused by jazz? Certainly not deeds of valor or martial courage.

In a recent letter to the author, Dr. Henry van Dyke says of jazz: "As I understand it, it is not music at all. It is merely an irritation of the nerves of hearing, a sensual teasing of the strings of physical passion. Its fault lies not in syncopation, for that is a legitimate device when sparingly used. But 'jazz' is an unmitigated cacophony, a combination of disagreeable sounds in complicated discords, a willful ugliness and a deliberate vulgarity."

Never have we more needed the help and inspiration which good music can give. The General Federation of Women's Clubs has taken for its motto: "To Make Good Music Popular, and Popular Music Good." Let us carry out this motto in every home.

Anne Shaw Faulkner, "Does Jazz Put the Sin in Syncopation?" [c.1920s] from *The Journal of the Century*, compiled by Bryan Holme and the editors of The Viking Press and the *Ladies' Home Journal*, (New York: A Studio Book/The Viking Press, 1976) 104.

[JAZZ] IS AN ORGANIC ENTITY which has different, though related, significances at different times. A concrete point of departure on the beginnings of jazz is *A Pictorial History of Jazz* by [Orrin] Keepnews and [Ben] Grauer Jr. On looking through the early photographs one notices

changes taking place in the style of photography. The very earliest photographs fulfill the minimal function of the photograph. The members
of the bands are assembled so that they can all be seen. They carry their
instruments. In many cases they wear uniforms: the uniform of the
band. The individuals are assembled on the basis of them being members of a band. The individual band members look as though they have
been made uncomfortable by being photographed; clearly, the photograph is not being used by them (individual by individual) for exhibi-
tionist self-advertisement. The photographs could almost be photographs
of convicts, i.e., photographs of those who would prefer not to be photographed. Photography is itself new and its application to colored
people rare. Even in 1939 photographic services for colored people in
the South were poor as is evidenced in the well-known letters from
Bunk Johnson to Frederick Ramsey Jr., on his inability to send Ramsey
photographs of himself—"I'm pretty sure that you all know just how
everything is down South with the poor colored man. The service here
is really poor for colored people."

However, a band as a whole is a larger economic possibility than
an individual, and New Orleans, in the last century, afforded colored
people greater freedom than most other areas in the South. To be photographed itself conferred status. Slavery is only 30 years behind the
recording of these assemblies. The band gives the negro status in his
own eyes. The band is to be identified with the liberation of the negro,
although this value is double-edged. The band's dress style is military
and bands and music were an important part of the liberating armies.
The musicians' instruments are in all probability instruments left over
from disbanded military bands. They have, then, a symbolic significance, as well as conferring status as pieces of property possessed
as signs of personal skill or expertise. These photographs conceal a shy-
ness, a lack of social confidence in the photographic situation, but also
a preparedness to stand and be photographed because of what the band
and being a member of it signified.

As jazz spreads, so as to take in wider audiences, so the style of
photographs in the Keepnews and Grauer pictorial history change. The
main bulk of examples, in the changed style, occur in the early 20s, but
the style can be found several years either side of this period. This sec-

ond batch of photographs testify to the musicians as socially acceptable performers of some accomplishment. The air of social acceptability is induced by a conscious photographic style. The bands are posed. It is no longer sufficient to have everyone present and so make sure they can be seen. The content of the photographs is now carefully arranged. The whole effect is one of neatness, precision, plus shades of dignity. The ensemble is chic. The fashionable style of the 20s, involving a preference for whole shapes bounded by clear contours, all slightly exaggerated by a penchant for the slender, invades the photographic presentation. The performers, then, are presented within the framework of what is fashionable, of what is of the moment. For this reason, they are presented as acceptable and desirable. They are part of *the scene.* Where the photographs are of colored musicians they are presented as members of the chic ensemble, this is to say, that the clean, conceptual contour of *band* bounds the presentation of the performers. In these photographic sessions we are not treated to off-duty poses, the performers remain part of a fashionable decor. They are surrounded by a galaxy of gleaming instruments; they are the players of these instruments. The kind of playing which results is suggested by a distinction within the photographs of this style. Many are of performers sitting in their places on the bandstand; they come across as smooth and well-behaved. In other words they know their place. They are not slaves from Congo Square in New Orleans.

However, just as many of the photographs are posed shots of the band in action. The action is simulated. The overriding compositional structure owes nothing to realism. The emotional content of these photographs is one of rakishness and excitement. The smooth, well-behaved colored musicians indicate, in these photographs, the kind of music they play, or, and perhaps better, the kind of music they don't play. The more formal pose is undermined by the more anarchic one, though the anarchic pose is not genuinely anarchic; the orgiastic impulse is still well-repressed, but, now, it is showing. The musicians don't play stiff, formal music, they play music which is of 'now', which is fashionable, which repudiates the past. The bands advertise themselves as being *Creole,* which strictly interpreted means, or meant, of Latin origins, though born in the Caribbean, and therefore, not of African origins. However, the concept of Creole in employment was a connived duplicity feeding off its literal meaning. Today the ordinary understanding of *Creole*, if not its dictionary approved meaning, is that of being light-colored and of the Caribbean (lacking thereby a clear racial meaning). This movement in the concept came about as the result of people of various racial origins passing themselves off as Creole. The ordinary understanding of the concept gives up authoritarian literalness and yields to transparent social fact. When the Grauer/Keepnews photographs were taken, the literal interpretation of *Creole* was not totally debased by social abuse, and it could still signify social acceptability. This is not to say that anyone really believed that the members of Kid Ory's Creole Jazz Band were Creole, it was just more acceptable when everyone engaged in the transparent fantasy that they were. In terms of fashionable acceptability it was also imperative that they should not be Creole; the important fact was that *they should appear to be but yet be known not to be.* Here, we have an idea emerging that I shall make a lot of, namely that one enormously important life-project for the negro in the USA had been *living in order to dissemble.*

Creole band was part, therefore, of an acceptable image. In addition, the bands in the photographs appear in evening dress (there is even a band that calls itself the Tuxedo Jazz Band). We are, then, in a different world from the marching bands in their uniforms. Yet it is the same world, for it is known that many musicians appeared in both contexts. These photographs from the past, present a concrete record of a lived ambiguity. On the one hand the negro stands self-conscious but obdurate, affirming the fact of his existence; on the other hand he engages himself in dissembling Europeanness. However, what really is socially acceptable and integrates is the ambiguity.

To bring out with more authority the meaning of this ambiguity it is necessary to locate the social context for which the photographs are bits of evidence.

Much research has been done and many books written about slavery in the Southern States of which *Roll Jordan Roll* is one of the latest examples. A resume of all that evidence is not what I wish to reproduce here. Rather I wish to make concrete certain possibilities inherent in the Southern context before Reconstruction. Much of our retrospective thinking about slavery prevents us from reconstructing it as a lived situation. From assumed positions of moral superiority we vent our spleen upon the white master race (failing to note in this that there were many free colored who possessed slaves) and empathize with the suffering of the negro. We tend to conceptualize the situation in terms of tyranny, suffering and the unended struggle for freedom. What we avoid in this attitude is the seduction of contemplating what it was in nineteenth-century America to be European in origins (but to have forsaken Europe) and to own slaves originating from Africa (a continent shrouded in European consciousness by a European concept of savagery). In avoiding these thoughts, we avoid, as a consequence, locating what it was to be slaves responding to this situation. Clearly, there is not just one way in which this general social situation was lived out. Gervase is right to affirm *paternalism* as a general social project, but it is not this element which, it seems to me, is the most influential, or the most relevant in understanding the early significance of jazz. It is the general possibility of *debauchery* that I wish to show was *chosen*.

In its clearest, or least concealed form, we have the situation of white, male masters, overseers, etc., having their way with female slaves. The typical location for this is the plantation where males, with power of authority, had a free run of the field girls regardless of existing mock marital relations between slaves. What Sartre calls the practico-inert reinforces this propensity, for in and around New Orleans there were more colored females than colored males and more white males than white females (J. W. Blassingame, *Black New Orleans*). The paucity of white marriageable females in the New Orleans district had led in the eighteenth century to the king of France sending out female prisoners from Salpetriere, and to the Mississippi Company organizing the system known as "casket girls," whereby girls came from France with a small chest of clothing plus a small dowry for the purpose of marriage. . . . Against this background many permanent liaisons developed between white males and colored females, producing subsequently the social need for the category of free colored as a way of responding to the offspring of such permanent relationships. These relationships were attempts in the New World context to produce substitutes for European normality, building the substitutes out of whatever material was at hand. White female scarcity and the presence of black female slaves was, obviously, a determining practico-inert, which was accommodated in different ways. The practice of using black female slaves *as slaves* for sexual gratification was one prevalent way in which the accommodation was made. But against this sketch of the crude satisfaction of physical need, by means of utilizing whatever was to hand, we need to set other facts. For instance, the fact that white mistresses took up with slave men (Blassingame), or the fact that negro women were taken up for short durations on the basis of placage arrangements (i.e. the setting up of a mistress in an apartment). Moreover, slaves were allowed into masters' houses for collective celebrations, where they dressed up in fine clothes (i.e. European style finery), indulged in sumptuous banquetry and performed erotic dances, like the "carabine" and the "pile chactas." In Southern Louisiana Voodoo not only sustained itself but it drew whites into its practices, thus, in the 1850s, a New Orleans newspaper described a Voodoo ceremony as follows,

> Black and whites were circling around promiscuously, writhing in muscular contractions, panting, raving and frothing at the mouth. But the most degrading and infamous feature of this scene was the presence of a very large number of ladies, moving in the highest walks of society, rich and hitherto supposed respectable, that were caught in the dragnet.

From such facts arises an idea which goes beyond straight-forward physical need as provoked by a scarcity of females. The negro as negro engenders in white consciousness a desire for sexual excess and self-indulgence. The negro symbolizes for whites the obscene and orgiastic (if you like, the "eros principle"). It is partly for this reason that puritan whites were so insistent on brow-beating blacks into a tame Christian submissiveness. Such whites saw in the slaves' drums and their dances the possibility of the obscene orgy. On this basis, in many areas, the drum and the dance were banned. In Catholic areas, however, what repression there was was much less severe, and New Orleans itself is a clear example of this (thus the permitted activities in Congo Square).

However, in so far as whites allowed themselves to be drawn into a celebration of the orgiastic principle, they did not do so without various forms of concealment. I do not mean by this that their activities were clandestine (though often they were this as well), but that, for themselves in the activity, there was an attempt made to disguise an object of desire. . . . Thus, the orgy with blacks was a specific release, a release from repressive mechanisms in European culture. The object was *debauchery*. In more colorful language we might say the object was the rape of European ideology. For the European the orgy was a debauching. What concealed the object of desire, the Europeanised black, became the sexually exciting contradiction.

After emancipation the system of slave labor gave way to wage-labor. This change permeated all transactions, including sexual transactions. We move . . . from a situation in which black females are sexually utilized as slaves, to a situation in which they are utilized in various forms of prostitution. The significance of this, for New Orleans, was that at its height the district had 2,200 registered prostitutes packed into its 38 blocks. The total negro population in New Orleans at this time was around 60,000. In fact the spread of prostitution in New Orleans threatened to engulf the whole city until Alderman Sidney Story proposed that there should be "a certain district outside of which it would be unlawful for prostitution to be carried on." Emancipation, therefore, altered only the form in which sexual practice took place.

The red-light district of New Orleans is, of course, an obligatory subject in describing the formation of jazz. However, the specific content of the New Orleans brothel is not really attended to. The normal thing is to allude to the seamy origins of jazz so as to strengthen the claim that jazz is an authentic music, springing from real life situations. The New Orleans brothel is . . . an interesting phenomenon. It is not generally uniform, but there is a uniform conception emanating from the top which pervades most set-ups to a greater or lesser degree. The top is Basin Street, which is not to be confused with some seedy street in Soho. The most famous establishment on Basin Street was Mahogany Hall, run by a chubby negro woman called Madame Lulu White. Here, in its most obvious form, we have the contrast and intermingling of black and white, African and European; the contrast declaring itself

in the debasement of what is European. Thus, the house, which has
four stories, five grand parlors on the ground floor, 15 bedrooms on the
upper floors all with private baths, is called Mahogany Hall (i.e. a fine
European house but a black house). Its owner is addressed as though
French, she is Madame White, but though called White she is colored
(as a matter of fact she passed herself off as Creole). She is referred to
in a guide of the period (Souvenir Booklet) as follows,

> As an entertainment Miss Lulu stands foremost, having made
> a life-long study of music and literature. She's well-read and
> one that can interest anybody and make a visit to her place a
> continued round of pleasure.

[W]e see her set up an attraction within the context of European
culture . . . the magnificence of the house (in fact a rather brassy and
gaudy magnificence, gross copies of so-called finest European taste),
the pseudo-culture of its hosts, is all in aid of the various satisfactions
of prostitution. Mahogany Hall was not a lone exception. All the top
establishments were structured by these values . . . [T]he Arlington is
referred to in the famous Blue Book (nothing to do with Wittgenstein),

> The wonderful originality of everything that goes to fit out a
> mansion makes it the most attractive ever seen in this or *the old
> country*. Within the great walls of this mansion will be found
> the work of great artists from Europe and America.

Other establishments were run by Emma Johnson, known as the
Parisian Queen of America (to rape the Queen of Paris) and the Count-
ess *Willie* Piazza, where *Jelly Roll* Morton played piano (*Willie* and *Jelly
Roll* both being expressions referring to the penis).

The significance of these establishments is neatly summarized by
Clarence Williams talking in Hentoff's *Hear Me Talkin' to Ya,*

> And the girls would come down dressed in the finest evening
> gowns, *just like they were going to the opera.* Places like that were for
> rich people, mostly white.

These brothels for the rich were not exclusively inhabited by colored prostitutes. Many white females were also employed. This would have had a different significance from the colored girl parading in European finery, but it obviously fitted into the overall project. It is revealing to emphasize how different was the general sexual fantasy life of the period, as served by these establishments, compared with contemporary sexual fantasy. Sex in New Orleans, during this period, was far removed from the allure of kinky boots, Spider Woman and PVC. Even at the lower end of the New Orleans sex industry the style of sexual fantasy drew on the same sources. Thus, Louis Armstrong describes the girls standing outside their "cribs" dressed in "fine and beautiful negligees," in other words apparelled in erotica which worked through the associations of Europe and high class.

The top brothels were not the nests in which jazz was hatched. The music for these establishments was provided by piano players. They were known as *professors* of the piano, thus underlining the connection with European culture. Bands were not part of the setting because they were too obviously noisy and disruptive. There was no loud playing. The piano because of its bulk was property within property. It did not belong to the streets or the marching bands, and consequently, in the history of jazz, it had, at the beginning, a separate development. It is for this reason that early black playing of the piano expresses itself in compositional music, like rag-time, whereas in jazz proper we have to wait until Ellington for this to come about. The early, colored piano players were much closer to legitimate music than the instrumentalists in the street marching bands and dance bands, although this division was not absolute, as is evidenced by the different status of various instruments in the bands (e.g. the violin and clarinet were more closely associated with legitimate music than the other instruments). The piano comes into jazz, as jazz leaves the streets and enters the interiors. This movement is not simply the jazz band becoming sedentary, it is the influence of the jazz idiom and integral and attendant social attitudes upon the piano-players. One of the clearest expressions of this intersection is in the development of boogie woogie, where the left hand takes up the function of the guitar's rhythmic chording while the right hand fulfills the piano tradition of filling in so as to provide a total event.

I have now said something about the social context in which a certain project was lived out. A set of simplifying contrasts helps to clarify my meaning. Being white, as encapsulated in New Orleans social experience, was *bringing blackness into whiteness,* and thereby obtaining some release from being white, but at the same time *not being black* and remaining white. The project was contradictory, it was to be white, but not be white and to be black but not to be black (all of this from the standpoint of those who were white), it was to *bring blackness into whiteness as a whiteness* but at the same time *that which entered as a whiteness had to be a blackness.* We might say all of this constitutes the *American setting* or, at least the white American setting. The European grip on America is not strong but for a while a rather garbled version of European style is an inspiration, especially with certain powerful social classes. The American experience is the way in which this grip is gradually dismantled. Europe is a fantasy, and in the fantasy Europe is "debased" and this is central to being American. This can be represented in economic terms for American capitalism as the powerhouse, which is the ultimately effective destroyer of the pervasiveness of European culture. But all of this, at present, from the standpoint of white Americans. What is needed is an account of this complex from the other side. To approach this I shall return to an adjunct of my main enterprise, that adjunct being the formation of jazz.

In schematic form to be black is to be committed to double dissembling. First there is *the being black,* but the having *to appear as white* though revealing blackness through the white pose. This is the demand white society makes on black. The demand, however, is twofold. It is the demand that what *is* black *makes itself white* through dutiful behavior (dutiful, white laboring classes) but that it remains black, i.e. slave, third-class citizen, non-equal. This demand is the exploitation of the blacks' productive capacity. Secondly, there is the more seductive demand (seductive to those demanding) that the excitement and release of blackness be offered through a disguise of whiteness. The black then *dissembles whiteness to have his blackness exploited,* but this is the external demand, and what we need to specify is how the demand is interiorized. It is interiorized *by dissembling the dissembling.* That is to say, the negro makes bland naivety at imitation indistinguishable, at an interpersonal level, from cynical mockery. If there is an awareness of this duplicity there is a tendency for whites to connive at it, because the desired object *blackness* is not simply shades of Africa and savagery, but the send up of uptight whiteness (this it seems to me is a contagious cultural influence).

If all this sounds like an analysis of the Black and White Minstrel Show, it should be remembered that Minstrelsy was very popular at this time, and it was a context in which all these contrasts and ambiguities were played out in stark caricatures. For instance, the walk around at the conclusion of a Minstrel show involved the Cakewalk, which was socially acknowledged as an impudent imitation of European, good posture and correct walking (of course we all move like negroes now, you know, "float like a butterfly, sting like a bee"). The blacked up whites also celebrated the negroes' phallic potential. Thus, they sang of being able to bend trees until they had humps like camels, or of their being able to pull a steamboat out of the river with their fishing rods, or of how they could sail down the Mississippi on the backs of alligators which turned into sea serpents, which they then rode for miles underwater without breathing. Apparently when one of these minstrels found his entrance to a river blocked by a giant catfish he simply sailed his boat right at its mouth and turned it inside out (how could any woman resist?). For the negro then, the dissembling whiteness was made in the form of dissembling the dissembling. To be a negro was to be two-faced. The formation of jazz is one important area in which we see this happening.

In the work songs and early blues we are dealing with material which, as all experts accept, was designed to be ambiguous. There is the meaning of the song which is acceptable to the European overseer, and there is the sardonic, send-up meaning (sometimes clandestine message) which delights the singers. An attitude is being bred here. It is that of not meaning what you say, and *living to say what you don't mean*, while at the same time implying what you mean and *living to imply meaning*. Success as a negro amongst negroes is measured by your success at dissembling. The Blues makes light of suffering so as to underline it. In the early jazz the perfectly acceptable European melody appears to be present, and to be holding the piece together, but something else is intertwined within it, which is something saying something else. Here, we are dealing with what is now called "improvisation," but in the early days of jazz it was known to everybody as *"faking."* (Perhaps we have run full circle when we get to Coleman Hawkins wondering whether or not Ornette Coleman might be faking and thus might not be for real.)

In the early jazz the improvisation feeds off the melody and its harmony. In this way the acceptable statement is transformed. European standards of strict tempo are evaded, with the accents coming off the beat and the stressing of weak beats. This produces a music which is shifty and evasive rather than open and straightforward. I often feel that musicians brought up on classical music who, when trying to play jazz, meet insuperable difficulties do so because their training has been one of always trying, honestly and openly, to be in the right place at the right time. In a lot of jazz you have got to let things slip a bit only to redeem yourself at the last moment, like the clown on the tightrope. The important thing is, according to European standards, to be in the wrong place, but to know how to get back in line (note how Charlie Parker is revered for his extraordinary capacity for doing just that). Here is the source of the sense of release that the early jazz offers; i.e. a release from an on-the-go, goal-orientated, rule-bound, repressive consciousness. In this connection the attraction of primitive Africa and African rhythm seems more a cultural image surrounding the music than a feature of its intentional content. We have, in the music, the standards and the slipping from them, and for the musician, I am suggesting, the important thing is the living out of the ambiguity.

There is one other very important predisposing factor for the way in which the black response to white society shapes itself in the living project of making jazz, and that is the fact of the frequent making of music by black males for the social intercourse of white males and colored females. Many books covering this period refer to black masculinity or "manliness" being under threat in the Southern social situation. I'm not sure I really understand what this means, but, certainly, the subsidiary role of entertainer, at these functions, would explain the pro-

duction of a concealed though ribald irony. For reasons stated this ribald element was not unwelcome to the audience. Marothy provides a
concrete illustration of this in discussing glissandi or slurs in jazz,

> The glissando effects (whose actual significance is naturally
> not restricted to the comic) produces a unanimously comic im-
> pact on the bourgeois audience, because here an excessive sen-
> timental expressivity and also its reversal were clearly to be
> observed.

. . . The theme of jazz musicians passing ironic musical comment
on the prelude to miscegenation is one that outlives the New Orleans
period. The Cotton Club where Ellington was resident for all those
years was based on the appeal of sexual fantasy surrounding the cou-
pling of blacks and whites. Marshall Stearns in *The Story of Jazz* describes
a typical tableau.

> The floor shows at the Cotton Club, which admitted only
> gangsters, whites and negro celebrities, were an incredible
> mishmash of talent and nonsense which might well fascinate
> both sociologists and psychiatrists. I recall one where a light-
> skinned and magnificently muscled negro burst through a
> papier maché jungle onto the dance floor, clad in an aviator's
> helmet, goggles, and shorts. He had obviously been "forced
> down in darkest Africa," and in the center of the floor he came
> upon a "white" goddess clad in long golden tresses and being
> worshipped by a circle of cringing "blacks." Producing a bull
> whip from heaven knows where, the aviator rescued the blonde
> and they did an erotic dance. In the background, Bubber Miley,
> Tricky Sam Nanton, and other members of the Ellington band
> growled, wheezed, and snorted obscenely.

I am now in a position to declare my main point with more obvious
intelligibility. To begin an exploration of jazz with the presupposition
that it is an art, or is a music of "high aesthetic value" (the latter claim
is typical of books on jazz, reflecting, I suspect, the actual borderline
status of jazz) where one is committed to these values, prevents one

from feeling jazz as hostile to oneself and a rejection of oneself, but, at the same time, feeling it as an undermining of oneself by being a release from oneself. Prevented from finding this interaction of objectives one fails to locate the white presence in early jazz. Early jazz is as much made out of white, commercial demands of black musicianship as it is made out of black musicianship itself. Jazz is a commercial music from the beginnings. It is not as though the commercialization of jazz only gets under way with the Original Dixieland Jazz Band and beyond. It is true that as the record and radio industries develop so certain concepts of jazz are spread by the abstract hand of capitalism, and that prior to this commercialization is under more concrete control. This isn't the difference between folk and commercial music, any more than the difference between the New Orleans underworld and Capone's Chicago is the difference between folk culture and muscular capitalism. Being a musician in New Orleans was to have a trade, like cigar making or carpentry. If not full-time it was a supplement to one's income. Even the playing at funerals, for the various lodges and secret societies, was on a commercial basis, and the music only became "hot" (as they used to say of early jazz) after the band had been paid and they were on their way back to town.

The social perceptions of jazz as art have been various both in location and motive. In trying to bestow honors on jazz they have failed, as far as previous forms of jazz music are concerned, to understand its intentional practice and thus its significance in its own social context. Of course, as I have tried to suggest, the application of art theology to jazz has often taken place on the basis of self-deception. The description "art" has often been the cloak under which jazz has been contemplated for its actual significances. However, again for various reasons, these actual significances have undergone large transformations through contact with the theoretical practices of bourgeois society. The net effect has been the absorption of jazz and its history into the fringes of the art process in society. Perhaps the fact that jazz has been anti-European, anti-white, anti-bourgeois, anti-art accounts for its peripheral rather than central position (i.e. as something difficult to integrate into the art tradition). With the absorption of jazz into the art process has come the decreasing significance of jazz as a catalyst for popular, mass experience. Moreover, through this identification the jazz process has run itself into a cul-de-sac. The art interpretation has not sprung from the clear perception of unprejudiced, morally sympathetic minds, but has grown out of the social needs of specific social groups and from the way these needs have meshed together. It has proffered misunderstandings of jazz, and has led to the death of jazz as popular experience and to its decline as any kind of developing social process. In other words there were other possibilities for the jazz process. Its route has been a chosen route, it has been nothing other than the practice of persons. The choices made are explicable and intelligible, but, I venture, it would have been better for the life of jazz if the jazzman's "piss off" response to the "cultural" interest in what he was doing had been meant rather than assumed as a theatrical pose within the "cultural context." Art is a value the masses should resist, not just ignore.

Roger L. Taylor, *Art, an Enemy of the People.* (Atlantic Highlands, NJ: The Humanities Press, 1978) 89–155.

THE WORD JAZZ IN ITS PROGRESS toward respectability has meant first sex, then dancing, then music. It is associated with a state of nervous stimulation, not unlike that of big cities behind the lines of war . . .

By 1926 the universal preoccupation with sex had become a nuisance. (I remember a perfectly mated, contented young mother asking my wife's advice about "having an affair right away," though she had no one especially in mind, "because don't you think it's sort of undignified when you get much over thirty?") For a while bootleg Negro records with their phallic euphemisms made everything suggestive, and simultaneously came a wave of erotic plays—young girls from finishing-schools packed the galleries to hear about the romance of being a Lesbian and George Jean Nathan protested. Then one young producer lost his head entirely, drank a beauty's alcoholic bath-water and went to the penitentiary. Somehow his pathetic attempt at romance belongs to the Jazz Age, while his contemporary in prison, Ruth Snyder, had to be hoisted into it by the tabloids—she was, as *The Daily News* hinted deliciously to gourmets, about "to cook, *and sizzle, AND FRY!*" in the electric chair.

By this time contemporaries of mine had begun to disappear into the dark maw of violence. A classmate killed his wife and himself on Long Island, another tumbled "accidentally" from a skyscraper in Philadelphia, another purposely from a skyscraper in New York. One was killed in a speak-easy in Chicago; another was beaten to death in a speakeasy in New York and crawled home to the Princeton Club to die; still another had his skull crushed by a maniac's axe in an insane asylum where he was confined. These are not catastrophes that I went out of my way to look for—these were my friends; moreover, these things happened not during the depression but during the boom.

In the spring of '27, something bright and alien flashed across the sky. A young Minnesotan who seemed to have had nothing to do with his generation did a heroic thing, and for a moment people set down their glasses in country clubs and speakeasies and thought of their old best dreams. Maybe there was a way out by flying, maybe our restless blood could find frontiers in the illimitable air. But by that time we were all pretty well committed; and the Jazz Age continued; we would all have one more.

The Jazz Age had had a wild youth and a heady middle age. There was the phase of the necking parties, the Leopold-Loeb murder (I remember the time my wife was arrested on Queensborough Bridge on the suspicion of being the "Bob-haired Bandit") and the John Held Clothes. In the second phase such phenomena as sex and murder became more mature, if much more conventional. Middle age must be served, and pajamas came to the beach to save fat things and flabby calves from competition with the one-piece bathing-suit. Finally skirts came down and everything was concealed. Everybody was at scratch now. Let's go—

But it was not to be. Somebody had blundered and the most expensive orgy in history was over.

Now once more the belt is tight and we summon the proper expression of horror as we look back at our wasted youth. Sometimes, though, there is a ghostly rumble among the drums, an asthmatic whisper in the trombones that swings me back into the early twenties when we drank wood alcohol and every day in every way grew better and better, and there was a first abortive shortening of the skirts, and girls all looked alike in sweater dresses, and people you didn't want to know said "Yes, we have no bananas," and it seemed only a question of a few years before the older people would step aside and let the world be run by those who saw things as they were—and it all seems rosy and romantic to us who were young then, because we will never feel quite so intensely about our surroundings any more.

F. Scott Fitzgerald, *The Crack-Up*, Edmund Wilson, ed., (New York: New Directions, 1947) 16, 18–19, 21–22.

Pre-Bop Swing

L ike the "Jazz Age," the "Swing Era" was an artificial identity used to target an essentially white middle-class youth market into consuming swing band records, attending dances and concerts, and buying into an identity commensurate with the commercial culture of pop music. That culture had become a well-integrated industry whose extensions and affirmations were circulated and recirculated through radio, recordings, magazines, and movies (including the short-lived "soundies," filmed performances of hit records or records needing promotion, displayed on jukeboxes specially built and more expensive to operate). Tangential but equally important style-related markets developed. Desirability was transmitted through peer-culture manifestations and advertising in magazines directed at teenagers, a category in the process of becoming a commodity archetype, entering into full marketability at the end of World War II.

As in the Jazz Age, the "Kings" of swing were not African-American players and arrangers like Fletcher Henderson, who wrote many of Benny Goodman's most distinctive charts, but first-generation white Americans born of immigrant parents: Benny Goodman, Glenn Miller, and Artie Shaw. Goodman was an odd symbol to define an epoch for WASP youth jitterbugging down theatre aisles. Goodman's roots in rowdy *shtetl*-based *klezmer* dance music, often evident in his and Ziggy Elman's improvisations.

This was also the period of Duke Ellington's most ambitious work, of Fats Waller's exuberantly casual pianistic brilliance and wry foolery on network radio. Count Basie's band, a swing machine from Kansas City, was rumored to be one of the lesser units in an incredible upsurge of creativity and invention occurring nightly in that city. This period, associated with juggernaut white swing bands, was also one of brilliantly intricate and eloquent small group jazz. This accelerated moment between wars shared the binary events of boogie-woogie's basic, propulsive, obsessive energy and the stunning (often unfathomable) genius of Art Tatum's solo piano virtuosity—a transitional period marked both by progress and re-creation, of impressionistic European harmonies refigured to express jazz expansionist borrowings and spine-scraping honking party music. Two clear options for tenor saxophone expression were offered by Coleman Hawkins and Lester Young, a preview of the Hot versus Cool ideologies spawned after World War II in the aftermath of Bebop's cyclone.

Like the Jazz Age, a product of and for middle-class white consumer culture, the Swing Era has been replayed over the decades in movies, record reissues, and on forums of TV nostalgia as time-widened divas (thrushes, chick singers) sing anthems associated with their historic participation in monumental hitdom, fronted by young and elderly uniformed musicians moving their horns back and forth in unison for geriatric dancers on the dance floor speckled by spangles of light rocketing off the glass-chipped globe above them. A nostalgia for those to whom the moment belonged and to successive generations convinced via mass mediation of Swing's socio-historic cohesion. The music becomes the emblem of an era that, after years of merchandising, is all one has to know of American cultural life at the edge of a World War.

Like any durable tale, it's easy to remember in its essentials, becoming cultural truth continually reproduced in so many reassuring modes, continually refined, simplified into a shadowless domain of Technicolor utopian nostalgia. Like any telling, it's a version turned into an institution, a desk on a floor of the culture bureaucracy, manufacturing mementos of itself as belief-sustaining memos for the disciples. Frank Mathias' memoir of playing with a local swing band, the Kentucky Kavaliers, is particularly trouble-free, reading like a movie novelization. My childhood memories of the Swing Era came after the fact. My first hearing of the Benny Goodman 1941 Carnegie Hall concert was in the fifties when it was "discovered" and issued in the new 12" LP format. The movies of the fifties shaped my mythic sense of the Swing Era: the serene Technicolor Glenn Miller epic with Jimmy Stewart as mild-mannered innovator Miller and June Allyson as his love-saint wife. Somewhat more testy, yet equally happy-ending inevitable, was the bio-pic of Benny Goodman starring Steve Allen as the introverted musician only able to express his "real" self through the licorice stick. Along the way, such delirious awfulness as *The Gene Krupa Story* with gum-chewing, reefer-sucking Sal Mineo as the drum-driven Krupa.

Jazz as a film subject has been essentially a reiteration of white sentiment, distance, and mythopoetic tendencies (curiously neither im-
proved nor transcended by African-American Spike Lee's recent *Mo'
Better Blues*). The divisive function of racism as a practice was filtered
out of the celluloid myth-stream dream of jazz. The fact of black was
presented in stereotypes of the simple-minded, servile, therefore harmless darkie, or the sleekly sexual, sinister hep cat, veiled in code of
language and movement, dangerous. One of the most durable jazz
presences in film was Louis Armstrong who, over the decades, appeared
in a variety of disguises—cannibal, bartender, Crosby's bug-eyed
companion in an abandoned house, barefoot on a cotton bale. A monumental smile as if pushing into some unknown gravity; his rumbling
voice talking or singing or laughing, gargling crunchy gravel, his instant
sweat and big, white handkerchief polishing his smile. Everpresent on
film, radio, or television, Armstrong remained a smiling, shining,
ebullient cipher everyone knew.

—DM

JAM, JIVE AND JELLY ARE THREE WORDS that can be found in the *Big Book of Swing* word dictionary. However, to save you the trouble of looking now, here's what they mean:

Jam is ad-lib, improvised music—in essence, it's jazz inspiration at the moment of playing; it is, in the opinion of many music critics, the life-blood of Swing.

Jive is Harlem talk, an inspired language that has contributed unique nuances and shades of meaning to our native vernacular.

Jelly means "on the cuff," "for free," something for nothing.

These three words all tie together in explaining the contribution of the American Negro to American music. Born of slavery and of limited economic opportunity, his access to music was difficult. There was singing, of course. He had a natural instrument for that, the voice. But to get a horn or a drum or piano required money. Then, assuming that this was acquired, getting a teacher was still a more difficult problem. Musicians were few and far between. Thus, he found the path to music strewn with handicaps. It was necessary, in order to get the wherewithal, borrow, to be "on the cuff." It was only natural, when musical education was highly informal and catch-as-catch-can, that improvisation and experimentation should occur. Here was the basis of what was later to be called jelly and jam. And out of the work of untutored, self-instructed musicians—improvising, living "on the cuff"—came the tendency to devise new words, new terms, new expressions that would give the mind images of the new experiences and a new way of life. This was the beginning of jive talk.

Swing was mothered in New Orleans over half a century ago. Music was a way to make a living and that city became the "home of the blues."

The Negro could seek adventure and escape from hard realities if he was a musician. He could get "up North." Homemade instruments were widely used. After a youngster had managed to earn a few dollars through his playing on one of these, he wandered around among the hock, swap and junk shops until he found a second-hand instrument. When he played the "blues," he came by them naturally. They were an obvious by-product of his environment; yet, with it all, the music proved that nothing could blot out his instinctive joy of living, his ability to laugh as well as cry. His music was eloquent evidence.

Love of music traveled from father to son.

The jazz tradition grew. Small combinations were formed. They would play for hours without music, "jamming" spirituals and other melodies they had been taught by their parents. Some played in restaurants. Others trouped with traveling shows.

From their midst have come some of the greatest men and women of Swing.

The music has been rough and loose, full of spirit and originality. It has been easy-going, loud, possessed of a heavy, steady beat. It has been packed full of improvisation. It has told the story of the Negro, his trials and sufferings, his laments and his laughter—and it has told the story in a style that is uniquely that of a people possessed by a profound musical and emotional heritage.

In the world of popular music, of Swing, the Negro has thrived and has earned for himself an eminent place. He is known, respected, beloved. His playing, singing, composing, arranging is enjoyed by millions of Americans of all races and creeds. From New Orleans his music went upward and Eastward to New York, to Harlem, to radio, recordings and the screen. Every entertainment medium has felt the impact of his work, has gained from his contributions, has been able to offer more to more people because of his genius for starting with his ingenuity and elaborating it into the music that folks dance by.

Bill Treadwell, *The Big Book of Swing,* (New York: Cambridge House Publishers, 1946) 37.

I WALKED DOWN AVENUES AND IN THE SIDE STREETS; when I grew tired, I sat down in the squares; nothing could happen to me. And if my feeling of security was not absolutely serene, it was on account of that fear in the hearts of people whose skin was of the same color as mine. If some rich businessman is frightened when he ventures into sections where people go hungry, that is understandable: he walks in a world which does not accept his own and which may triumph over it someday. But Harlem is a society on its own, with its middle class and its proletariat, rich and poor, unmelded in some revolutionary movement, wishing to integrate themselves with America, not to destroy it. These people will not suddenly roll forward in a flood heading for Wall Street; the unreasonable fear they inspire must be the reverse side of some hatred or remorse. Clamped to the heart of New York, Harlem weighs on the good conscience of the white people in the same way that original sin does on that of the Christian.

Among men of his own race, the American cherishes a dream of good humor, goodwill and friendship and even puts these virtues into practice. But they wither at the gates of Harlem. The average American, so anxious to be in harmony with the world and with himself, knows that beyond these barriers he assumes the hated features of the oppressor and the enemy; and it is this appearance which strikes terror into him. He knows himself to be hated, and this thorn in his conciliatory heart is more unbearable than any concrete danger. And all the white men who have not the will and courage to work for fraternity try to deny the very existence of Harlem and forget about it. It is not a threat to the future, but a wound from which they are suffering right now. It is an accursed city, a city where they are cursed, and, in fact, it is themselves they are afraid of meeting at the street corners. Because I am white, this curse weighs heavily on me also, no matter what I may think or say or do. I dare not smile at the children in the squares, nor do I feel I have a right to wander in the streets where the very color of my eyes typifies injustice, arrogance and hate.

It was more on account of this moral uneasiness than of fear that I was glad Richard Wright was accompanying me to the Savoy tonight; I should feel less suspect. He came to fetch me at the hotel, and I noticed he was not looked on kindly by the people in the lobby; if he were to ask for a room here, he might be told that there were no more available. We dined at a Chinese restaurant downtown, for it was likely they would refuse to serve us uptown. Wright lives in Greenwich Village with his wife, who is white and comes from Brooklyn, and she told me that when she walks in their neighborhood with her little girl, she hears the most unflattering remarks. While we were searching for a taxi, people looked darkly at this Negro accompanied by two white women; there were taxi drivers who flatly refused to stop. After that, how could

I hope to mingle quietly in the life of Harlem? I felt a kind of stiffness that made me feel guilty.

While Wright was buying tickets at the entrance to the Savoy, two sailors called out to Ellen and me, as sailors the world over call out to women at the entrance to dance halls, yet I felt embarrassed as never before; I should have to be offensive or else equivocal. But Wright, with a word and a smile, arranged everything; a white man would never have found just the right word and the right smile, and his intervention, though natural and simple, would only have aggravated my embarrassment. I climbed the steps with a light heart: Wright's friendship, his presence at my side, seemed to absolve me tonight.

The Savoy is a huge American dance hall, and in no way exotic. On one side the floor is bounded by a wall against which the band is placed; on the other side are boxes with tables and chairs, and beyond is a kind of hall like a hotel lobby. The floor is carpeted, and there are people sitting in armchairs, looking bored; they are non-drinking customers; they pay only to enter, and in the interval between dances women knit as though at a country dance. We sat in one of the boxes, and Wright put a bottle of whiskey on the table; the whiskey is not sold, but patrons can bring it; we ordered soda water, drank and looked on. There was not a single white face. Although this place is as open to visitors as Lenox Avenue, only a few jazz enthusiasts and foreigners feel the urge to venture there from downtown.

Most of the women were young, in simple skirts and short pullovers, but their high-heeled shoes had sometimes the look of cloven hoofs; the light or dark tan of their skin suits their bare legs better than nylon stockings; many were pretty, but, above all, each was alive. How different from the strained coldness of white Americans. And when these people dance, their animal vitality is not choked by the armor of Puritan virtue, and you understand how sexual jealousy can enter into the hatred that white men in America carry within themselves. However, only a small percentage of lynchings, riots, etc., have a pretext of sexual basis. Although envy goes even further, it is said freely and without spite: "Those people are freer and happier than we." There is some truth in this. What gaiety, what life and freedom in all this music and dancing! It struck me even more in this dance hall, which had about it something of home and everyday life.

In Paris, when Negroes dance with white people in the rue Blomet, they are too self-conscious. But here they are among themselves; they have worked all day and have come in search of amusement with their boy-friends; they do not aim at creating an effect. Many of the young women belong to decent families and probably go to church on Sunday morning. They dance simply and in a way natural to them; one must relax completely and be possessed by the music and rhythm of jazz; and it is also this relaxation which gives vent to dreaming, emotions, naturalness to a degree unknown to the majority of Americans.

Of course, the prejudiced pick an argument here: why should one try to change the conditions for Negroes if they are happy and absolutely free? It is the old argument of capitalists and planters: it is always the workers, the natives who are happiest and most free. Although the oppressed escape the power of the idols which the oppressors have set up for themselves, this privilege is not sufficient to justify oppression.

I listened to the band, I looked at the dancers, drank whiskey; I was beginning to like it. I was feeling fine. The Savoy is one of the biggest dance halls in New York, that is to say one of the biggest in the world; there was something very satisfying in this. And the band is also perhaps the best in the world; at all events, nowhere else does it sound more authentic; the truth is there in the dancing, in the heart, in the whole life of the assembled people. When I listened to a dance band at home, when I saw Negroes dancing, the perspective was never altogether true; it suggested something different, a reality which might attain to greater fruition and of which it was but a doubtful reflection. But tonight I felt its message, I touched on something which was linked to nothing but itself: I had emerged from the cave. From time to time I felt the fullness of spirit in New York which contemplation of a pure idea gives to a freed personality; that was the greatest miracle of my journey, and it was never more dazzling than today.

April 11th
I showed N. the Bowery, the Jewish neighborhood and Chinatown. We went to have cocktails with our friends, the L.'s, and, after dinner in a

French restaurant, A. E. took us to hear Sidney Bechet and his saxophone on Fifty-second Street. He is one of the last musicians to play
in the pure, New Orleans style; he had been famous in America and
had also played in France, but in Paris he killed another colored musician in a brawl and was in prison for a year, during which his hair
turned white; he was now an old man with a deeply-lined face. A pianist
accompanied him, but the team did not draw, and the night-club was
deserted. There were only three young people at a neighboring table,
listening intently . . . they listened the way people pray.

But Bechet could not have wished for an audience more worthy of
his genius than the woman with the black face and white apron who
appeared from time to time through a door behind the platform. She
was the cook—a stout woman, perhaps in her forties, with a tired look
but with tireless eyes; with her hands flat on her stomach, she strained
toward the music with a kind of religious fervor, and little by little her
tired face was transfigured, her body sketched out a dance rhythm, and
she danced, motionless; she was filled with peace and joy. She had trou-
bles and misfortunes, but now she forgot them, forgot her dish-cloths,
children, and ailments. Without past or future, she was filled with joy,
the music justified the whole of her difficult life, and we felt justified
with her; she danced, rooted to the spot. The smile in her eyes was foreign to white men's faces, where gaiety shows only in a grimace of the
mouth. And, looking at her, one understood the meaning of jazz better
than by listening to Bechet himself.

It is evident that white Americans understand jazz less and less.
They do not make it their daily bread as I had thought. There is a deadly
innovation, called "Music by Muzak," which performs music to order
at any hour of the day. In factories, during working hours, floods of
music are released throughout the workrooms, and every public place
has its jukebox. The American, whether eating, working or resting, wal-
lows in music, even in taxis, thanks to the radio; there are some who
go so far as to carry portable sets, ridiculously cheap to buy.

More serious is the fact that even those who pretend to like real
jazz have made it synthetic, and as Negro musicians can earn their living
only by playing to white audiences, they have to join in this perversion.
When you compare Bechet, the little bands in New Orleans, old Arm-

strong records and Bessie Smith with fashionable jazz, you realize that Americans have emptied this burning music bit by bit of all human feeling and content. Whether it was mourning, sensuality, eroticism, work, hope, joy or sorrow, Negro music always expressed something, and "hot music" was the feverish, passionate form of this expression; the present was exalted in concrete form, that is to say, weighted with some feeling, some situation linked to a past and a future. The Americans turn away, with contempt, from the past. ("What, you're still interested in Faulkner?" a publisher said to me with horror.) The future of the masses lies in the hands of a privileged class, the Pullman class, for whom the joy of enterprise and large-scale creation is a prerogative. Because it is a void, it can express itself only by exterior signs: it must be "exciting." What pleases Americans in jazz is that it expresses the passing moment, but, as this moment is something abstract, they also demand abstract expression; they want noise and rhythm, nothing more. Of course, noise and rhythm can be artfully and scientifically orchestrated in such a way that the present is endlessly reborn from its own death, but the meaning of the old jazz is entirely lost.

A. E. told me that the most modern kind of jazz, "be-bop," shows this divergence even more clearly. Originally, it was "hot music" pushed to extremes, an attempt to express quivering, palpitating life in its most fragile and feverish state. But white people have made of this inner fire an exterior trepidation, and the Negroes have copied them; they have kept only breathless rhythms that no longer have any meaning. Transition into abstraction is not limited to the field of jazz. Again, in picture galleries and while reading certain books by young writers, I was struck by the general character of this phenomenon. Cubism and surrealism are also emptied of their content, and only the abstract pattern remains. These forms which were living languages in Europe, and which were destroyed by their own vitality, are found here, intact again, but embalmed, produced and reproduced mechanically, without people realizing that they have lost their meaning. In this country, so eagerly preoccupied with concrete civilization, the word Abstraction is always on my lips. I must know why, more precisely.

Simone de Beauvoir, *America Day by Day*, Patrick Dudley, trans. (New York: Grove Press, 1953) 36–40, 241–243.

THE SAVOY BALLROOM IS ON LENOX AVENUE and 140th Street, in the dark heart of dark Harlem. It's fabulous and wonderful, and it gets in your blood. If the pale but desperate prose which follows seems impossible to believe, don't blame me. Just try the Savoy yourself once. Stronger men have been carried out of the place, babbling.

I got there late, as is my custom, paid seventy-five cents admission and twenty cents more to have my hat and coat storaged. While I was hurrying up the stairs I heard a battery of brasses blaring "Flat Foot Floogie with the Floy Floy" into infinity. And the first thing I saw, on a huge oblong of a dance floor, was some four hundred black dancers going stark mad. Men were lifting women way up, throwing them down, flinging them over their shoulders, tossing them over their heads, hurling them to arm's length, yanking them back, shaking them like wet mops. The floor was a mass of glazed expressions, grins and teeth and popping eyes. Hands flew out in all directions—waving, flaying, stabbing the air. It was a surrealist's nightmare. As the dancers soared up to delirium they cried out in tongues: "I—*I'm* goin'!" "He-e'll do it!" "Go-o on! Go-o *on!*"

I saw girls grab men around the waist and slide to the floor like epileptic snakes. Maidens clasped hands behind men's necks, moaning with joy, while their feet dragged and their bodies wriggled to the drum-beat. I saw an Amazon in a red sweater get a standing scissors on her enchanted partner, throw her head back til it trailed near the floor, and dance with her arms. A blissful buck heaved his lady across his suspend-ers while she kicked ecstatic rhythms into space. Frenzy ruled that ball-room, and if you think I'm exaggerating you might as well stop reading right now. This is only the beginning.

I noticed a pack of swing-addicts standing in front of the band-stand, in a coma. They were just watching the musicians, paying hom-age to the discords with radiant faces. Another group of bipeds was anchored right in the middle of the dance-floor, closer to the *Sturm und Drang* than anyone else in his (or her) right mind should have been. They yelled, clapped their hands, and shouted encouragement to the black bacchantes, which was ridiculously superfluous. I was sure one of them would be felled by a clout from a flying arm or foot at any moment, but they escaped unscathed. This encouraged me. So I went up to a Nestle-colored gentleman perched on the rail which separates the dance-floor from the recuperating area, and said: "Can I go on the floor without a partner?"

"Whaffo' yo' need a partner?" he asked at once.

"I mean I just want to go on the floor and watch."

"Jes' suit yo'self, Mister."

I thanked him and went onto the floor. He shouted after me, "Jes' suit yo'self, Mister! We all does." I have never forgotten that.

I ducked under a meteoric arm, bounced off a flying leg, and joined the brave little band in the center of the floor. It was like being at the center of a particularly violent tornado. Not more than two feet from me an uninhibited mob broke into a dance oriented around the theme of indigestion: they clawed at their bellies, twisted their faces, and let mocking screams and laughter pour from their throats. Then, at a secret signal and with marvelous precision, they slid into a slow-motion step, so slow it was hard to believe. Then someone clapped hands, someone gave a Tarzan call, and the group went into an acrobatic furor. The whole maneuver ended with the she-devils taking an impulsive hop, skip and jump to their swains' shoulders, gripping the men's necks with their thighs, and laying on with hands—howling all the while. I was bewildered.

There were a few white girls cavorting with gentlemen of the opposite hue, and several white men dancing with tawny-skinned women in lovely gowns. The women, I learned, are hostesses—three passionate dances for a quarter. They were gorgeous creatures and they carried themselves regally. One of them wore a white rose in her hair: she looked like a princess from the Malay. I saw a sad little Filipino shuffling with a girl whose color was bituminous. They were very serious about it; they seemed all weighted down by problems. I saw middle-aged burghers from Harlem hopping around in a fever, hunting for their youth. One sepia-toned behemoth made the floor tremble with her prancing, and all the time she gurgled to a tiny man lost in her shade: "You man . . . *you* man . . . you *man!*"

The dancers' clothes were, if anything, more bizarre than their dances. They wore every variety of garb known to modern man, from sweaters to evening gowns. Color goes berserk up at the Savoy and it starts from scratch. Orange, purple and scarlet were in the ascendancy.

Suddenly the music stopped. There was a collective "Yahhh." But before I could catch my breath, a second orchestra, welcomed by a howl from the masses, roared into action. (A banner identified them as "Christopher Columbus Swing Crew.") A drum announced the beat with a deep boom-boom-boom. The extroverts stood around for a moment, intent, immobile, letting the rhythm get in their blood. Then someone yelled—and hell broke loose all over again. A man seized a woman with a Comanche whoop and began to twirl as if he believed in perpetual motion. A couple began to wrestle. Two coryphees went into a cakewalk. Couples joined the alarming cotillion until the floor looked like a chiropractors' brawl. One opaque Nijinsky grabbed his partner in an admirable half-Nelson and hauled her down the length of the floor (two-thirds of a block), twisting her from side to side while her heels beat a tattoo on the hardwood. It was beautiful.

Then a long ecstatic "YEeaaahHH!" sounded, and an answering "OOooohHH!", and bodies flamed into action, and red ties and orchid dresses swung through the mass of black faces. The brasses crashed out, the drum did jungle tom-toms, and hundreds of bodies twirled and leapt and spun. I had a premonition that if any of it stopped, for a single instant, the whole world would fall to pieces.

Leonard Q. Ross, *The Strangest Places*, (New York: Harcourt, Brace and Co., 1939) 179–184.

1930 Jazz

rocked me in my cradle, While Papa was in
    the madhouse, Mama
      on welfare,
Billie was at the Savoy with Count
    Basie singin' Swing it, Brother
Swing and I kicked my bootied feet
    in time to Teddy Wilson.
Papa, walk Tremont Street again
    in the fog, let your bald head shine
      like a full moon
        between bars.

Stop this diddle daddle.
　　There is time for nonsense, romance
　　　　and forgetting.
　　Deep rhythm stimulates me, hot
　　　rhythm captivates me,
　　　　　to the next fix,

New York, Boston, San Francisco.
　　The scene widens as the years
we walk with a cane. Dont stop
　　　to diddle daddle, stop
　　　　　this foolish prattle.
Come on, swing me Count.
　　Swing it, brother swing.

[1967]

John Wieners, *Cultural Affairs in Boston: Selected Poetry and Prose 1965–1985*, Raymond Foye, ed. (Santa Rosa, CA: Black Sparrow Press, 1988) 76.

I WANT TO WRITE THIS DOWN BEFORE JOE GOES. Joe Turner, I mean. There was never any singer in my life like Big Joe, as the albums used to call him, or what was that other word they used about him? BOSS of the Blues? Words of that kind. But whatever it was that he was called by promoters, jacket-writers, cliché-loving pop writers, it was the sound of his voice that got to me in the most delicious sense when I was about 17 years old and went off to the University of North Carolina as a be-wildered freshman.

Somehow it was down there, in the Southland, the northern part of it, that Joe's voice began to penetrate me. This was in 1939, 32 years ago, and I feel that my being in the south when I first heard Joe, al-though North Carolina and especially Chapel Hill was a most liberated place, that the memory and flavor of Negro life in the south helped make Joe's sounds that much more poignant to me. At any rate I fell in love with that voice when I first heard it singing blues on what must have been early 78 rpm Atlantic labels. Later, when people began to get very sophisticated about blues singing, I often heard it said that Joe was an urban blues singer who toned down some of the harsher, rougher aspects of authentic blues. I imagine there's some truth in that, but it never undid what his voice had done for me; once he had planted those sounds with his particular brand of mellowness into my ear and into the rest of me, nothing that could be said about him could erase the memories, or stop that voice from echoing and re-echoing in my imagination. It conjured up a rolling richness, a flow of nonstop sexy satin, the like of which I had never heard before in any singer black or white.

When I finally met him in the early 60s up at the Apollo Theater in Harlem I almost knew that voice by heart. It was a voice that I fucked to in later life, beautifully, not that I was always beautiful in bed but that it was a beautiful experience, it was a voice that I danced to with black tricks in my tiny pad on E. 10th St., it was a voice that always cheered me up when I heard it. I've heard black maids, housecleaning women, tell me their work went quicker when they heard Joe coming out of the box. The early Joe was, of course, simple blues with its repetitive form, and now that I hear new black voices coming out of the same chant-gospel-blues tradition, opening up the form, getting rid of some of the repetition, I realize that Joe was restricted by that tradition he had inherited perhaps too unquestioningly.

Let's not forget that he was a club performer, not an intellectual, not a musical theorist, a guy hustling for his bread and honey with his voice. Shake that money-maker, Joe! So even though it is the one voice I love above all others out of the contemporary blues tradition, because of the sounds, texture, the lovely humor and passion and inflection that he gets—every time I try to hum a line along with Joe on the record player he always crosses me up because I can never predict which way his voice is going to go, which makes him constantly interesting—I also recognize the corset that he was bound into by the rather set cotton-growing sonnet form that was imposed on him.

I sometimes think Joe's voice will last as long as there are ears. But as blues and black music become ever more complex, the comparative poverty of the form he worked in is going to put black on black, so to speak, that is, it's going to put black marks on a great black voice. Guys like Ray Charles, B. B. King, Junior Wells, Eddie "Cleanhead" Vinson, Howlin' Wolf—god, there are gangs of them, sometimes reach out further in the form than Joe. But nobody ever really struck that exquisite combination of zest and laughing-even-while-it-hurts lust, at least to my particular ear, that Joe was able to do when he sang about rocking some chick in her Hollywood bed, or his boogie-woogie country girl, or the chains of love that bound him, or any of the easy, rolling things that he slid down on and took off on. It's extraordinarily difficult to try to communicate the exact quality of music through uninflected language on the page. But my own existence has been bound up with that of Joe Turner's for a longer time than some of our dead kids in Vietnam ever lived on the planet and I think it's quite an unusual love affair we've been having ever since I was 17 and lost my cherry to him.

Eastern mystics often talk about being centered as my ex-wife, Eleanor Goff, did, a woman who knew dance, the body and music as centrally as anyone I've ever met, and Joe certainly kept his head when a lot of people close to him in spirit lost theirs. Yeah. Even when you hear the quake in his voice for new pussy, a feeling in his voice for a new Cadillac and new vines, heard that unappeasable yen for living sensuously, you always hear the note of reality in the background too. I guess that's what I've always liked so much about him—going all the way with pleasure without doing himself in as Bird did, as Bud Powell did, as so many fanatic preachers of ecstasy in jazz and jump music have finally fallen victim to their own uncontrollable flood of sensuous experience. Joe wanted to live. There was a self-preservational quality about it which kept him moving and if you take blues and then later rock-blues as living history, if that doesn't sound too pretentious, as a chronicle of people's real lives, then Joe's self-preservational streak was not unlike Louie's. They both had to move on and go through all the stages of life—young manhood, middle age, old age—and sing them out as best they could. Louie's powers declined quickly, and I don't see Joe moving ahead soundwise either. I'm just about to get a new out-of-print 1967 album that he did and I'll know better at that point whether he's really taken a step forward in the last five years. I know his ears must be wide open to all the new sounds that are coming up now that we've taken the cover off all of black music, especially black singing music, in this country, and these new sounds must be gassing him. But as to whether he can still translate them into his voice remains an open question for me.

I'm going to close this testimonial to my friend and turntable lover without having heard this album, though. I think it's fitting that I say what I have to say right now for him. But whether or not he's able to break those mechanical formal blues chains that seem more to bind him to me now than ever, now that the forms—what you can do with these—have opened up, whether there was, damnit, a lack of imagination in cracking that mold, though he did remarkable things inside of its boundaries, I still defy anyone to say that it was not a voice unlike any other. Lordy, it stood out—stands out—like a flower of special hue. And when I finally go out on terminal cancer, or whatever new diseases they can dream up, and tell my hip doc to slip me a tab of acid, I also want him to get me one of those little $19 Zenith record players and a stack of Joe Turner's albums and I'll say goodbye sweetly, riding on Joe's wings.

Seymour Krim, *You & Me*, (New York: Holt, Rinehart & Winston, 1974) 133–135, 145–146.

RADIO LISTENERS WHO TUNED IN the Blue Network's Chamber Music Society of Lower Basin Street last Sunday night heard a mammoth left hand beating out the solidest bass in U. S. pianism, a right hand doing fine and jubilant things. The hands were those of the great Thomas Wright ("Fats") Waller, short-time student of Leopold Godowsky and lifelong admirer of James P. Johnson, the great professor of Jamaica, Long Island. Even a tyro in such matters might easily guess what experts have known for years: that Fats Waller is the pay-off in the classic American jazz piano style—full-chorded and hallelujah.

Of late the Waller hands have not been idle. In the motion picture *Stormy Weather*, they caused a battered piano to romp in rare fashion. For the Broadway musical *Early to Bed*, the Waller right hand picked out the tunes. This week, back in Manhattan after a trip to Canada, Fats Waller was cooking up some new numbers.

He has cooked up some good ones before. Among them: "Ain't Misbehavin'," "I've Got a Feelin' I'm Fallin'," "Keepin' Out of Mischief Now." Waller has collaborated with many a lyricist. Some of his best results he turned out with Andy Razaf, his favorite poet next to Long-fellow. During one rewarding session in retreat at Asbury Park, New Jersey, the two men turned out "Zonky," "My Fate Is in Your Hands," and "Honeysuckle Rose" in two hours. Razaf had enticed Waller into his mother's Asbury Park home for a production session away from the nightspots. Says Razaf: "She's a wonderful cook and Fats loves to eat. We had a show to write and I figured that would keep Fats away from the bars. He could set the telephone book to music."

Keeping Tom Waller away from bars is a difficult feat. His capacity for both food and drink is vast. A Waller breakfast may include six pork chops. It is when he is seated at the piano that he most relishes a steady supply of gin. When his right-hand man, brother-in-law Louis Rutherford, enters with a tray of glasses, Tom will cry, "Ah, there's the man with the dream wagon! I want it to hit me around my edges and get to every pound."

That requires a lot of alcohol: Waller is five feet ten and weighs over 270 pounds. That mass helps to account for the great strength of his basses, and makes his playing look as magisterial as it sounds. Whether he plays a stomping "Dinah" or lazy variations on "When My Baby Smiles at Me," no other pianist gives quite his impression of com-manding ease. Musicians he plays with sense it instantly, ease up them-selves.

In 1932 Fats balked the depression with a rapid month in Paris. There his enthusiastic friends included Marcel Dupré, one-time organist of Notre Dame Cathedral. With Dupré, Fats climbed into the Notre Dame organ loft where "first he played on the god-box, then I played on the god-box." In Paris Fats also came into cultural contact with a fellow pianist and expatriate named "Steeplehead" Johnson. Fats got home from the French capital by writing Irving Berlin for funds.

Few who had funds could ever refuse him. With a piano, a bottle of gin, and a hot weather handkerchief, he is one of the most infectious men alive. With his wife Anita and their two musically gifted sons, Maurice, fifteen, and Ronald, fourteen, he lives in an eight-room En-glish brick house in St. Albans, Long Island. The house has a Ham-mond organ, a size B Steinway grand, and an automatic phonograph with fifteen hundred records. Next to Lincoln and FDR, Fats considered Johann Sebastian Bach the greatest man in history.

Once, a dewy-eyed young thing stopped Fats and inquired, "Mr. Waller, what is swing?" Said he: "Lady, if you got to ask, you ain't got it."

Weldon Kees, *Reviews and Essays, 1936–1955*, James Reidel, ed. (Ann Arbor: The University of Michigan Press, 1988) 69–71.

I DID NOT MIND LEAVING CARLISLE as much as I minded leaving what I had going for me in nearby Maysville. This little Ohio River city, thirty miles to the north, had been my birthplace in 1925, and nearly all of my mother's side of the family still lived there. I was related in various degrees to hundreds of people there, including Rosemary Clooney, who had been born in Maysville three years after I was. My mother, Nancy Browning Furlong, had been a Maysville schoolteacher who delayed marriage until she was thirty-five, then married a forty-three-year-old salesman named Charles Mathias who, as a typical drummer of his day, had gone through life unmarried, getting by on a shoeshine and a smile. My younger brother Charles was born in 1928 and that rounded out our family of four. But Maysville now entered my life in a way which would stamp a musical theme on my army career and greatly increase my chances for survival. Late in December, 1942, I received a phone call from Clarence Moore, a dance band leader in Maysville. His band, the "Kentucky Kavaliers," played throughout northeastern Kentucky and southern Ohio. I held the phone in stunned delight as he said he had heard that I was a good sax man—"Could you come and audition with us?" I barely managed to utter a hoarse but happy, "Yes Sir!"

Was I a "good sax man," as Moore said? I did not know. I remembered getting my first tenor sax back when I was twelve years old. My mother had cashed in $120 worth of her World War I war bonds to buy it. Its gold lacquer shimmered in a "red crushed plush" case, the most exciting thing I had ever seen. My identity was soon tied up with it, and I worked hard to win a spot in the Carlisle High School band. At several state contests I was criticized by the judges for "affecting jazz techniques," showing fine talent, but "going astray." I could not help "going astray," for I imitated every great sax man I heard on the radio— Coleman Hawkins, Ben Webster, Flip Phillips, Jimmy Dorsey. Each night I huddled over the Crosley radio at home, more alert to the music than anything I studied at school. My parents sighed, but I sat there, listening and yearning as radio announcers brought me "the great Benny Goodman band from the Hotel Sherman," or "Tommy Dorsey from Castle Farms" or "Glenn Miller from Frank Dailey's Meadowbrook." This was the Swing Era and I was part of it. My generation was part of it, too, but I yearned to play that music myself, to share the work of a sax section as it swung the lovely ballads and exciting jump tunes of the day.

My pulse pounded wildly as I walked in for my audition. The other musicians were seated behind blue stands with *Kavaliers* stenciled on the front. "God," I prayed, "let me pass; let me belong." Moore seated me behind the second tenor parts, kicked the band off, and after several numbers told me I was hired. He was disturbed that I could not double on clarinet but I promised fervently that I would learn to do so "or die trying." A wild elation swept through me as I left the audition. I had everything I wanted.

I returned home in triumph. I was no longer "little Frank," the kid trapped in such a slow growth cycle that the fame and fortune of football and basketball had passed him by. "Are you really going to play with the Kavaliers?" old girl friends asked, but with a delicious new interest in their voices. "Sure," I replied, relishing the questions and the perfume as the sweatered bobby-soxers clustered about me. Questions were blunt. "How much will you make?" June Stewart asked, though all wanted to know. "I get six dollars a dance—that's for four hours—as much as I make working a whole weekend at Krogers!" This caused a ripple of "Gollees!" to run through the crowd. We were all frugal children of the Great Depression, and six hard dollars for four easy hours of work was cause for amazement. But on the sidelines there lurked the males, puzzled now but greening with envy as the former duck began preening himself like a swan!

Most of us can look back to a time of perfect harmony, an unforgettable skein of months when formerly discordant parts of our lives suddenly blend together, as if deftly arranged by a master musician. My life during the first eight months of 1943 fits this description. I had more money than I needed, new friends in every town within range of our band, and complete acceptance in front of every juke box in Maysville. And there were the girls—new ones, lovely ones, interesting ones—clustered like butterflies around those drugstore juke boxes. "Frank, what do you think of that new record over at Kilgus's Pharmacy, you know, the one everybody's talking about—Glenn Miller's 'Moonlight Cocktail'?" I had to have an opinion, for I was a musician, and even if I had never heard the song, I fabricated an answer. "Yeah, that's a great one, typical Miller sax voicing. We'll have it in the Kavalier book real soon." My opinion was usually the last word on the subject. I did not fully realize that there were really two subjects, music being only the first one. "Frank, you just know so much; why don't we walk over to Kilgus's and listen to it—together." This second subject, romance, was part of the music, at least for the girls. It was all one subject for them. I abandoned all dry analysis of chord structure and embouchures in such pleasant situations, content to sense the soft, sweatered presence beside me in the booth, sip cokes together, or get up and jitterbug in a flash of bobby sox and saddle shoes. Nevertheless, music was a separate subject for musicians, and I was studying and practicing hard to guarantee my spot in the band.

Gradually I learned to double; at least I could play the clarinet parts on most of the printed "stock" arrangements. Tough ones, like the clarinet chorus on "Josephine," I committed to memory. There were thirteen other musicians in the band, and I watched and learned from them. I chuckled when the leader broke up a fight on the dance floor by calling up "The Star Spangled Banner." Everyone, including the fighters, stood at a respectful attention; it was war time, and this clever use of social pressure ended the fight. I learned that "Stardust" would get a slow dance started by forcing couples out on the floor—it was "everybody's song." An experienced leader like Moore knew how to keep a dance going once it started. The trick was to call up sets tailored for each type of crowd, ones that did not wear the band out, and that fit the time and place. A typical "Set" would have two ballads, a waltz, and a "jump" number: "Heaven Can Wait," "Mood Indigo," "The Waltz You Saved For Me," and "White Heat." At least once during a dance we would answer please to "turn the drummer loose!" After a long drum solo, heads would nod knowingly as the crowd agreed that "he sounds just like Gene Krupa!" We were always pleased at this response, for we tried to sound like the big bands of the day. In our segment of the Ohio Valley the dancers expected to hear things they heard on juke boxes, and they wanted them played exactly as they heard them. We obliged them, seeking out stock arrangements based on the originals. I was learning rapidly and piling up experience I could have gained in no other way. If the time ever came when I had to fall back on this experience, I would be ready. The time was not far off.

Frank F. Mathias, *G. I. Jive: An Army Bandsman in World War II.* (Lexington, KY: University of Kentucky Press, 1982) 3–6.

THEIRS WAS NOT THE ONLY FOLK MUSIC in those cotton camps. The many Negro families there added a different musical dimension. Their music deeply impressed young Jim Rob. It is likely they played the only other type of music he had ever heard up to that time. He had heard it since he was old enough to remember anything, from black neighbors near the farm where he was born. Above all, the horns the Negroes played fascinated him. "They generally always had trumpets and guitars, and I will never forget how well they played them." Years after this experience, he combined the frontier fiddles his family played with the instruments the Negroes played in those cotton shanties. "I combined them," he said, "because I've loved horns since I was a little boy."

It was significant that [Bob] Wills learned much of his music style directly from blacks. Many other white musicians learned from them, but generally from afar, via radios or recordings, never really touching their lives, rubbing elbows, sharing their sorrows, joys and poverty working alongside them, and living in their culture as young Jim Rob did. He said he never played with many white children, other than his two sisters and younger brother, until he was seven or eight years old. Negroes were his earliest playmates, and his father enjoyed watching him jig dance with black children. It was a study in coordination and rhythm, especially as both white and black musicians provided the appropriate music. Jim Rob did much more than learn rhythm with the blacks; he got a *feeling* for it, a feeling that enabled him to lay down a beat, create a tempo, and develop patterns for dancing that astounded musicians in his band who were much better trained than himself.

In the cotton camps, the children often competed in jig dancing contests, and both blacks and whites enjoyed listening to the music and watching the dancers. They soon forget their poverty and the hard day's work as the whole camp was swinging. Later in the evening, when things had quieted down and the children were in bed, the sound of a trumpet could be heard coming from one of the Negro shacks, wailing out the blues. Often the Negro women would join the wail of the trumpet or the strains of a guitar and cry out a blues song. These blacks had an endless blues repertory. While working, one of them would begin to hum or sing and before long the whole field would be alive with the sound of the blues. They could sing off and on all day and never sing the same song twice. "I don't know whether they made them up as they moved down the cotton rows or not," Wills said, with a twinkle in his eye and an approving smile on his face, "but they sang blues you never heard before."

Now that blues has become a major influence on popular music and have become more sophisticated than the rural blues Wills admired it is easy to overlook the importance of the blues as a nineteenth- and twentieth-century folk music. In the cotton camps and cotton fields in the early years of this century there were two important strains of American folk music, both rural in origin and development—frontier fiddle music, such as that played by the Wills family, and Negro blues. Young Jim Rob Wills stayed close to his own family's music for the next twenty years; but in less than twenty-five years he bridged the gap between the two folk musics and combined white frontier fiddle music with Negro blues and jazz to develop a music and style of his own. Wills's music was the confluence of these two streams. Before Wills brought them together in the 1930s, both streams underwent some change, as the tributaries of popular and other musics flowed into them. Nevertheless the main streams were basically folk.

Because James Robert became a famous fiddle player, the influence of frontier fiddle music on his career is well known. What is not known, or at least not fully explored and appreciated, is the extent to which Negro folk music later characterized Wills's music. He often told close friends and members of his band, for instance, that he learned a great deal about rhythm from the black cotton pickers. These rhythms became a permanent part of his own music. Still another characteristic Wills and the blacks had in common was the uninhibited way both expressed their souls in music. Later, when their music was heard on radio and recordings, those better trained in music would frown on the "folkish" and "jazzy" way they took liberties with musical rules and played and sang more from feeling than from training.

Wills and the Negroes were themselves in their music, and they expressed a way of life that many Americans wanted to forget existed. In some ways, they were protesting both against society and against formalism in music. Even when they were not aware of this, their music provided an emotional release. In many areas of the American life at that time there was revolt against formalism: Thorstein Veblen in economics; Oliver Wendell Holmes, Jr., in law; Frederick Jackson Turner and Charles A. Beard in history; John Dewey in philosophy and education. There were other revolutionaries in thought and action in the tumultuous Populist-Progressive era. By the 1930s the folk musics of those cotton camps would help change, if not revolutionize, many areas of American music. Smokey Dacus, Wills's first drummer and longtime member of his band, summarized his contribution to American music: "Bob Wills took music out of the straitjacket." If this is too much to say of any one person, it is not suggesting too much to say that Wills's generation, the Jazz Age, did more than any other to remove America's musical straitjacket.

One must guard against making those cotton camps appear romantic and idyllic. There was little romance in the fact that entire families (all who were able and old enough to pull a cotton sack and many who were not) worked twelve to fourteen hours a day in a cotton patch. The shacks were generally cold, vermin-infested, and grossly overcrowded. Doubtless, some of the men who played fiddles, trumpets, and guitars had hands so chapped from wind and weather and cut by sharp edges of cotton hulls they could hardly play. The women who sang the blues probably did it from a blue soul. Their bodies were weary from picking cotton from sunup until sundown. Then they had to cook a meager meal, feed their families, and clean up the shacks. They washed their families' clothes by drawing water from a well, heating it in a washpot outdoors over a wood fire, and scrubbing them on a rubboard. This did more to irritate sores caused by cotton hulls than it did to clean the clothing. Human nature being what it is, there were race problems between whites and blacks (and the Mexicans who were sometimes there), as there are today. Often all the two races had in common was their bigotry, poverty, ignorance, and love of music. At best it was a life of mere survival, and there was very little in those cotton camps that the people who lived in them would have thought romantic. Everyone, black and white, got out as soon as he had the opportunity. Long before these people began to make their voices heard and better their lot through the ballot box in the 1930s, their music had already liberated many of them. Jim Rob Wills, like many others in the South and Southwest, was liberated from the poverty and deprivation of the cotton culture by the folk music he had learned so much about in that culture.

Charles R. Townsend, *San Antonio Rose: The Life and Music of Bob Wills*, (Urbana: University of Illinois Press, 1976) 3–6.

I FIRST MET BENNIE MOYLAN ON THE TRAIN, going to a job in Racine, Wisconsin. His appearance didn't startle me—and at that time I always carried a lot of chip on my shoulder anyway. He was around my height, 5-10", full of face in a lean sort of manner, nice smile. Jack Daly, a guitar player, introduced us.

We were four characters on that job. Moylan played sax, clarinet, a little trumpet, and sang. Jack Daly played guitar, and fooled around a bit on the piano during intermissions. Sleepy Kaplan played drums, myself on piano.

Sleepy really earned that name—talk about a guy moving slow! We'd decided to play cards one night after work; Sleepy said he'd take a shower and be right out. After about an hour of waiting we gave up. But what kills me is the night I called him up for a job, and his dad answered the phone. I asked, "Is Sleepy there?" He answered: "There's nobody slipping here!" in a real heavy Jewish Brogue.

Bennie tried to play tenor sax like Louis was playing trumpet at that time—which was about 1930. He honked on it, got a tone like Pee Wee [Russell] gets on clarinet, only considerably heavier. And he sang beautifully. Crosby reminds me of Bennie, only Bennie was hearing Louis all the time, and that's what would come out of him.

There's not much I can remember about that job in Racine except playing and listening to records and drinking.

After that job in Racine we came back to Chi and Bennie and I would hang out together. I had the use of a small organ—you know, the kind arrangers work out on, or the kind the Salvation Army uses— and I'd become pretty good at it. It's not an easy instrument to play on, with a beat. Bennie and I would stay home, or visit friends, and play. Once we went out on a strip of sand—you could stretch it a bit and call it a beach—and sat and played till we were scared off by the cops.

Time passed—I got a job at a dancing school—that is, a joint where the fellows came to get acquainted or make dates with the gals. The last thing anyone does at a dancing school is worry about the art of dancing. I took Earl Wiley with me on drums, Earl Murphy on banjo, Leroy Smith on clarinet (and he played all the jazz tunes of Oliver and Jelly Roll like you would on trumpet—melody clarinet). When Leroy left us, Bennie joined us. I vaguely remember Wingy [Manone] hanging around, Dave Tough sitting in. The job ended too soon again.

And then Murphy got us a job at a spot about thirty miles out of Chi. A lot of swanky people came there. Someone drove us out there and we played for the boss. We had a band—besides playing as much music as any four pieces I've heard would produce. Bennie sang, Wiley could do a dance, soft-shoe, that would kill us. Murphy sang—and I'd written a song for a gangster that was very popular among that set. And when the boss found out I was the author—I sang plenty too—it was a dirty ditty—we were in. Ask me about it some time when we're alone.

After the audition the boss gave us all we wanted to eat and drink, also $100 to get a car, so we could drive there and back. Oh, yes, we were hired. We got a good salary, all we wanted to eat and drink. That's how it was when we started.

But how we could drink! In a few days the bartenders couldn't take it. So new rules were laid down. A pint of gin when we got there, a pint of gin on the way home; in between a few drinks at the bar. Mind you, we were up there playing when we had to. One night we were all packed up, in the car ready to drive off, when a few of the boss' cronies came in, wanting to hear my song. We got out the banjo and gave it to them right out in the yard, chorus after chorus. And he paid off, and we all split.

But that ride home! Going there we wouldn't fight much about who drove the car we all owned, but coming back everyone was a race track driver. And shortly I developed a bad set of nerves. We had a couple of close calls that I'd like to forget.

One day our place was held up. We were all on the stand playing when it happened. I found out later the hoodlums broke the doorman's head a bit, and ruined the chap's arm just to impress us. And then one of them slid across the dance floor up to the band with a gun pointed at us. "Get off and lay down, face forward." Needless to say, we did.

We'd just drawn fifty bucks to pay the union with, and Bennie had it in his pocket. "Get up!" The band got up. "Empty your pockets!" Then Bennie did something I'll always remember. "Man, we ain't got nothing, we're musicians, we're always broke—man, you know that . . ." The hood sort of laughed and passed us by, but went down the line and took every one else's bank roll. Also, they escorted a couple of girls out of the washroom. Those guys meant business. They also took everyone's car keys. It was a mess. All we could do was step to the bar and drink—on the house. And I wrote another verse to my tune about "Did you ever meet the hold-up man well, into this cafe he ran, pointed his gun, get off the stand." After that the band was really set with the boss; we could have had anything.

But like all good things it came to an end. We started taking advantage a bit; we'd be late, and that would murder the boss. Once we had to lay Bennie off for four days, "rest him up a bit," figuring he'd need the job and would behave when he got back.

So we got Bud Freeman to take his place, just to help us out. But Bud wasn't happy in our sort of band. He heard notes, harmonies, we didn't play. And as for us, well—Bud was no Bennie Moylan. Bud made pretty runs and knew his horn, but Bennie was Louis on Gut Bucket. Bennie honked on his tenor, he had a whiskey tone. He was in a groove that couldn't be mistaken. We sent for Bennie to come back.

Three fellows in the band—all but me—had Irish in them, and you've heard of the fighting Irish. Well, when it got so bad that we took to talking of fighting between ourselves (this all the way home, of course), and when Wiley pushed me through a plate glass door, just while emphasizing a point, I decided I needed a rest. Tut Soper took my place. But pretty soon I was back, too—pretty soon we lost that job.

I worked on a couple more jobs with Bennie. One, during the depression, paid us all $10 a week, and our drinks. And the only reason I mention it is because the second night we were there, the boss called us over and told us we'd have to make other arrangements about the drink department.

Too bad Bennie never recorded. Bennie and I made a few of the ten-cent variety of records while we were in Racine, but they warped on me and though I tried my damndest to dub them, it was impossible.

I believe Bennie died at 27. He was in the hospital but wouldn't stay put; got out of bed saying, "Man, I'm not sick!" He was too strong to stay in bed; but it licked him; Bennie went.

So you want to talk of tenor sax giants—so you go out and hear someone running up and down the scale, or play "Body and Soul," and you say, "Oh, my God!" Well, we said that, ten, fifteen years ago, when you had to be damn good before one of the boys said that about you.

Some time, when you catch Dave Tough drinking and being himself, ask him about Bennie Moylan. Or else ask Earl Murphy. You'll hear about a guy who could make you cry when he sang, and turn around and play some low down music on his sax (rubber bands and strings attached) like you won't hear being played anywhere today.

Art Hodes, "Blues For Bennie" [1944] from *Selections from the Gutter: Portraits from the Jazz Record*, Art Hodes and Chadwick Hansen, eds., (Berkeley: University of California Press, 1977) 32–33.

Roy Eldridge, Little Jazz

A fake ID won't get you
into the Metropole.

That epithetical "little" must've
implied something synecdochial
together with a downright
shortness.

Eldridge was a quintessence:
as Billy Ternent says,
"the guy who could squeeze
anything out of a trumpet."

His playing contains no stunts or slurs.
Each bitten phrase is meted out with specific dignity,
matched to the man's compact decorum.
Where the trumpet blares, architectonic soarings—

the high notes, those saturated chomps and splays,
    occasioned
(in Kenny Clarke, for one) a concomitant reach in rhythm
(the high-hat cymbal
rose in prominence)—

with an aspiration like of the Chrysler Building
pierce the night air.

[The Metropole, of course, is where R. E. played "All Star"
sessions during the 50s—I used to stand outside (under age),
listen & watch under the marquee.]

[1989]

Bill Berkson, *Intent*, vol. 1, # 3, Fall 1989, 27.

MONDAY NIGHT WENT UP TO 52ND ST FOR JAZZ. Heard Bill De Arango's quintet, the guitar player in *Esquire Jazzbook*. He's good, but it's gone to his head, his publicity, I think. Sidney Bechet was across the street and I went in twice, but both times he was not there during a break, and I didn't hear him yet. It was getting late, almost 3 AM, and I went home. Last night went to Eddie Condon's, and heard some good stuff too. Condon is really a commercializer, with ratty eyes and tiny ears, and I don't much like him. But the others were fine. Joe Sullivan, the piano player, plays during the intermissions. He's the one in our Sidney Bechet album that has three piano solos by him, Timothy, and Chimes. Chimes is the best, the one you and I both like. I requested some numbers and got to talking to Sullivan. He was drunk and somehow very pathetic, and he got mad at me over some obscure remark about blues, and asked me what the hell I knew about jazz, and I said only records, and he said you cant know them from records, and was this what he had spent 12 years for? 12 years listening to all the old ones, Hines, and Johnny Dodds and Baby Dodds and Jimmy Noone. I got a big thrill out of hearing him mention those names. I apologized to him and agreed I was just a punk and had never heard them except on records, and told him how it made me feel to hear those names that I had on all my record albums and loved so well and that I didn't blame him for getting pissed off. It ended up I bought him a drink and we shook hands and he started calling me J.J. and I promised him an autographed first edition of *Eternity*, in about two years. He was like a kid, so pleased I was going to send him a book I'd written, and wanted me to come back some more.

James Jones, *To Reach Eternity: The Letters of James Jones*, George Hendrick, ed., (New York: Random House, 1989) 112.

Crazy and Cool

The two most complex and contentious sections of this book are on the Jazz Age and the Bebop Era. Arguments activated in the twenties return somewhat modified in the mid-forties and fifties to express the challenges of postwar music. In both eras, jazz and jazz culture were used to exemplify what was bad or good about the overall culture. War's impact on the creative impulse can be a partial explanation: the First World War was premised on traditional banners of Honor and Duty, chivalric ideals confounded by mechanized impersonal death delivered by automatic weapons, poison gas, airplanes, and telegraphy. The loss of ritual warfare; the gain of de-centered selves described by relativity, psychoanalysis, and evolution; the erosion of faith in the continuity of Heaven and Hell and its substitute faith in visible progress; materiality instead of spirituality: all these initiated a process of art production and consumption reinforcing the ever-renewing Modern. Jazz, in the light of the now/then argument, was described as devolution into savagery or ascent into unfettered moments of endless novelty and self-expression. The imperative of upholding a manageable lid on Culture acceptable for white middle and upper classes provided an escape hatch for its progeny to defiantly (often comfortably) transgress down the social scale. (The word "slum" enters public speech in the nineteenth century, but I haven't been able to track the point of origin for "slumming," i.e., eavesdropping on the poor and/or infamous for apparent and transparent needs.)

My earliest memory of culture clash came during the Bebop moment through caricatures in mainstream magazines like *Life* and *Look*, on radio comedy shows, in cartoons and jokes in newspapers and magazines (*The New Yorker, Collier's, Coronet*). As a young fan, I resented the uniformity of misreading which focused almost exclusively on styles of display (beret, shades, goatee, cardigans, suede shoes), lingo (crazy, man, go, dig, cool, etc.), the laid-back relationship to reality (the genre of [stoned] hipster jokes), dismissing the singular music as "noise" or "cacophony." The Abstract Expressionists of the period were also herded into the public bestiary. Suburban intrigue with otherness was further placated by TV's electronic impregnation: "wild savage" abstract artists were easily tamed by Donna Reed; beatnik Maynard G.

Krebs—"Like, work?"—was harmless, ineffectual. Urban postwar intellectuals such as Anatole Broyard, Bernard Wolfe, and Norman Mailer wrote challenging, overburdened essays on the complex relationship of "alienated" white intellectuals and their use of black culture as a way out of the ravages of Progress and its hardball politics of divide-and-conquer, or a way into a more "natural" world where centuries of physical and emotional slavery were danced away. No matter how transparent Mailer's "The White Negro" reads to post-structural postmodern eyes, it was seen in its time as furiously transgressive. ("Seen," that is, by the rather contained intellectual spheres of Manhattan, Chicago, and San Francisco.) European ambassadors of Existentialism, Jean-Paul Sartre and Simone de Beauvoir, saw American racism clearly in the rural South or avant-garde Manhattan. They wrote unimpeded by guilt; de Beauvoir is particularly sensitive to the issue.

Broyard directly addressed the impact of drugs on jazz and hipster life, constructing a grass-framed aesthetic distinguishing hipsters from upwardly-mobile martini-powered squares. The parochial and one-dimensional battle of Hip versus Square, Square versus Hip, quickly played out in mainstream media. But in the cultural criticism of Dwight Macdonald, Mary McCarthy, Robert Warshaw, and Harold Rosenberg, a postwar (and post-Stalin) Left asked difficult questions about racism, and mass-media's power to manufacture meaning, history, and therefore truth. Waldo Frank's late twenties criticism anticipates Adorno/Horkheimer's oracular rants against the industrialization of Art that became more fully developed in the post–World War II intellectual milieu. As earlier, intellectuals allied themselves with one side or the other via jeremiads against mass-mediation or in zealous reception of the persistent play of meanings in popular cultural forms. Art's forts and castles were being challenged, reclaimed, and redefined, just as Man's inherent "goodness," damaged by the Holocaust and the Atomic Bomb, was being questioned. (Maybe postwar abundance, white flight to suburbia, compulsive conformity can be read as by-products of moral terror and the contagion of the Holocaust and Atomic Bomb; maybe the period's two major art revolutions, Bebop and Abstract Expressionism, can be interpreted as conscious or unconscious responses to the Unimaginable becoming so rationally managed;

perhaps the nuclear energy of chain reaction was what Pollock hurled onto floor-long canvases; maybe Parker's power was an affirming reminder of what's lost if a culture's soul becomes too damaged to grieve or admit complicity in mass destruction; maybe the reclamation of jazz as a specifically black discourse and Bebop as a non-partying music (exclusive to initiates only, anti-pop, and, in a sense, anti-body, privileging the listener's ear and intellect, asking for the same involvement given to classical music), a music heard for itself in the same way Abstract Expressionism was asking viewers to look at paintings.

The "margins" of the postwar era were trenches of criminality around drug use; initiation into a drug was a rite of passage from the middle class to the outlaw realm. Marijuana was as common in jazz culture as alcohol; even publicly neutral Louis Armstrong was a hemp devotee. Some ambitious jazz historian might want to explore the role of specific drugs (including alcohol) in jazz culture; was there a qualitative difference in a musician's art traceable to his/her drug of choice? The Parker hagiography celebrates his supernatural capacity for voracious and unselective intake. Reading Dexter's petulant obituary of Bird is valuable on many levels, including buried plantation tensions about "gratitude." It makes one want to know more about the circulation of jazz history, myth, reputation (inclusionary/exclusionary) by newspaper critics, magazine reviewers, and record producers. Each, in their symbiotic niches, wields much primary and secondary power in manufacturing the art's history. In jazz print culture, drug use/abuse was always played down, euphemized ("health problems") in an attempt to present a wholesome picture of musicians. In jazz periodicals and album liner notes made a covert attempt to maintain "legitimacy" for jazz as a profession and product; a disingenuous history contradicting much of the everyday actuality inside the art. Curiously, where "legitimate" artists, writers, composers were celebrated for their tragic excesses, jazz musicians were being reinvented as straight-arrow "professionals," useful, clean-cut, no different than the "[men] in gray flannel suit[s]."

Central to the performance and reception of Bebop was Charlie Parker.

I've included a range of responses to Bird, from poets to record producers. Kenneth Rexroth, like Weldon Kees, wrote from the particular cultural politics of San Francisco. I realize most of the writers on Bird I've included were associated with San Francisco—Lew Welch, Jack Spicer, Rexroth, Kees (Stuart Z. Perkoff is identified more with the Venice community in Los Angeles)—so it's appropriate that San Francisco was "birthplace" or, as Rexroth would have it, re-birthing place for the jazz and poetry attempt. (Rexroth claimed to have first instigated the form in the twenties in Chicago, reading poems to the backbeat of speakeasy jazz players.) That jazz "speaks" to other artists and they, in turn, "speak" or "sing" back to it doesn't always mean that dialogue is possible. Often it's another well-intentioned misuse of jazz, devotional but often off the mark. During the brief rise and fall of the Beat Generation, poets (myself included) read poetry in nightclubs accompanied by jazz musicians. Some—Rexroth, Lawrence Ferlinghetti, Kenneth Patchen, and Jack Kerouac—recorded their efforts. To my ear, the first three failed to either swing or sing. They recited or declaimed verse while a jazz combo vamped behind them. A jazz ensemble played arranged compositions for Patchen to enter into in a manner akin to Schoenberg's use of *sprachstimme*. While there was a formal musical setting for Patchen's work, Ferlinghetti and Rexroth seemed separate from the music, the jazz only background to the poem, not interactive with it. I thought Kerouac was the most successful, grasping the jazz "spirit," both on record and in his writing. His sessions of haiku call-and-response with tenor saxophonists Al Cohn and Zoot Sims are wonderful examples of dialogue absent in the other records. (Even backed up by Steve Allen's pedestrian cocktail jazz piano, Kerouac overcame the music's distracting lacklusterness with an élan intrinsic both to his performance style and relationship with language and jazz sensibility.)

When I think of the "spirit" of jazz I mean improvisation and the willingness to improvise. In and out of control at once, a conduit of/for invention. Present tense. Awake and alert to the cues and clues the music allows. Receiving and transmitting. At once.

—DM

[THE ATOM BOMB] WAS THE FINAL TOUCH in terms of human misery, devastation, and destruction in a world that had just seen the ugliest war in the history of mankind, World War II. [Some] people were lucky enough to come out of it with their skins intact, and their emotions pretty well ripped up. I know mine were, and I know Wally [Berman] had his private hell about the whole deal.

We were sustained by the literature of people whose history is a lot older, who endured much more than we did on a continuing basis, who were more at ease with their passion in describing their feelings about the hard times, the pain and the suffering of being a creative, sensitive person living in a society, while at the same time isolated from that society by virtue of your feelings about the status quo. In our case, the French poets, [and later] the Surrealists and Dada, gave us continuity at a time when, without that body of stuff plus our own jazz blues, I don't think any of us would have made it. We'd have all been candidates either for an insane asylum or suicide. We would not have been able to believe in ourselves enough to continue.

Wally and I probably both had our lives saved by jazz music. [We identified with the world of jazz and blacks], the pain, the roots. We shared persecution . . . I like the word "soul" if it's understood the way I mean it, as a feeling of the heart that can be shared—smoking a little weed, going to jazz clubs, meeting jazz musicians, getting into the idiom . . .

Jazz in this city [Los Angeles] was divided up into two parts of town—the Westside and the Eastside. During the early days there were places on the Eastside where typically only guys like Wally and myself would feel comfortable, because they were essentially black, not yet black and tan, or black and white, but black clubs . . . Ivy Anderson's Chicken Shack, the Double "D" Breakfast Club, the Ritz Club. One of the best places was Lovejoy's . . . small, tiny clubs, as most after-hours joints were, where these great musicians would come to relax and play. Two of the best-known clubs [on Central Avenue] were Mrs. Brown's Little Harlem, which was way out on 164th, [and] the House of Blue Lights. You could go in these after-hours spots and, for the right price, either the owner or one of his henchmen or somebody would send you a bottle and you'd keep it under the table and pay a dollar and a half for a glass with some ice in it.

The main club [on the Westside] was Billy Berg's Club Capri, which [in the early 1940s] was located at Pico and La Cienega. I was only about seventeen or eighteen years old when I first went to that club. In a thirty-day period at that club, you could have heard Slim and Slam—Slim Gaillard and Slam Stewart—two of the greatest names in jazz at that time; Lee and Lester Young, two brothers—Lester, of course, on saxophone, and Lee, his brother, playing drums. They had their own quintet. Billie Holiday, the Daniels Brothers, the Spirits of Rhythm, an incredible group of men, and Leo Watson, who was the forerunner and teacher of any scat singer who came after him.

I think we [Wally and I] were both "turned out" by musicians. It was like a ritual, initiation. You come around the club, and you're cool, and you meet a musician or a few musicians. You're able to express to them—you blow a little bubble back to them for what they've given you. Think about a couple of artists, having acculturated themselves to the history of art and literature, finding themselves living in a society which neither understood nor desired it, and considered anybody who was interested in it an oddball or weird because you didn't do the conventional things. And you meet other artists, in this case musicians, who didn't know a goddamn about Baudelaire, Apollinaire, or Surrealism, who could look at what you did or listen to your poem and dig it. I would consider those musicians that we knew personally, who turned us out, introduced us to the life, the way they lived, their suffering, their pain, as brothers in a world of creativity.

Wally and I both knew Charlie Parker. I can remember reading Bird a couple of my poems. He liked them a lot. We were in the studio when Bird recorded "Lover Man." He had gotten very hot during the session and took off his shirt. It was raining, really heavily, outside. Bird was very erratic, a genius in his lifetime—not always, but sometimes. People who are in worlds that nobody has ever been in before, like a Bird, like a Picasso, any original thinker or creator, are charting new courses, and it can be very overwhelming at times.

Robert Alexander, *Lost and Found in California: Four Decades of Assemblage Art*, (Santa Monica: James Corcoran, Shoshana Wayne, and Pence galleries, 1988) 57–58, 60.

RED SLIPPED THROUGH THE DOOR. The crowd had spilled over from the main room into the corridors. The hipster ranks opened a way for him. The horn glinted in the catchy light. Recognizing not a single face, Red heard them saying, "Ready like Teddy! Not dragged at all. Real happy —you can see it in his eyes. Just got the Word from upstairs. Ready to romp, man!" Red made his way through the strange room and vaulted onto the bandstand. He was aware of a slim, correctly-dressed young man in the late twenties, with a quiet, handsome face, straight dark hair, and thoughtful brown eyes. Zaida's discoveries often seemed to run to type. Red turned to the microphone.

"Thank you, thank you, thank you everybody"—he told the crowd, falling into his imitation of a stock master of ceremonies, not his line at all. "You are so *very* kind. As you know, my band and myself was brought out all the way to Hollywood here by the management of the Hi De Ho at tremendous expense." He paused until somebody chuckled. But this was too serious a matter for real yocks. The chuckle gave way to reverent silence. "Sorry about the plane being late, folks," he went on, as if there weren't a single thing he could do about airline efficiency. Tactfully, he did not name the carrier, but this information spread through the house, so that no one present was apt to ride *that* line again. "But we all present and accounted for now and we here to entertain you with a new little number we brought out with us all the way from the Apple. Called—" pause—"Seein' Red!"

"*Yes!*" That part was a smash. The crowd dug in. Red turned his back on the house and faced the rhythm section. A martinet had replaced the ingratiating master of ceremonies. He wasn't jovial in the least now. Blood had risen to his face. He crouched and began bobbing to show the tempo he wanted. "Seein' Red, men!"

Slim Cook and Bernie looked in dismay at Hassan. The drummer made a helpless gesture and flung back at Red, "This the up blues?"

"No, no, man," Red scolded. "Seein' Red is the chords of I Got Rhythm." He gave them a look as if to ask, three thousand miles for this? "We in B-flat now. Let's get off."

Chuey Figueroa, a fat musician with a round baby face, stood blandly aside, faintly amused by the whole thing, his alto saxophone cradled gently in the crook of one elbow. He knew the tune.

"Up, up, up!" Red urged. "Come on, Hassan, bring it *up* to *me!*" He continued to bob, his lips quivering in a rage to get at the trumpet.

Hassan glared back, his wrists flying ever faster. Even he had forgotten those fearsome tempos of the Street, or how hard Red could come on, those times that he really wanted to, when he had an impression to make, or some interloping musician had to be cut down once and for all and shown who was boss. But the real problem was the piano. "I Got Rhythm, Bernie. B-flat, man!" (. . .)

Bernie Rich was conditioned to a more orderly type of performance. Of course, practically everybody knew the chords to I Got Rhythm. Bernie Rich knew them. Bleakly, they flashed through his mind's eye—B-flat, C-minor seventh, F seventh, B-flat, C-minor seventh, and so on. Except that he had not the faintest notion of the new riff based on these chords. It had not been among any of the Red Travers records to which he had listened again and again at Zaida's apartment. Nor had he the faintest idea of how a trumpet could be tongued at the insane tempo Hass was now setting up.

Hassan's ride cymbal began to vibrate, pumping its shimmering sound across the bandstand. He was playing six notes to the bar, And-One-TWO, And-Three-FOUR, but the notes seemed to run together so that the big cymbal, with light splashing off its gentle coolie-hat curves, had a musical pulse of its own. The stick flew in the drummer's wiry wrist and fell against the alloyed metal, hammered to paper thinness by the craftsman who had forged it. Hassan's fingers maintained the stick in suspended motion, like a juggler with a stream of balls flying. The sound came in waves, one close behind the other, until all the air in the night club was dancing to its airy sound. To the backmost corner, where the curious cradled their highballs and the hip huddled over their glasses of iced coffee, past the velvet rope and out into the street, the shimmery sound ghosted and gathered in its thrall. Hassan began to add little percussive figures, muffled thuds on the bass, pistol shots on the snares, jungly throbs on the tom-toms, puffs of air lightly caught between the surfaces of the high hat and charged with a bubbly froth of sound, truncated press rolls that were like thunder heard briefly and at a distance—his mosaic of skilled, subtle sounds.

The tempo was more of a quiver than a beat. Hassan sounded an admonitory rim shot and Red spun out of his crouch and came up, facing the crowd, dead on mike, with his mute inches away. Like the partner in a clever vaudeville act, Chuey Figueroa was right there at rendezvous with the alto saxophone. The two instruments almost touched. Nestling one another, they breathed into the microphone, softly and in unison, the subtle phrases of Seein' Red, a grim parody on the old Gershwin tune. Dead at the end of the 32-bar statement, Chuey let out a bubbling laugh and stepped away. Red flipped the mute out of the bell and dumped it down on the top of the piano with a clatter and turned the horn toward Bernie.

Red had him under direct fire. The bell of the trumpet shone like a great headlight. For Bernie it was like the first time when, as a child, he had ridden a roller coaster at a beach resort, and the free-rolling cars, released by the starter, had drifted to the foot of the first big incline. Then, all at once, from somewhere underneath, they were seized up by a hook running on a conveyor mechanism which began hauling them forward and upward with terrifying and irresistible force. Everything that had a moment before seemed on the point of flying apart was now gathered together by a sure hand. The trumpet continued to hammer him down with its metal tones.

Red played an entire chorus with only the three notes of the triad. But he varied them infinitely, altered their intonation and attack, bent and fitted them into various positions of the bar structure, creating a whole series of rhythmic patterns and levels, each more complex than the other. Bernie's knees banged against the under side of the piano. He could feel the cross rhythms powerful inside himself. People had stopped talking and drinking. Even the square waiters had downed trays. Dark and primitive forces were set loose in the room.

Red held the trumpet with one elbow wedged to his side, the other winged out and loose, so that his wrist was higher than the valves and he could fan them with his fingers. When he crouched, or turned, or leaned back to point the horn at the ceiling, he preserved exactly the same position, the same embouchure. Man and instrument moved in a solid block. In one piece. He blew with his cheeks hard packed from compressed air, a glazed look on his face, his throat distended like a bellows. Spewn forth from the trumpet's bell a festoon of notes, each perfectly in place and tied to the next, uncoiled and hung quivering over the tables and the crowd, the longest melodic line Bernie had ever heard, an entire thirty-two bars without a break in continuity, without a pause for breath. A complete unanimity existed between the fingers and lips, and the mind which moved with such breathtaking speed among the ancient bones of harmony of the old Gershwin standard. The technique in itself was prodigious, yet always subjected to a greater creativity. Never in the long solo did he suffer it to exist for itself. Not once did he embellish with a mechanical device or easy trumpet figuration. Every turn, triplet, arpeggio, grace note, smear, slur had its place in the final tonal and rhythmic fabric of the solo.

They played Seein' Red for almost fifteen minutes. During that time no one else took a solo. It was all trumpet, one chorus piled on to the next, variation upon variation, surprise topped by surprise. Bernie's wrist muscles had begun to lock on him and even Hassan looked a little desperate. Toward the end Chuey Figueroa came in for a series of chase choruses where eight-bar sections were traded back and forth between trumpet and saxophone. Red took every phrase that Chuey played and rephrased it instantly. Chuey would shake a series of notes out of the gleaming cornucopia of his alto, then step back and cock his head, only to wag and smile in wondering disbelief as Red turned them all inside out. They finished the chase and Red took charge once more for a final dizzying ride into the upper register, pinching off high notes as easily as if he were playing a fife. He came diving out of that last flight dead on cue, and the group was back on rails, tracked dead in on the unison-and-out. The final note hung aloft, like a streamer, over the house, and the crowd, stunned into some moments of silence, suddenly broke loose and began yelling. The applause continued, deafening. Red chuckled, adjusted his mute, waited, quiet and easy. Then called a new tune. And the mood changed.

Ross Russell, *The Sound,* (New York: E. P. Dutton & Co., Inc., 1961) 47–52.

CONTINUOUS CHECKER GAME GOING ON in the dressing room between me and Charlie Parker—We play to see who pays for the food—Bird eats all the time—in between shows (he don't care)—He always loses—no way he can win against me—The best most anybody can

get from me is a draw—Bird don't believe this he thinks it's luck—
We're playing this game—it's even he don't want to quit—the intermission act is off—my show's next—"Let's play and blow the show"—
"I'm with you man"—"groovy"—we're both on heavy shit—spaced
out—Bird carries the checker board up on stage—nobody knows
what's going on—"Your move"—The guys in my group—breaking
up—We're cookin' my first number—Bird's studying the board—
makes an exchange—picks up his horn blows a wild chorus—gets a
hand—I jump one of his—sing the lyrics "Who put the Benzedrine
in Mrs. Murphy's Ovaltine"—Everybody's diggin' the game—shouting—"Move it man"—cheering—"Get it on Bird"—"Play it cool Hipster"—We're playing the whole show—people laughing—high
jiving—"Git it man"—"Don't hit no clinkers"—"Watch out"—"Lay
it down" "That's it"—"Let's call it a draw Bird"—"My man"—We
laugh—rock the joint.

Harry 'The Hipster" Gibson, as told to Arlena Gibson-Feller, "From the Hipster:
The Story of Harry 'The Hipster' Gibson," from *Sulfur 17*, vol. 6, #2, 1986, 16.

CHARLIE PARKER WAS A SPOILED BRAT. In Kansas City, where he was
growing up in the 1930s, he was called a "mommy's boy" by musicians
who quickly tired of his thinking only of Parker. And years later, in
New York at Birdland when he reigned as the uncontested king of the
alto saxophone throughout the world, an advertising executive [Cy
Schneider, account executive of Carson-Roberts, Inc., an extremely
knowledgeable jazz buff who has written many liner notes for Norman
Granz down throughout the years] hurried into the club one night, did
not see Parker on the bandstand and prepared to leave and return later.
But then he saw Charlie, in a telephone booth with the door wide open:
the Bird was urinating.

Writers for every jazz magazine and music trade paper as well as
those for mass-circulation magazines have wasted hundreds of thousands of words concluding that Bird died of frustration because (1) his
genius was appreciated by only a few, and (2) his colleague Dizzy
Gillespie got all the credit for introducing modern jazz and became
bop's high priest.

Parker may indeed have been frustrated. Most everyone is today.

But Parker's miseries started much earlier, perhaps as far back as 1933, certainly by 1934, when he was fourteen years old and attending Lincoln High in Kansas City. There he played a baritone horn, whenever he showed up. Ed Mayfield and other of his schoolmates at Lincoln have always tried to be tactful in speaking of little Charlie's childhood, but that he tried to bully others, borrow "lunch money" that was never repaid, and brush off schoolmates who tried to be friendly in favor of older boys who took him on benzedrine parties, is documented.

Those who played alongside Parker say he was smoking marijuana in high school, where he was a perpetual freshman until he quit and turned to music full time. The late Bob Simpson, a fine trombonist, and Lawrence Keyes, the pianist who is still active, were both more advanced musicians than Parker at fourteen. Parker demanded, never graciously, that they teach him chords. The late and lovable Freddie Culliver, who in 1940 recorded beautiful tenor solos with Harlan Leonard's band on Victor-Bluebird, was a far more polished and musicianly saxophonist. Little Franz Bruce, alto, Johnny Jackson, alto, and Jimmy Ross, another Leonard sideman, likewise were regarded as far more skillful jazzmen than Parker. They were all his age.

But Charlie, for all his surliness and bad habits, could charm the leaves from the trees. When he wanted something, he got it. His mother, Mrs. Addie Bailey Parker, widowed when her son was seventeen, went without necessities to provide for him. She also supported Charlie's half-brother, John Parker, although he was not her son. But Charles, as she always called him, was the pet.

Parker married his first wife, Rebecca Ruffin, when he was sixteen. Their marriage lasted two years and in that time young Charlie turned to narcotics. A sleazy little crumbum named "Little Phil," whom we constantly encountered in jazz clubs and at rehearsals, was the salesman. He was locked up later, but much too late to deter Parker and certain other youngsters from acquiring the most despicable deadly habit there is.

I did not meet Parker until he started working with Jay McShann and the Harlan Leonard band in Kansas City in 1937–38 (neither was employed regularly, so Parker rehearsed and gigged with both) while I was a reporter-rewrite man on the Kansas City *Journal-Post*, a correspondent for *Down Beat*, *Metronome*, and *Orchestra World*, and a stringer for *The Billboard*. Parker was ever the personality kid, and he would pick your billfold from a rear pocket while showing you how to finger a high E on the side keys of his alto. If you caught him, he would laugh it off and hand the billfold back.

"Little Phil" not only lurked about furtively, but there were girl-pushers as well. McShann and Leonard chased them away. They would meet with the personable Parker later. Apparently his mother still was unaware of his use of heroin, but she knew how he beat his first wife, Rebecca. And she eventually learned how he would constantly hock the new saxophone she had bought him with money earned from scrubbing floors, then get it back with money he "borrowed" from McShann, Leonard, and the musicians with whom he worked.

Tired of the road by now, Parker continued his con man traits. He frequently used a dime store ring to lure young girls to his pad. Sometimes, Hines' sidemen say, the Bird actually went through a marriage ceremony to get what he wanted. That ruse has, of course, been used by musicians, salesmen, and travelers for a thousand years. But Bird bragged about his deception. Hines' musicians desperately tried to keep him straight, but it was a losing cause. He missed shows in theaters. In ballrooms he failed to show, or fell asleep on the stand, his cheeks puffed out as if he were blowing his horn.

[In] his next phase . . . he worked the joints and boites of New York's Fifty-Second Street with scores of musicians, made his first bop records, formed his groups, left his second wife Gerry and wed Doris Sydnor, made his first trip to California for the ill-advised and egg-laying run at Billy Berg's nitery and, sadly, more and more demanded narcotics.

In Los Angeles, depressed as he had never been before because of the Californians' apathy, Bird returned to his hotel room one evening, set fire to it and wound up in the Camarillo sanitarium northwest of Los Angeles.

He was there for more than six months. His incarceration, of course, was page one streamer news in all the music sheets. Most mu-

sicians thought he was through. The late Freddy Webster had come
out of Benny Carter's band and lost his mind. So had Bobby Moore,
a promising young trumpeter with Basie. Back in the 1920s Leon Rap-
polo had wigged-out and spent the remainder of his life in an asylum.
Other cases musicians knew about were purposely unpublicized.

At Camarillo, Bird was allowed to meet his wife Doris three times
a week. They fixed his teeth, which had always been bad. But mostly,
he rested.

There followed the greatest, most illustrious, and most creative period of the Bird's short life. He still "borrowed" money from everyone
with whom he had contact. No one ever recalls his reimbursing anybody. But he was as straight as he had ever been. Camarillo had bene-
fited him. His records of this period on Dial included *Bird's Nest, Cool
Blues, Relaxin' at Camarillo, Cheers, Carvin' the Bird* and *Stupendous*—all made
in Hollywood after his release—and on Savoy *Chasin' the Bird, Cheryl,
Buzzy,* and *Donna Lee,* cut in June 1947, after he returned to New York.

Charlie had always been a heavy drinker, even while dependent on
narcotics. And musicians who were working with him in this pre-1950
period will sadly relate how junkies and pushers of heroin flocked
around the Bird almost constantly. Charlie frequently warned young
musicians of the horrors of narcotics and sometimes missed work
drinking himself into a stupor, apparently trying to evade the "horse"
habit. But, like so many addicts, he gave in, and was back on the tread-
mill to hell by the summer of 1947. There was, his friends apologized,
just too much pressure to resist.

The French jazz buffs Panassie and Charles Delaunay, long-time guid-
ing lights of the Hot Club of France, split about this time in violent
disagreement over the course jazz was taking. Delaunay, son of a brilliant French artist, forthwith produced the 1950 International Jazz Festival in Paris himself, intending to concentrate on the newer bop and
cool musicians. Bird got an invitation.

Delighted, eager, and perhaps inspired, he went to Sweden first,
played about a week there, then went to Paris and soared off on a mad,
wailing, drunken binge of at least three days and missed the festival
completely. Delaunay, it seems, had paid the Bird in advance!

By 1954, Bird was without any question the most publicized musician alive, in the trade mags. The public still knew nothing of his phenomenal talent, or his eccentric behavior, but musicians throughout the world carefully followed his every move. Yet, he endured periods when he had no money in his pockets, none in the bank, and none in sight. He survived another trip to California in 1952 but failed to attract patronage aside from musicians in both Los Angeles and San Francisco.

He said he would turn atheist, but they didn't have holidays.

There are some who insist that Parker's suicide attempt (drinking iodine) was an act, and that he merely smeared iodine on his tongue with cotton in September 1954. It gave him admission to New York's public Bellevue Hospital (for the second time) and perhaps a rest and a chance to think things out for two weeks.

[. . .] Bird's record at Bellevue was eye-opening: Psychometric testing indicated a high average intelligence with paranoid tendencies, a hostile and evasive personality with manifestations of primitive and sexual fantasies associated with hostility and gross evidence of paranoid thinking. The diagnosis during his second stay was simple: acute alcoholism and undifferentiated schizophrenia. A spinal tap was performed. Colloidal gold curve proved negative, and blood Wassermann was two-plus positive. Notes on his medical chart indicated that the patient was "lazy" and kept bothering nurses for doses of paraldehyde . . .

So much for the Bird's pathetic physical condition just six months before his death. His ulcers were painful and he had survived at least two heart attacks, one a blockbuster. His liver was bad. He had gained sixty to seventy pounds over his early days in New York.

Parker's last days were not happy ones. Like Bolden, Oliver, Beiderbecke, Berigan, and other outstanding jazzmen before him, Bird had nothing to show for all his ability, and the long arm-jabbing years of music and addiction. More and more he was seen around New York looking aged, and shabbily dressed. More and more did musicians and fans "lend" him money.

He knew his time was limited, and he told some of his friends he wouldn't be around much longer.

Parker's estate, consisting almost entirely of royalties still accruing to him as a composer and recorded performer, is being contested and fought over by various parties. But the Yardbird is gone. His mother—and never was one more devoted to a son—mourns him as she did in 1955. With the years, the Parker legend, like Beiderbecke's, spreads to every corner of the world:

How he would line up six to eight doubles of Old Grand Dad on a bar and gulp them all down just before going on the bandstand . . .

How he answered Dr. Freymann, three days before he died, when the physician asked him if he drank liquor. "Sometimes," the ailing Parker answered straight-faced, "I sip a little sherry before dinner . . ."

How he horsed around in Kansas City, in his late teens, goosing musicians on the stand, stealing packs of cigarettes from their cases, and invariably greeting a cub *Journal-Post* reporter who didn't think Parker was anything special with a smiling but sarcastic, "Greetings, Dexterious! . . ."

How his appetite for the opposite sex was inexhaustible, averaging out to three "servings" a day, according to his loyal and attentive manager, Teddy Bloom . . .

How Norman Granz, whom Parker never spoke of in complimentary terms, paid all the expenses of the funeral, shipment of body, and burial, and hoped to keep it quiet . . .

How he was listed in magazines and music books for twenty years as "Charles Christopher Parker" until his mother finally protested and vehemently denied the middle name ever existed. His headstone simply lists his name as "Charles Parker, Jr."

How Bird's revolutionary playing will live forever, although there were as many musicians who disliked it, didn't understand it, and didn't want to hear any more of it as there were those who called Parker a genius.

There will never be another like him.

Dave Dexter, Jr., *The Jazz Story: From the '90s to the '60s*, (Englewood Cliffs, NJ: Prentice-Hall, Inc., 1964) 145–147, 149, 150–151, 152–153, 154–156.

LIKE THE PILLARS OF HERCULES, like two ruined Titans guarding the entrance to one of Dante's circles, stand two great dead juvenile delinquents—the heroes of the post-war generation: the saxophonist,

Charlie Parker, and Dylan Thomas. If the word "deliberate" means anything, both of them certainly deliberately destroyed themselves.

Both of them were overcome by the horror of the world in which they found themselves, because at last they could no longer overcome that world with the weapon of a purely lyrical art. Both of them were my friends. Living in San Francisco I saw them seldom enough to see them with a perspective which was not distorted by exasperation or fatigue. So as the years passed, I saw them each time in the light of an accelerated personal conflagration.

The last time I saw Bird, at Jimbo's Bop City, he was so gone—so blind to the world—that he literally sat down on me before he realized I was there. "What happened, man?" I said, referring to the pretentious "Jazz Concert." "Evil, man, evil," he said, and that's all he said for the rest of the night. About dawn he got up to blow. The rowdy crowd chilled into stillness and the fluent melody spiraled through it.

The last time I saw Dylan, his self-destruction had not just passed the limits of rationality. It had assumed the terrifying inertia of inanimate matter. Being with him was like being swept away by a torrent of falling stones.

Now Dylan Thomas and Charlie Parker have a great deal more in common than the same disastrous end. As artists, they were very similar. They were both very fluent. But this fluent, enchanting utterance had, compared with important artists of the past, relatively little content. Neither of them got very far beyond a sort of entranced rapture at his own creativity. The principal theme of Thomas's poetry was the ambivalence of birth and death—the pain of blood-stained creation. Music, of course, is not so explicit an art, but anybody who knew Charlie Parker knows that he felt much the same way about his own gift. Both of them did communicate one central theme: Against the ruin of the world, there is only one defense—the creative act. This, of course, is the theme of much art—perhaps most poetry. It is the theme of Horace, who certainly otherwise bears little resemblance to Parker or Thomas. The difference is that Horace accepted his theme with a kind of silken assurance. To Dylan and Bird it was an agony and terror. I do not believe that this is due to anything especially frightful about their relationship to their own creativity. I believe rather that it is due to the catastrophic world in which that creativity seemed to be the sole value. Horace's column of imperishable verse shines quietly enough in the lucid air of Augustan Rome. Art may have been for him the most enduring, orderly, and noble activity of man. But the other activities of his life partook of these values. They did not actively negate them. Dylan Thomas's verse had to find endurance in a world of burning cities and burning Jews. He was able to find meaning in his art as long as it was the answer to air raids and gas ovens. I believe his art became meaningless to him. I think all this could apply to Parker just as well, although, because of the nature of music, it is not demonstrable—at least not conclusively.

Thomas and Parker have more in common than theme, attitude, life pattern. In the practice of their art, there is an obvious technical resemblance. Contrary to popular belief, they were not great technical innovators. Their effects are only superficially startling. Thomas is a regression from the technical originality and ingenuity of writers like Pierre Reverdy or Apollinaire. Similarly, the innovations of bop, and of Parker particularly, have been vastly overrated by people unfamiliar with music, especially by that ignoramus, the intellectual jitterbug, the jazz aficionado. The tonal novelties consist in the introduction of a few chords used in classical music for centuries. And there is less rhythmic difference between progressive jazz, no matter how progressive, and Dixieland, than there is between two movements of many conventional symphonies.

What Parker and his contemporaries—Gillespie, Davis, Monk, Roach (Tristano is an anomaly), etc.—did was to absorb the musical ornamentation of older jazz into the basic structure, of which it then became an integral part, and with which it then developed. This is true of the melodic line which could be put together from selected passages of almost anybody—Benny Carter, Johnny Hodges. It is true of the rhythmic pattern in which the beat shifts continuously, or at least is continuously sprung, so that it becomes ambiguous enough to allow the pattern to be dominated by the long pulsations of the phrase or strophe. This is exactly what happened in the transition from baroque to rococo music. It is the difference between Bach and Mozart.

There is one difference between Bird and Dylan which should be pointed out. Again, contrary to popular belief, there is nothing crazy or frantic about Parker either musically or emotionally. His sinuous melody is a sort of naive transcendence of all experience. Emotionally, it does not resemble Berlioz or Wagner; it resembles Mozart. This is true also of a painter like Jackson Pollock. He may have been eccentric in his behavior, but his paintings are as impassive as Persian tiles. Partly this difference is due to the nature of verbal communication. The insistent talk-aboutiveness of the general environment obtrudes into even the most idyllic poetry. It is much more a personal difference. Thomas certainly wanted to tell people about the ruin and disorder of the world. Parker and Pollock wanted to substitute a work of art for the world.

Technique pure and simple, rendition, is not of major importance, but it is interesting that Parker, following Lester Young, was one of the leaders of the so-called saxophone revolution. In modern jazz, the saxophone is treated as a woodwind and played with conventional embouchure. Metrically, Thomas's verse was extremely conventional, as was, incidentally, the verse of that other tragic *enragé*, Hart Crane.

Parker certainly had much more of an influence. At one time it was the ambition of every saxophone player in every high school band in America to blow like Bird. Even before his death this influence had begun to ebb. In fact, the whole generation of the founding fathers of bop—Gillespie, Monk, Davis, Blakey, and the rest—are just now at a considerable discount. The main line of development today goes back to Lester Young and bypasses them.

Kenneth Rexroth [1957], "Disengagement: The Art of the Beat Generation," from *World Outside The Window: The Selected Essays of Kenneth Rexroth,* Bradford Morrow, ed., (New York: New Directions, 1987) 42–45.

WHO SAYS THERE NEVER WERE ANY STREETS OF GOLD IN AMERICA? In 1944, I found one. I had learned from an issue of *Down Beat* that Biff Anderson was back in New York. I sought him out again. I told him I'd been trying to understand bop, and was hopelessly confused. He told me that was tough shit. I told him he was the one who'd advised me not to even *try* playing Tatum piano, that bop was the new thing, and that was what I should be learning. He said That's right. So where am I supposed to learn it? I asked. Nobody's teaching it, Biff, there aren't any bop solos in Braille, there aren't even any *Tatum* solos in Braille, what am I supposed to do? (I was using the little-blind-bastard ploy that hadn't worked on my grandfather with Vesuvio; it didn't work on Biff, either.)

"Look," he said, "I don't know you from a hole in the wall, I got enough problems of my own, I don't need a blind man hanging around me all the time asking questions."

"Biff," I persisted, "if you saw me walking down Broadway with a cup full of pencils, you'd take pity on me, wouldn't you?"

"Oh, sheee-it," he said.

"Biff, all I'm asking you to do is take me around a little, help me to understand the style, okay? And then if I decide I want to play bop . . . which is what *you* advised me to *do*, right? am I right?"

"Yeah, yeah," he said.

"Then all I want you to do is give me a lesson every now and then. Or even if I decide to play Tatum, okay? I just need some help, that's all. I can't take it off the records anymore, I'm not getting anywhere."

"Where in hell you want to go, man?" he asked.

"I want to be the best jazz piano player who ever lived."

"Oh, sheee-it," he said again.

"I can't pay you much for the lessons, Biff."

"Ain't gonna *be* no lessons," he said.

"Fifteen, twenty dollars a week maybe, that's what I was paying the man who taught me classical music . . ."

"Man, you one hell of a pushy blind person, you know that?"

"I've got to be," I said.

He was quiet for a long time.

Then he said, "I must be out of my fuckin' mind."

Fifty-second Street was pure gold. I very nearly suffered a cardiac seizure the first time Biff took me downtown and I learned (he had saved it as a surprise) that Tatum was playing at the Famous Door, with a bassist and a guitarist as his sidemen. We got there at ten, and I sat there in ecstasy till two in the morning, when Biff took me up to meet Tatum. The next night we went to hear Sidney Bechet, an old-time New Orleans soprano sax player, and the night after that Biff took me to hear Coleman Hawkins at the Onyx. Biff had played with Hawkins many years back, and he told me this man could shake down the Empire State Building with his horn. Man, he shook me to the roots. He was playing with two young musicians who had cut their chops on bop, a drummer named Max Roach, and a trumpet player named Howard McGhee. Biff asked me to pay particular attention to the drummer, who had learned from Klook Clarke (another new name to me), and I listened to him very carefully and did not like what I heard. The next night we went to the Downbeat and listened to Red Norvo on the vibraphone, and the night after that we caught Eddie Condon playing Chicago-style jazz, and Biff introduced me to him, and later told me that he was the one who'd said, "The boppers *flat* their fifths; we *drink* ours." For the next six months, or seven, or eight, Biff and I walked from door to door on the Street, and then taxied downtown or crosstown to every jazz joint he could find, listening to the main attractions and the intermission bands. For me, it was like rushing through an encapsulated chronology of jazz from its earliest beginnings to its then current form, all the giants and near-giants assembled, blowing for all they were worth in cabarets stinking of booze and smoke—Bobby Hackett, Don Byas, John Kirby, Pee Wee Russell and Bud Freeman and Zutty Singleton and, of course, the Bird—who was playing at the Three Deuces with a band that spelled Erroll Garner, who was the feature attraction.

I hated what the boppers were doing. I'd hated their music on the few records I'd heard, and I hated it all over again hearing them in person. I cursed Kenny Clarke, who, Biff told me, was the first drummer to stop playing time, hated the klook-a-mop explosions that erupted unexpected from bass drum or snare like mortar shells in an undeclared war. I hated those flatted fifths the horn men were playing, though Biff told me he'd first heard them played on a *piano* as far back as 1940 (while I was still laboring over Chopin) by a man named Tadd Dameron, who was also one of the first to play in what Biff described as "the legato manner," using his English accent, which I learned was both defensive *and* derisive. I think he hated bop as much as I did, but he was stuck with it, he recognized it as the wave of the future, and like my Uncle Nick, he wasn't about to buck the system. I hated Gillespie and I hated

Parker and I hated Powell and Wallington, Pettiford and Monk, and the whole damn gallery of men who were, it seemed to me, forcing me to change my path even before I'd firmly placed a foot upon it.

To me—I was eighteen and eager and excited and ambitious— these men were doing this deliberately, were trying to screw up my life, were out to get *me* personally. I wasn't far from wrong. They were out to get Whitey, though he was known as Charley in those days. They were playing music they thought the white man could not steal, changing the names of songs so that when they played them with strangely revised charts, they would be unrecognizable to square Charley—"Ornithology" was "How High the Moon"; "A Dizzy Atmosphere" was "I Got Rhythm"; "Hot House" was "What Is This Thing Called Love?"; "Donna Lee" was "Back Home in Indiana." The machine-gun chatter in the early stages of this war was an idiomatic cliché vocalized as "Bu-REE-bop," or "Du-BEE-bop," and probably deriving from Gillespie's "Salt Peanuts," a tune with a I, VI, II, V chord pattern and a Sears Roebuck bridge. Salt-PEA-nuts—the tonic, the octave, and the tonic again. The "Salt" was an eighth note on the second beat of the bar, followed by an eighth-note rest. The "PEA" was an eighth note on the upper tonic, and the "nuts" was an eighth note on the tonic below; beamed together they comprised the third beat of the bar. And there you were—"Ru-BEE-bop" or "Bu-REE-bop," later shortened to "bebop" or "rebop," and finally to "bop" as the definitive label for the new jazz.

Freed from the need to express themselves in an archaic musical tongue, the boppers invented a shorthand verbal language as well, and this became the coinage of everyday communication. A word like "ax" was first used to describe a horn of any kind, but its scope rapidly expanded to include *any* instrument, even the guitar and piano, which are about as far removed from an actual ax as a giraffe is from a water buffalo. The word "gone" was initially an abbreviation of the expression "out of this world." If you are out of this world, why, then you are literally gone, no? But it was also used in brief exchanges such as this:

"So I'll see you Tuesday, man."

"Gone."

The "gone" meant "okay," or "all right," or "agreed," and was frequently used interchangeably with the word "crazy," which also expressed approval, and which was sometimes linked with the word "like."

"Like three bills for the gig, cool?"

"Like crazy."

"Like" was probably the most overworked word in the new jazz vocabulary. If, on the battlefield, soldiers (black *and* white) were using "fuck" in its numberless variations—"pass the fuckin' ammunition, you fuck, or fuck if I give a fuck what fuckin' happens"—so were black musicians at home using "like" with every fucking breath.

"I was like walking along, when I dug this wigged-out chick, she like gassed me."

"Like I'm short of gold, you got like a pad for me tonight?"

"Like, dig, man, you puttin' me on?"

"Like I got eyes for like retiring like in Paris."

"Like gone, man."

"Like I like *love* you like."

Like *I* like *hated* it, man.

I hated the music, which I thought was simplistic, crude, mysterious, irritating, architecturally inept, and utterly without warmth or feeling. I figured the only reason Bud Powell was playing such primitive stuff was because he had tiny hands, as Biff had pointed out, and couldn't reach those resounding Tatum chords. Tatum had riches to squander; he threw gold coins into the air, rubies poured from his ears, he swallowed emeralds and belched black pearls. Bop seemed impoverished to me, and the boppers—for all their dexterity—made music I considered emotionless and cold. I know a lot of jazz players who assign colors to keys. B flat will become brown, F will be green, E pink—meaningless references for me. I think instead in terms of warmth or lack of it. D is my favorite key, but only because it represents the *feel* of sunshine, and not because I think of it as saffron or burnt umber. Keys, as a matter of fact, have never meant very much to me. The problem confronting me each time I sit at the piano is not what *key* I'm going to play in, but only what I'm going to do with the tune. If I'm going to bomb out in E flat, I'll bomb out in G as well. As far as I was concerned, the boppers were bombing out in all twelve keys, and if they were playing in *any* color at all, it was the opposite of black, which most of them were; the music they made was cold and white. Dead white. I listened to it, and I thought this can't be it, this can't be where it's going, this has got to be a fad.

I hated them for systematically and maliciously (I thought) destroying a sound I had loved instantly and without reservation from the first minute I'd heard it; I hated them for their exclusivity, which I did not recognize as naked hostility until that day years later when Rex Butler put me down on Broadway; I hated them because they caused me to long for acceptance into their inner circle, where they spoke a childlike code, easily cracked and therefore no code at all, and yet impossible to imitate without incurring derision from them. Actually, I was missing the point, and it took me a long time to realize that Charlie Parker had been right. He understood, intuitively, that jazz as it was being played had come as far as it could ever go. There was no longer any way to modify or refine the existing system; it had to be completely demolished. He had reevaluated the entire harmonic and rhythmic structure and decided—not consciously; none of these decisions are ever conscious—to return jazz to its purest form.

I did not know what to do. I had given up classical piano in favor of jazz, and hardly registered as an alien before my adopted country exploded in revolution. I now had the choice of sticking with the Tatum style and perfecting it (eating cake, so to speak, while the rabble was clamoring at the palace gates), or learning to play a music I did not like or even understand. I could either go it alone, play solo piano if I chose—solo piano *already* had its head on the chopping block, and George Shearing would lop it off forever in 1947—or I could learn to play with other musicians in small ensembles where the piano player was a part of the rhythm section and, except when taking a chorus, was expected to feed chords to horn players. I had no idea that running down a chart for a horn player could be excitingly heady stuff when the horn players were inventive geniuses like Parker or Gillespie. I did not realize that the bass line of the thirties had indeed been a prison, or that Powell or Wallington and many, many others were freeing the right hand from those cop-put pentatonic runs, more suited to the playing of the bagpipes than the playing of piano. In bop, the concentration on the right-hand blowing line—the truly creative line, the invented melody line—was intense. The very system of using hollow shells in the bass demanded that the right hand be innovatively restless at all times, free to express ideas and feelings. And the left hand was no longer rigidly playing the rhythm, but was playing *against* the rhythm—and that was freedom, too. I didn't realize this when I first told Biff I'd made up my mind. I only knew that I could either go it alone, or if I could learn to play music with other men in . . . well, a family. If it happened that the family was black, and perhaps angry, that was something I would have to cope with. This was America.

I made the American choice.

Evan Hunter, *Streets of Gold*, (New York: Harper & Row, Publishers, 1974) 282–288.

[TED FOX] *Let's talk about Bechet. How did your relationship with him begin?*

[ALFRED LION] We were living in Berlin. My mother was in the theater set, the movie set. She was like a jet-setter in a way, and she was very good looking. One day she told me she met a very strange man. A gorgeous-looking man with a turban and two big white dogs with him. She said, "We stopped and talked, and he told me he was a musician, and invited me to come see him play." She took me to where Bechet was playing; this was very early, it must have been 1922. I was a kid. It was called the International House or something. On different floors were different types of music. There was an American bar with pictures of cowboys and such. And there was Sidney with his soprano sax, dressed up like a cowboy. So years passed and I went to New York. One day I heard something about Sidney. Somebody tipped me off he was living somewhere uptown around 125th Street. I met him, and he was very nice. I mentioned my mother, but he didn't remember, he'd known so many women in his life. He wasn't doing too much. He'd had a tailor shop. I said let's get something to eat. So we went to an Italian grocery store for some sandwiches. There was a little room behind a display with a couple of tables. So we sat down to eat the sandwiches. We looked around and one of the walls had toilet paper stacked up to the ceiling. He said, "Now we're really in the shithouse." I asked him why he didn't make records. He said he wanted to make "Summertime" for RCA Victor and they told him no. They said, "That's not something for someone of your color." Sidney was a little pissed off. I said, "Make it for me, make it for Blue Note."

Tell me how your friend Francis Wolff came over to join forces with you.

Frank came over in 1941. He lived on the same street in Berlin. A very nice, swanky section. We met on the street and got acquainted. He was always nicely dressed, but not Germanic, he dressed like the Americans, or English. He was also a jazz fan. That was very early. You know you have friends in your life, but maybe only one friend really. Frank was that person for me. We were together day and night for almost thirty years. We were friends for fifty years. I left Europe fast when I noticed things were not going the right way. Frank was there until he got caught in the Hitler thing. The Gestapo came to his apartment. I was working feverishly to get Frank out. His brother and sister got out to England. I got him out on the last boat. The Gestapo came to the boat shed as it was leaving and examined everybody again. He thought it was all over, but somehow he was passed and he got to New York.

He had no recording experience either, did he?

No, he was just a record collector. Like me. I had the company started, and had done a few records. We got together right away as partners. He stayed in my place. I was working for an import firm and Frank had no job. He met a woman photographer with a little studio. She shot bar mitzvahs and weddings, and occasionally she sent Frank out to take some pictures. Between the two of us we made a living.

How did you two work together and divide responsibilities?

It came very naturally. I'm the kind of person who likes to run out and do things. I was the horse and he was the cart. All those things that I didn't want to be bothered with, Frank picked up. The business end of it. He did a lot of the detail things like the books, and taxes, and royalty statements. I saw the musicians and tried to get the sessions together. But he wasn't just sitting with the books. Frank was a jazz man. We always discussed things together. And he knew all the musicians, and the musicians all liked him because he was a very soft, nice person. You know how when two people are together all the time they start to look alike? People used to ask me about my brother Francis.

You always seemed to encourage especially free sessions. Do you think that helped lead to the bebop revolution of the forties?

The music we recorded in the beginning was a little different already from the usual. It had a certain flavor that stuck out from the other things that were more set already. This was in the Swing Era. That's when I met Ike Quebec. He was playing for Cab Calloway. It was a popular band with some fabulous musicians. Ike took Ben Webster's place after he left. I heard him play some solos and I said, my gosh, the man plays so beautifully, but he gets two choruses all through the evening and he's finished. I said to myself let him stretch out, let him play. I brought him in to Blue Note and we became very good friends. We had girlfriends together, and went out to make the scene together. I felt more comfortable uptown. Anyway, when bebop came along Ike was just as confused about it, in a way, as lots of other guys. When bebop came along a lot of famous players stopped and said, I can't play like that, I can't think like that. Ike had open ears and everything, though he was a member of the old school. But the both of us went to different sessions. We went often to 52nd Street to see Dizzy, Milt Jackson, Max Roach, and others, and they were improvising and playing the new way. It was so free, almost like Dixieland in spontaneity. Of course they weren't playing Dixieland, but it was a free music. Ike realized it was a new way of thinking.

So although you did not immediately understand bebop, because of your instincts you were receptive to it?

Yes. Receptive, of course. But I didn't dig it all the way. I'm sorry, I didn't, and I'm not the only one who didn't. Then I started to hear. I was always interested in drummers. I love drummers. So when I heard Max Roach I said, "Yeah, it's different." But I didn't know what it all was because I'm not a musician, and I could never read a note. All those years I had Blue Note I went by my ears and by my feeling. So I didn't know what they were doing with different timing and so forth, I just heard the difference. But it started to click for me. I could hear it better. Ike came to me and said, "There are some good pianists around. Why don't you listen to them?" One was Thelonious Monk, and the other was Bud Powell. So Ike and I went to see Monk, and when I heard him I keeled over. I said, "That guy's so different—the compositions, the beat." I loved him, and that's how we started with Monk and bop. Then Bud came up the same way. He was fantastic, and I went for that.

You recorded Monk in the forties before anybody had.

Nobody else had! It was such a struggle because people thought we were nuts. Nobody wanted to buy the records. Except for a few like Ira Gitler. There were other big critics who didn't want to hear about Monk. We couldn't give Monk away. But we made some records. And we made some records again! The hell with it. I thought, "I've got to get this all down on records." I went uptown to Harlem with the records. All those people who are supposed to be simple, no culture, they said, "Hey, this guy's good." Then he made "Round Midnight" and oh boy! They put that on the jukebox. What a personality he was. He played the same way in the forties as he did later on. He never became a big technician on the piano. But he had his own thing. He had twenty-seven compositions, and I wanted to get it all down. We recorded everything he had. He didn't compose very much more after those.

Ted Fox [19855], *In the Groove: The People Behind the Music,* (New York: St. Martin's Press, 1985) 106–109.

WHILE GAINING ADHERENTS THROUGHOUT THE WORLD, [jazz] ran into increasing resistance from the Puritan American conscience. The general public saw in jazz, and the audience for which it played, a threat to accepted social standards. During the First World War, jazz became the cultural safety valve for the sexual and aggressive emotions which had become intensified by wartime hysteria. During the reactionary "return to normalcy" postwar period, Prohibition created within the American population an even larger rebellious minority. The "speak-easies" in Chicago and New York nurtured the Jazz Age. The sphere of influence of jazz was widening.

However, this music, indigenous to America's strange national and racial mixtures, and embodying in its very form the democratic idea of unity through diversity, found more serious consideration in France, in particular, and Europe, in general, than it did at home. Despite the increasingly large audience for jazz, and the impressive number of white as well as Negro musicians within its ranks, jazz had become so intimately associated with society's outcasts that it remained outside the artistic experience of most American people. There are several reasons for this. Evidently, the American psychological factors of race supremacy and Puritan conscience could not tolerate the return to primitivism which Europe embraced in all its art forms at this period. The general cultural level of American art was so conservative that even the new within the traditional forms of composition was rejected, as for example was Charles Ives, in favor of slavish copies of European nineteenth-century music. However, European composers like Milhaud, Stravinsky, and Hindemith looked at jazz with perspective and saw in it great possibilities for the revitalization of traditional forms of music.

The dangerous tendency has been, especially in France, to restrict jazz to the primitive New Orleans music and to consider any development after that an unwelcome deviation from the African core. The critical jazz fans in Europe, and the small, rabid group in the United States who refuse to hear modern jazz as a natural evolution of the music they so enthusiastically embraced, usually cling to the stereotyped myths of jazz: that only an uneducated creative mind can play jazz, that it expresses only the raucous and primitive elements of American culture, that it is solely a Negro expression.

The addition of European elements does not arbitrarily mean bad jazz. Duke Ellington proved this by handling the classical elements in jazz with such originality that his compositions remain the most authentic jazz expression in traditional forms of compositions.

Jazz has always been a hybrid music. What most people do not realize is that the history of the harmonic conception of jazz has paralleled that of composed music, except that jazz has lagged about twenty years in its exploitation of harmonic ideas discovered by European composers. Even today contemporary jazz is years behind the new harmonic concepts of contemporary composers, but the gap is fast narrowing. It is important to add that in this parallel growth there have been occasions when jazz contributed heavily to traditional forms of music by the originality of concept and emotional expressiveness.

The non-Negroid elements which appeared in swing were not a complete compromise of the jazz tradition, but indicative of the gradual integration and expansion of the Negro in the American culture. When the jazz musician became aware of the symphonic form and classical musical devices, it was as natural for him to absorb this music and reflect it in jazz, as it had been for his earlier exposure to traditional marches, popular tunes, and hymns to be reflected in the rag form and the blues.

Adapting the harmonic concepts of the romantic and especially the impressionistic composers, and utilizing classical musical devices in arrangements, the jazz musician combined folk, popular, and classical elements to produce swing. The "head arrangement" gradually gave way to written big-band arrangements, free counterpoint to the repeated riff, and the heavy two-beat accent to the smoother syncopation of swing, which specialized in easy dance tempos. The change in style answered two needs. It gave the public acceptable dance music, vocalists, and well-arranged "pop" tunes from Tin Pan Alley. It offered the searching jazz musician the whole heritage of European harmony and orchestration, while it still retained enough of the hot core of jazz through its soloists to attract many of this country's most talented musicians. The result was a delicate balance between popular commercialism and creative jazz.

By 1941, the ambivalent character of swing became increasingly evident. The importance of the star vocalist and the arranger was exploited for mass consumption. The improviser, who had sparked the swing band with his creative solos, carried on the old tradition by organizing small "combos."

Among the jazz experimenters in the forties was a group in New York which extended the choruses of the swing era into a specialized form of improvisation. Ignoring the original melody (which the initiated knew without reiteration), these musicians improvised their own themes based on their own alteration of the chords of standard tunes. They demanded that audiences listen. Tempos were set for instrumental performance, not for dancing. This music, called "bop," was a radical protest, not only against a world in war, but against the growing commercialism that threatened the extinction of an American art form.

For its audience bop attracted a comparatively small, but fanatically loyal, group of intellectuals, artists, and malcontents, who felt in the tense new music some of their own revolt from a society that had betrayed them. While the general public sought *escape* in popular vocalists, hill-billy tunes, novelty bands, and vulgarized interpretations of rhythm and blues, the restless protest fringe was seeking *expression* of its discontent. Part of that expression was fulfilled in the controlled, masterful, emotional realism of bop.

The continuity of jazz history had been violently disrupted by World War II. Musicians who had served their apprenticeship by playing all kinds of jobs in all styles of jazz and were approaching the age for serious contributions to jazz were in the service. There was a demand for entertainment and a dearth of competent musicians. Crusading bop was the center of creative activity. Consequently, the newcomers to jazz patterned their music so directly after Parker, Gillesipie, Davis, and the other leaders that much of the music of this and of the postwar era degenerated into an endless repetition of bop cliches. Thus, the complex, highly individual styles perfected by Parker and a handful of great bop musicians unwittingly determined the course of jazz history. Their return to "raw emotions" is a saving landmark in the tradition of jazz.

Bop and, later, "cool jazz" were extreme reactions against the vulgar escape music that thrived on the hysteria of the times. While the cool-jazz men can be condemned for alienating the public, it has been their uncompromising attitude toward their music that has kept jazz alive and creative during the postwar eclipse.

Though jazz has just struggled through a period of rejection and disfavor, many of us who were overseas during the war returned to the United States with confidence in its future as an important contribution to world music. We had witnessed for ourselves the powerful symbol of freedom jazz had become in Nazi Germany—and the role it had played toward liberation in the French Underground, Sweden, and England. There was a vitality in jazz—a basic universal dream implicit in its free expression of the individual—that made it an important music not only to Americans, but to the world. Many of us talked of a renaissance of jazz of world-wide nature. We see this dream materializing in the work of new jazz artists in Canada, England, Australia, Germany, France, the Scandinavian countries, even Japan—in fact in every country in the world which allows free expression.

There is need now for historical perspective and a conscious acceptance of the jazz tradition. The returning veterans who crowded the music conservatories to study under the G. I. Bill offered us a new hope. Many of them were jazz instrumentalists who would soon apply their knowledge of polytonality, atonality, counterpoint, and composition techniques to jazz. I do not mean to imply that the music scholar outweighs the natural musician in his contribution. Many of the jazz greats have been completely unaware of their roles, and in their freedom from classical restraint have succeeded so well in expressing their own individuality that they have touched upon the universal. At the grassroots level today are folk musicians who remind us that all of our preoccupation with form, technique, and analysis is but an attempt to speak within the art rules of music the same message they sing in poetic simplicity.

As a musician I feel free to explore the whole area of my musical heritage—from African drum batteries to Couperin, Bach, Jelly Roll, Stravinsky, or Charlie Parker. As a human being I feel free to explore the whole area of human emotions. If I am successful as a musician, this mixed musical heritage is projected into the future in a manner worthy of the name "art form."

Jazz offers the medium for expressing the conflicts and dreams of the people in an emotional language they comprehend.

Today the jazz artist is faced with an artistic dilemma. How far shall we deviate from the folk characteristics of jazz? Shall we change the steady 4/4 or 2/4 beat, which for so long has been the pulse of jazz? Do we break with tonality? Shall we expand the restrictive 32-bar form? How much of the techniques of composition can we utilize without losing the spontaneity of the group improvisation? Is the structural, harmonic, melodic, and rhythmic framework of the standard tune too limited for the advancement of contemporary jazz?

I hope that in answering these questions the audiences and the musicians of the future will remember the dual role of jazz as a folk as well as an art music, as a fusion of African group consciousness with the Renaissance concept of individualism.

In jazz the audience is an essential participant. How it participates is a variable determined at the moment by the empathy established between listener and improviser. The emotional impact of the music depends as much on the sympathetic, responsive ear of the listener as the free imaginations of the musicians. Commercialism exists when the artist and the audience impose upon themselves restrictions, determining the emotional and intellectual level of their communication. The first challenge of a jazz performer is to unify the diverse responses of an audience so that it becomes an entity. Co-creation exists in this timeless area of subconscious communication when the improviser becomes the articulate voice of the group. The compassion of this inspired moment of unity is the reason for jazz and for its continued existence.

In a little more than a half century the cry of protest has become the voice of liberation, and the musical dialect of an American minority has the possibility of becoming a universal music for all people.

Dave Brubeck, "Jazz Perspective" [1951] from *Perspectives U.S.A. #15*, Spring 1956, 22–28.

I PICKED UP THE DOUBLE REISSUE OF BRUBECK TRIOS and recalled how I needled every crevice of those Fantasy 10-inchers till you could almost see light through them. Some of his heads on those tunes, when not too consciously "classical," still shine. Tea For Two is one. I just got a flash of the wallpaper pattern in that attic room of my folks' house where I first listened to those sides snapping brushes across my first snare drum (a Slingerland black & gold-flash model). No wonder I never learned to dance! Or prove geometry propositions. Ancient frigates sailing toward purple clumps of weed . . .

All the old Brubeck quartets, up until Morello joined, are well worth the rehearsing. Especially the live recordings. Jazz Goes to College is an album I've never tired of. Even its acoustics (via early amateur tape) have a presence (before Columbia fucked it up with phony starey-o) that sounds to me like the sound of meditation itself, maybe because I think it was this precise album that I learned to listen *into* music on. I even love to ponder the most whacky poundering mad-grit Brubeckian key-gnashings, where it sounds like he's trying to carve out harmonies with axe-point from *inside* (if only he had a rhythmic sense equal to his harmony-head). I don't think I know a more intense all-out *improvisation* than his Balcony Rock solo. I mean, you can talk about swing, fingerpopping et al, but that slow build up through some of the maddest cornerturnings of idea, his way of using riff structures to layer strange heavy chordal bunches that even got Cecil Taylor at that time. And Desmond I've come to appreciate (hardly the word) even more since my early fascination with the group. I see him as an unequaled *melodic* improviser. His solo on Little Girl Blue (Jazz: Red Hot & Cool) still kills me. And his Carnegie Hall variations on For All We Know, a gorgeous tune with that altered change at the end. Outside the Bru Band a favorite Desmond is the Warner's First Place Again album, pure melody out of air on the perfect touch of Percy Heath and Jim Hall. But so many . . . Even the later albums, where he's fighting Morello for a lot of the time, have perfect Desmond melodics. And the sadness of that last tour when he had almost no breath left, could only play short phrases. On the concert broadcast by Public Television he played a whole solo on A Train *totally* composed of tiny quotes from other tunes.

Joe Dodge's bass drum. A sound to reckon with, still. Best recorded example: that opening shot on A Train (Jazz Goes to College). I once asked him how he could possibly get that sound, like a door slammed at the end of a long hallway. He just pointed to the batter head, the calfskin totally hidden beneath masses of moleskin bandages and adhesive tape repairs.

There's still a lot of retrievable mystery in those long solos, "my own catastrophes" Brubeck once called them. Massed harmonic wisdoms, sometimes he seems almost to forget rhythm entirely, so bound down he gets in the chordal depths. I can recall fifties Brubeck concerts where you'd get that "I saw him inside" feeling of total committed improvisation. The main reason he was such a hero-model for me as a kid. One could take universe in hand and make it over (on the fly) into a run to the end of (the) night. Literally everything else faded away from those moments of solo which grew huge in time and even space. Later I began to see the frat-boys spilling beer on their Bru discs and gave 'em a sneer. What could they possibly hear? Collegian popularity must've been some colossal mistake? It's impossible not to feel superior at some point in your life? The look and manner of those Bru guys, especially when not playing?, must have made them acceptable enough to fifties lounge-sitters. But when I watched Brubeck playing I saw the possibility of madness.

Meditative space of the long Brubeck feel. I remember watching him build up those big structures. Serious digging-in and platforming the space beneath you with wielded notes. Brubeck some kind of chordal carpenter. Desmond the sluice-gate for tensile exhalation. Brubeck with a real hold on narrowing & thickening the line. The tension of sequence as a sentence structure. Improv meant you went at it HARD, clang down of hands, use your legs too. High-wire walker tipping a lead bar for monstrous balance. And then, suddenly chorus-end amazement of your position, raise brows and blow pianissimo, sing and let the dust settle in the blackbox. The crowd will wait behind the lights. Pin drop to babble roar of Brubeck audiences in a few seconds flat. Risks as coefficient of high-paying oneniters. I hear fifties Brubeck always in a closed-in echoing four-square hallspace, pin-point on the black varnish corners, Brubeck arrayed in a huge hunch, his head disappearing below the Baldwin sign, Desmond's hands clasped over a tiny brass glow, his tight smile closed-eye punning on his hands, Joe Dodge chugging his used-car bassdrum blanks with a very hip configuration of angled elbows and ducked head behind light hornrims. A clangor boxed in quiet. They had their structures of jazz to climb, no matter the uptown derogatories of hardbop nothing putdowns, the endless replays of their least interesting tune. They belong in no "stream," anomalysville forever. I see them in the fifties heights, making planes to Oroville, taking pictures of airports, numberless choruses of On The Alamo tending and pending in their brains, signing autographs with regular-guy smiles while within it's all innards of risk and "weird" musics to get up on and speak your piece before TIME covers slam down on everyone and the vista wastes into middle-aged Morellos at every bus station grinning and slapping five.

Clark Coolidge (personal correspondence with the author).

I AM THE LAST INDIVIDUAL IN THE WORLD. His claim was no longer hard to understand, but behind it lay the unanswered question: How could a man be so alone and unambitious and still be so confident and content? There was a secret somewhere within him. There had to be.

Between sets at Fack's Jaeger found himself alone. Coming out of the back room after a drink and standing in the shadows along one wall, he could see and feel countless eyes watching him. They wanted to meet him, buy him a drink, talk to him about jazz, find out how he liked San Francisco and what he thought about Chet and Brubeck and Shorty. They wanted to know him so that later, over campus coffee, they could say, casually, that they were talking to Ross Jaeger the other night and he said San Francisco was a great town, he would like to live here someday, and that Brubeck was way the hell out as far as piano went. Jaeger knew what was hidden in the glances because the eyes had been the same at The Zouzou, at Berg's, at Birdland and The Deuces and The Silhouette, at every place small enough to bring him close to the audience. Sometimes one of them would drift over and ask for his autograph, and when he signed, every now and then they would be encouraged into inviting him to join their table. And in places like this, where he knew no one, he accepted gratefully but did not dare show it. He had his pride. It would not do to impose himself on anyone who looked at him like a celebrity.

So, inevitably, there were times when they stared at him but did not ask, while he noticed them but could not ask, and presently he would climb to the piano and play for them again.

All the first week it was the same at closing time. The others in the quintet were fifth-raters who had so much respect for him that he was never asked to join them; they assumed that Jaeger had his own life to lead, and that after playing with them all night he had had enough of them. And, just as he felt toward the audience, Jaeger secreted his isolation and made no attempt to impose himself on them.

So he would leave Fack's alone and drive his Hertz Cadillac to an all-night chophouse down the Peninsula along its El Camino Real, where, still brilliantly awake, he smoked over bottomless black coffee and ate cheese or bacon omelets. Then he would go back to his hotel, take a scalding shower, and fall asleep with The Sporting Green of *The Chronicle* folded on his chest.

The second week brought relief. It started with a guest-spot on an afternoon record program, and the same night he got a call from Flip Phillips, who was opening at The Blackhawk. San Francisco was opening like a night-blossoming flower.

Phillips knew good people in the city. Together Jaeger and he would meet at either one of the clubs after their shows and head out for apartments on Russian Hill or ranch-low homes across the Bay. Only twice did the sleepy-eyed tenorman pack his saxophone for a night of extra-curricular jamming with Jaeger on piano. For the most part their hosts let them relax and treated them like any normal friends. Jazz conversation was not compulsory, and it was a tonic to be able to sound off about politics and advertising and winter baseball trades and the shortsightedness of the tract-home building boom in California and why Los Angeles should be expelled from the state for giving it such a bad name.

But the evenings always ended. The fog rolled from the sea like a glacier of wool, muffling the sun and orange bridge girders and pastel-sided houses, mirroring asphalt with dampness, making blurs of faces and headlights and morning neon, and finally, as always, bringing with it another day and the time when Jaeger was again in his room alone.

Dressed in a white terrycloth robe and with slippered feet braced against the windowsill, he wore memory in his eyes and cigarettes in his mouth. The cigarettes were from the carton Helen had given him before leaving. She had opened each package and one by one put every cigarette between heavy red lips. The oil of her lipstick had dried and was now tasteless, but he felt the touch of her each time he bit the darkened end.

Stanford Whitmore, *Solo*, (New York: Harcourt, Brace and Company, 1955) 159–161.

blues for billie holiday

I.

soft & quiet are the rooms in which
the lady of day chants her runes & riffs.
reverence &
peace to the sound.

an anguish ended. call
it a life. a lonely bed,
robed, defiled,
too frightened to take her last fix.

the singer of songs, stilled.
the beautiful throat, clogged.
the hottest flesh, chilled.

2.

life is that disease
we are infected with at birth.
we die of it with ease
& become earth.

the earth does not care
about the body's scars.
to it all is air,
& stars.

o earth, our mother, enfold
this twisted & beautiful soul.
let her become a bird, or a tree.
let her be one with thee.

3.

mirror, mirror, in my soul
who is the guiltiest of all?
mirror, mirror, in my eyes,
where does peace & penance lie?
mirror, mirror, in my flesh
whose name is written across the glass?

        man /
            giant numbskull dingo junkie slob
            angel killer cesspool bone & blood
            bird ocean moon fire earth knife
            skin torn death born eyes scorn jazz horn life

            o Goddess, grant him
            o poets, chant him
            o demons, taunt him
            o love, haunt him

4.

billie dead
in a cold bed.
paid up dues
no more blues

now she flies
thru the eyes
touches each face
in close embrace

she can sing
anything.
she can rest
has passed the test

you & i
have yet to die.
while she flies
we live more lies.

the lady sings
of truth & sorrow
the lady of day
the lady of tomorrow

[1976]

Stuart Z. Perkoff, *Visions for the Tribe*, (Denver: Black Ace/Temple of Man/Bowery 25, 1976).

FIVE YEARS ON THE STREET THAT NEVER SLEEPS, and I never sleep. I'm beginning to smell bad to myself. Five years, Ruthie is still carrying my music, one club to another. We play the cocktail hour, the shows, the afterhours joints, round the clock—never go home. And it's union scale, just fifty-six dollars a week. Some life! And the future . . . I see Maxie Kaminsky, the Dixieland trumpet player—he's taking the subway. Ten years older than me! a great musician! riding the subway! We

still live on Ruth's money, still send mine home to Florence and the
kids . . . but there's four of them now . . .

Billie's moving around in the next dressing room, at the Deuces.
I'm changing my shirt—you sweat buckets, doing a show . . .

"Hey, Hipster, it's about time for my medicine"—she's calling
from next door—"Come over and help me, would you?"

Lady talks the way she sings. Molasses with something bitter in it.
Slow, no hurry, then everything together—then nothing. Breaking over
a word, like a hurt animal . . . I can't listen to her sometimes—that pure
sorrow.

"Yeah, baby," I say, "I'll be right over. Just changing my shirt . . ."

She's real sad today, sad and slow, because she hasn't had her medicine. She's just in her underwear—reaches into her pants grabs the cel-
lophane bag of powder. The room smells like her, bitter—even with
all the rotten gardenias. White women smell sour—black women, bitter. She's nodding. Can't keep her head up. Too much effort to live . . .

"Got to change my stash . . . Dreamed last night, they busted me,
man . . . I know they were following me today . . . one car . . . saw it
through the window every time I looked back . . . every time . . . Mama
said she heard clicks on the phone—I know they're bugging the
line . . ."

She's cooking a spoon . . . keeps striking matches . . . puts it in the
syringe . . .

"Aw, Billie, why the hell would they do all that? If they're gonna
bust ya, they'll just bust ya."

"No, you don't understand. They playing cat and mouse. *Playing*
with me. You drive home with *me* some night! up to Harlem. I see them
kick the shit out of them old wino niggers, the old whores, anybody
they can get their damn *hands* on. Kick 'em in the stomach. Wail on
them, man, *wail* . . ."

She's winding a kerchief around her arm. Red silk.

"Hold that turnikey now. Hold it tight."

She's in slow motion . . . underwater . . . waiting for the veins to
pop . . . The track's all the way down her arm. Elbow to wrist. She's
searching in the middle. Gets the mark—pulls some blood up the needle . . . dark brown. She's on the vein. Presses down, hard. "Oh, yeah,"

she says, "oh, yeah!"

It's an explosion. She's buzzing. Her cheeks flush. You can see the pink. Her eyes shine—teary, strange—dancing! "Oh, yeah! That's what I'm talkin' about!"

"Come on, talk to me, I need company. You want a taste? You're just a little boy, you can't have too much. But I'll give you a tippy." She puts it on a nail file and holds it under my nose. A little of Billie's stuff got you really high. "Okay, one for you, two for me. You don't want to get no habit! Don't laugh. I mean it. I see you hanging around with all those bad junkies. You watch yourself!

"Man, I never would have started if it wasn't for those dirty pimps. They give you a shitpail full of it—get you working! pump your ass! I was just a kid . . .

"Man, I don't eat right any more. I used to be fat and smooth. Look at me. Won't eat my own mamma's cookin' . . . You know that Lester —that man! hasn't balled for months! . . . lies there dreaming . . . talking to his damned self . . . all morning long . . . Too much shit!

"And those bad dreams, those nightmares! Last night I dreamed I was busted . . . I could feel that cold cement floor under me . . ."

The band's playing downstairs—Ben Webster. As long as they take choruses, nobody's coming up to bother us. Billie sits on my lap, wraps herself around me like a cloud . . .

Somebody bangs on the door. "Go away! Who the fuck is that?" Billie says. "Who'd they let up here? We don't want to talk to nobody right now!"

"Lemme in! It's me! It's Dizzy, baby!"

"Listen, I don't want no Dizzy! I got to go on in a while. You too jumpy! You make me nervous . . ."

He's banging louder—using his feet. Gets his shoulder into it. He's a big guy, with a bull neck—when he plays horn, he blows up like a cobra—head! neck! shoulders!

"Dizzy! You stop that! Just go to hell with yourself! I told you I don't want no Dizzy! You damn crazy fool! Coming around, making people mad!"

He's through the door seeing red . . . eyeballs popping . . . two hundred pounds, and off his skull! Why didn't we let him in, that's what he'd like to know. He wants to talk . . . things on his mind . . . He's not just anybody! He's Dizzy! Can't he talk to Billie once in a while? And if she's so nervous, what the ofay piano player doing here?

Billie picks up a pair of scissors. She's high! a powerhouse! after his ass! quick! Dizzy flies around the room, running into walls, tripping, banging his shins, his head. "What the fuck's wrong with you, woman?" He gesticulates. "Put that thing down. It's *Dizzy!*"

"You fuckin' botherin' me! Give me a minute of peace! If it ain't the square johns, it's the damn musicians! John Hammond's down there. Fuck John Hammond! Don't want to see no John *Hammond*, no *Dizzy*, no *nobody!*

Dizzy got the message! He's in the corner, all over himself, trying to get out. The mirror's spilled on the floor—sparkling . . . Dizzy's breathing hard. "I just want to get out now, Baby! Lemme out the door! All right? . . . Never seen nobody get so mad! . . . Damn! . . ."

He's gone. Billie pushes the door into the jamb. It's completely haywire. A mess. She sits down, breathing hard—swears to herself . . . "That Dizzy was a sight! Thought I was gonna cut him! with the damned scissors!" She laughs a chorus . . . sweat pours on her face . . . She comes close, spills it on me. "Ben's still blowing," she says, "let's be nice to each other."

Harry "The Hipster" Gibson, as told to Arlena Gibson-Feller, "From the Hipster: The Story of Harry 'The Hipster' Gibson" in *Sulfur 17*, vol. 6, #2. 1986, 14–16.

(. . .) SO IT IS NO ACCIDENT THAT THE SOURCE of Hip is the Negro for he has been living on the margin between totalitarianism and democracy for two centuries. But the presence of Hip as a working philosophy in the sub-worlds of American life is probably due to jazz, and its knifelike entrance into culture, its subtle but so penetrating influence on an avant-garde generation—that postwar generation of adventurers who (some consciously, some by osmosis) had absorbed the lessons of disillusionment and disgust of the twenties, the depression, and the war. Sharing a collective disbelief in the words of men who had too much money and controlled too many things, they knew almost as powerful a disbelief in the socially monolithic ideas of the single mate, the solid family and the respectable love life. If the intellectual antecedents of this generation can be traced to such separate influences as D. H. Lawrence, Henry Miller, and Wilhelm Reich, the viable philosophy of Hemingway fit most of their facts: in a bad world, as he was to say over and over again (while taking time out from his parvenu snobbery and dedicated gourmandize), in a bad world there is no love nor mercy nor charity nor justice unless a man can keep his courage, and this indeed fitted some of the facts. What fitted the need of the adventurer even more precisely was Hemingway's categorical imperative that what made him feel good became therefore The Good.

So no wonder that in certain cities of America, in New York of course, and New Orleans and Chicago and San Francisco and Los Angeles, in such American cities as Paris and Mexico, D. F., this particular part of a generation was attracted to what the Negro had to offer. In such places as Greenwich Village, a ménage-à-trois was completed—the bohemian and the juvenile delinquent came face-to-face with the Negro, and the hipster was a fact in American life. If marijuana was the wedding ring, the child was the language of Hip, for its argot gave expression to abstract states of feeling which all could share, at least all who were Hip. And in this wedding of the white and the black it was the Negro who brought the cultural dowry. Any Negro who wishes to live must live with danger from his first day, and no experience can ever be casual to him, no Negro can saunter down a street with any real certainty that violence will not visit him on his walk. The cameos of security for the average white: mother and the home, job and the family, are not even a mockery to millions of Negroes; they are impossible. The Negro has the simplest of alternatives: live a life of constant humility or ever-threatening danger. In such a pass where paranoia is as vital to survival as blood, the Negro has stayed alive and begun to grow by following the need of his body where he could. Knowing in the cells of his existence that life was war, nothing but war, the Negro (all exceptions admitted) could rarely afford the sophisticated inhibitions of civilization, and so he kept for his survival the art of the primitive, he lived in the enormous present, he subsisted for his Saturday night kicks, relinquishing the pleasures of the mind for the more obligatory pleasures of the body, and in his music he gave voice to the character and quality of his existence, to his rage and the infinite variations of joy, lust, languor, growl, cramp, pinch, scream and despair of his orgasm. For jazz is orgasm, it is the music of orgasm, good orgasm and bad, and so it spoke in no matter what laundered popular way of instantaneous existential states to which some whites could respond, it was indeed a communication by art because it said, "I feel this, and now you do too."

So there was a new breed of adventurers, urban adventurers who drifted out at night looking for action with a black man's code to fit their facts. The hipster had absorbed the existentialist synapses of the Negro, and for practical purposes could be considered a white Negro.

Yet there is this to be said for the search after the good orgasm: when one lives in a civilized world, and still can enjoy none of the cultural nectar of such a world because the paradoxes on which civilization is built demand that there remain a cultureless and alienated bottom of exploitable human material, then the logic of becoming a sexual outlaw (if one's psychological roots are bedded in the bottom) is that one has at least a running competitive chance to be physically healthy so long as one stays alive. It is therefore no accident that psychopathy is most prevalent with the Negro. Hated from the outside and therefore hating himself, the Negro was forced into the position of exploring all those moral wildernesses of civilized life which the Square automatically condemns as delinquent or evil or immature or morbid or self-destructive or corrupt. (Actually the terms have equal weight. Depending on the telescope of the cultural clique from which the Square surveys the universe, "evil" or "immature" are equally strong terms of condemnation.) But the Negro, not being privileged to gratify his self-esteem with the heady satisfactions of categorical condemnation, chose to move instead in that other direction where all situations are equally valid, and in the worst of perversion, promiscuity, pimpery, drug addiction, rape, razor-slash, bottle-break, what-have-you, the Negro discovered and elaborated a morality of the bottom, an ethical differentiation between the good and the bad in every human activity from the go-getter pimp (as opposed to the lazy one) to the relatively dependable pusher or prostitute. Add to this, the cunning of their language, the abstract ambiguous alternatives in which from the danger of their oppression they learned to speak ("Well, now, man, like I'm looking for a cat to turn me on . . ."), add even more the profound sensitivity of the Negro jazzman who was the cultural mentor of a people, and it is not too difficult to believe that the language of Hip which evolved was an artful language, tested and shaped by an intense experience and therefore different in kind from white slang, as different as the special obscenity of the soldier, which in its emphasis on "ass" as the soul and "shit" as circumstance, was able to express the existential states of the enlisted man. What makes Hip a special language is that it cannot really be taught—if one shares none of the experiences of elation and exhaustion which it is equipped to describe, then it seems merely arch or vulgar or irritating. It is a pictorial language, but pictorial like non-objective art, imbued with the dialectic of small but intense change, a language for the microcosm, in this case, man, for it takes the immediate experience of any passing man and magnifies the dynamic of his movements, not specifically but abstractly so that he is seen more as a vector in a network of forces than as a static character in a crystallized field. (Which latter is the practical view of the snob.) . . .

It is obviously not very possible to speculate with sharp focus on the future of the hipster. Certain possibilities must be evident, however, and the most central is that the organic growth of Hip depends on whether the Negro emerges as a dominating force in American life. Since the Negro knows more about the ugliness and danger of life than the white, it is probable that if the Negro can win his equality, he will possess a potential superiority, a superiority so feared that the fear itself has become the underground drama of domestic politics. Like all conservative political fear it is the fear of unforeseeable consequences, for the Negro's equality would tear a profound shift into the psychology, the sexuality, and the moral imagination of every white alive.

No matter what its horrors the twentieth century is a vastly exciting century for its tendency is to reduce all of life to its ultimate alternatives one can well wonder if the last war of them all will be between the blacks and the whites, or between the women and the men, or between the beautiful and ugly, the pillagers and managers, or the rebels and the regulators . . .

Norman Mailer, "The White Negro," from *Advertisements for Myself*, (New York: Rinehart, 1958) 340–341, 347–348, 355–356, 357.

Broadway! Broadway!

Halloween is black and orange.
A song, as in "le clarinet du marmalade."
Some are happiest drowned
in a saxophone solo.

>   "Le jazz hot" rhymes à la Mallarmé
>   with tabasco: vide Bunk Johnson
>   astomp in New Iberia.

>   I saw Dexter Gordon play to six people
>   in a frayed suit. His golden horn had lost
>   its sheen. The notes gleamed.

Dexter in his brilliance.
Exquisite phrasing and perfect comedy.
A black velvet an
orange corona corona.

[1978]

Gilbert Sorrentino, *Selected Poems 1958–1980*, (Santa Barbara: Black Sparrow Press, 1981) 208.

WALTER SUTTON: You said you don't like much modern music. What is your feeling about jazz, and the attention that the Beat poets have given it?

WILLIAM CARLOS WILLIAMS: The Beat generation has nothing to do with beat, and they should if they're interested in jazz because jazz is always percussive. But in jazz music even the saxophone sounds are not advanced enough from the primitive to interest me at all. I don't like jazz. The artists in Paris rave about jazz, but it's too tiresome, it's too much the same thing.

SUTTON: There's not enough variability?

WILLIAMS: Not variability at all. Not subtle. And if you've got to be sexually excited by it, it shows you to be a boob. It merely excites; there's no subtlety at all . . .

SUTTON: From what you have said about jazz, and other things as well, it seems that the critics who have tried to classify you as a primitive may be off the beam.

WILLIAMS: I think so. I was very sexually successful, as a young man, but I did not believe in going so far that I lost my head. I wanted always to be conscious. I didn't want to indulge in sex so much that I lost my head.

SUTTON: This may be a distinction to make between you and the Beats, since I think that in Beat poetry there is often the desire to get beyond consciousness somehow—

WILLIAMS: Yes, I think so very definitely.

SUTTON: —through jazz or sex or dope, or whatever it may be.

WILLIAMS: Dope! That I have no sympathy for at all! I want to be always deeper intellectually—That's a bad term to use—intellectually—because it makes you think of the thinker, but I don't think that the thinker's thinking anything out any more than Kant thought out in his *Critique of Pure Reason*. What did he think he was coming to? Except futility. And I don't believe in the Beat. I've known some of the Beat poets. But they only confuse themselves. That is, an anti-Beat tenet of mine would be the variable foot. But what do they know about the variable foot? They've never thought anything about it. They don't even know that poetry is written in measurable feet.

SUTTON: Is that one reason why this poetry can be read with jazz? Because it doesn't have a beat of its own anyway, would you say?

WILLIAMS: That is a very good thought. I think it is because they want to be *primitive*. And they *want* to be primitive.

SUTTON: Self-consciously.

WILLIAMS: Yes, self-consciously. And they can't be primitive. The only thing they can be is more thoughtful than ever ... I've known many primitive people, but they are surprisingly complex when you get to know them. Their primitive natures disappear. They become quiet. We value them as individuals not because of their beat characteristics but because they are capable of becoming more like us.

William Carlos Williams and Walter Sutton from *Interviews with William Carlos Williams: "Speaking Straight Ahead,"* Linda Welshimer Wagner, ed., (New York: New Directions, 1976) 54–56.

(wife snoozin on the sofa/ dog under the table: little boy upstairs— pretty cool, I'd say.)

Some nota/ ah.

I.e., some of these warm days, you shd be picking up on, say, they
sd: New Sounds—I mean, say, as of this mo/ am sitting here listening
to some (real) nice things. Well, it is the matters of time (1) and variation (2): that cd interest you. It is not to suggest that a logos (this)
can be jumped to a logos (that)—but there are parallels. Many times
have thought (tho not without blindness) if, say, if: I cd put down a
series of lines, that wd string themselves, like the lines/ line: in Bach
(back/ & back): well/ wd be one sweet biz. Now with the matter at
hand—here is the gig. The Bird (also Chas) has strung his way thru
abt (now) 30 variations (on wax) of the one I GOT RHYTHM
(agreed)—where we have, as you will know, a series of (basick) chords
which can be extended in a strict (gripped) manner, inverted, wound,
pitched, & heaved, or let's just—go. so we go, like: la do de da: becomes
oo oo de la oo/ (oo) da ee oo/ (different but the same: like Coleridge,
yet). Well, it is something to hear, old sport, if against yr ear you is
placing, are, the basic sounds/ then these: well, back in Burma. sipping
my—tea. But timing: there we can learn, right from the pattern, without
more (ado). There is nothing being put down that can match/ that
timing: Bird's. It is: flight/ on sound & sense. Good stuff. Well, can't
say more, except that you wd do well/ to stay clear of: bop/ usual shit.
It aint the thing (the same thing)—but like the biz of the ( ) it was
bird taught me. And, to be true, the phrase like here, it is, is no different:
from there/ the same, a, a: push & sense, of: limit.

Well, to orient yrself: wd suggest you listen to any of the following.

Miles Davis:	Boplicity & reverse side.		
" "	: Move.		
The Bird	: Chasing the Bird	i got	
	: Cheryl		rhytmethe, . . .
	: Dont Blame Me		
	: Donna Lee	I got R/	
	: Billy's Bounce & so on? yes. There are a		
	great many/ but each of the		
	above: sd do it.		

The names to look for/ whenever getting this type:

                                                            musick/

Miles Davis, Chas Parker, Bud Powell, Max Roach, Milt
Jackson, Al Haig, &tc.
    But the above/ all yez know: on earth
    & all yez need: to know: to leave it.

me, i got eyes for asia.
(how you come on)

[Added at top of page:]
(later: perhaps not it/ but: for document and //: you will know/
that what makes the LINE in any of this, IS, most obviously, the
breath—it is a profitable analogy, for the problems of poetry, or just
so/the bird/within the limit of his sounds/ breath/ is attempting to
reach to: form/ from content: just so/ you/I: with our sound/sense:
and TIME. It is interesting, as document, to cite his KNOWING of
the problem. Tho it is assumed that all jazz (uh huh) has a (uh huh)
beat. (uh huh). Hmmmmm . . . Well, so has mary had er had: a little
lamb: I look to EXTENSIONS.)

[Fontrouse, Aix-en-Provence]
July 21/51

Dear Chas/

Still riding!
    And thinking:
        this whole gig rides
me as, just as, one item I had recalled, this morning, is: Chas Parker &
fellows, on a very simple song: After You've Gone.
                                            What that
is all about: one of those recordings done at a 'concert.' so that you get
noises, clappings, cheers, all thru same, & when any man, say, himself,
flips—the people fly out, seem to go out of their heads with same, &
so on.
                            At one point in sd
record, Chas Parker is gone, very damn truly, beyond any damn expect-
able limits of sd 'musick' and hangs there, just damn well hangs: & is
an almost blanket silence behind him, the rhythm section too surprised
to keep at it, etc.

And following, directly
—another (alto) rides in, so damn goofed with CP/s thing, he is off,
himself, riding, before, & long before, the people have quieted—so that
you hear, first, the sounds riding in, & out, on a chaos of clapping,
shouting, et al. To grow quiet, as it does, & the whole wt/ of this man's
wonder—then clear—as it is, & is, only, just an 'appreciation' of CP/.

Another, now thinking, & a very damn wonderful one it is: Slim
Gaillard, I think, who is, mostly, a joker—but has with him, that trip,
the Bird & Dizzy G/. And is, a talker, or thruout, they are talking, a
kind of: have to cut out, MUST . . . go, etc. And the thing: they are
swinging, this goofy little song, a kind of thing like a girl twisting her
skirt, or kid, kicking a stone, etc.

What all thru any of this: goofs met at least. The very damn wonder
of the whimsey, the damn fine lightness, & edge the best (& these are
Bird, Max Roach, Bud Powell, Miles Davis, et al) of them make—how,
always, the edge is, given, is always a doubling in on: the given, a kind
of *thing*, to be expended, to be brought round the hands, to have them
so shape round it, to *hold*.

I used to spend so many damn nights, talking, in
Boston, with same : musicians, et al, & some there : too much. How
one always backs up to it! Such damn pure delight—that in all speech
there is, all, play! And this, it is, again, what the best make of the gig/
musick : any occasion. IS, wonder.

Which I had in mind, then : that this issue, ORIGIN, boots itself home,
just so. Is, so very finely, such a continuum, & each man, excited,
brought into full play, by the man next to him.

(To ignore
the owl-eyed monstrosity with the French horn . . . . etc.
Mizziz : Foreskins)
Which is : BLOW / GO / MAN / GO!!!

(And damn well
ALWAYS : the end!)

[1950, 1951]

Robert Creeley [1950, 1951], from *Charles Olson & Robert Creeley: The Complete Correspondence*, vols. 1 and 6, George F. Butterick, ed., (Santa Barbara: Black Sparrow
Press, 1980, 1985) 1:155–157, 6:175–176.

... WHEN THELONIOUS SITS DOWN AT THE PIANO the whole hall sits down
with him and produces a collective sigh as great as his relief because
the diagonal progress of Thelonious across the stage contained something of the risk of piloting a Phoenician sailing ship with probable
grounding in sandbars, and when the ship loaded with dark honey and
its bearded captain reach the port the masonic wharf of Victoria Hall
receives it with a sound like air escaping from the sails as the ship's bow
touches the pier. Then it's "Pannonica," or "Blue Monk," three shadows
like masts surround the bear exploring the beehive of the keyboard, his
good rough paws coming and going among disorderly bees and hexa-
gons of sound; barely a minute has passed and already we are in a night
outside of time, the primitive and delicate night of Thelonious Monk.

Yet this is unexplained: A rose is a rose is a rose. We are becalmed,
someone intercedes, perhaps somewhere we will be redeemed. And
then, when Charles Rouse steps toward the microphone and his sax
imperiously shows us why it is there, Thelonious lets his hands fall,
listens a moment, tries a soft chord with his left hand, and the bear
rises, swaying like a hammock, and, having had his fill of honey or in
search of a mossy bank suited to his drowsiness, he leaves the bench
and leans against the end of the piano, where, as he marks the beat with
a foot and his cap, his fingers go gliding over the piano, first at the end
of the keyboard where there should be a beer and an ashtray but instead
there is only *Steinway & Sons,* and then imperceptibly his fingers set off
on a safari across the piano, while the bear sways to the beat, because
Rouse and the bass player and the drummer are entangled in the mystery of their trinity, and Thelonious makes a dizzying journey, barely
moving, progressing inch by inch toward the end of the piano, but he
won't reach it, you know he won't reach it because to get there he would
need more time than Phileas Fogg, more sail-sleds, more hemlock-
honey rapids, elephants, and high-speed trains to leap the abyss where
the bridge is down, so Thelonious travels in his own way, resting on
one leg and then the other without moving from the spot, teetering on
the point of his *Pequod* grounded in a theater, every so often moving his
fingers to gain an inch, or ten tenths, otherwise remaining still, as if on
guard, measuring the heights with a sextant of smoke and refusing to
go forward and reach the end of the piano, until his hand abandons

the shore, the bear gradually spins around, anything could happen in that moment when he is without his prop, when he glides like a halcyon bird on the rhythm through which Charles Rouse is casting out the last, long, intense, wonderful swashes of violet and red, we feel the emptiness of Thelonious away from the shore of the piano, the interminable diastole of one enormous heart where all of our blood is beating, and just at that moment his other hand falls from the piano, the bear teeters amiably and returns through the clouds to the keyboard, looks at it as if for the first time, passes his indecisive fingers through the air, lets them fall, and we are saved, it is Thelonious the Captain, we have our bearing again, and Rouse's gesture of moving back as he takes apart his sax contains something of the delivery of powers, of the legate who renders to the Doge the keys of Highest Serenity.

Julio Cortázar, *Around the Day in Eighty Worlds*, Thomas Christensen, trans., (San Francisco: North Point Press, 1986) 72–74.

JIVE MUSIC AND TEA were the two most important components of the hipster's life. Music was not, as has often been supposed, a stimulus to dancing. For the hipster rarely danced; he was beyond the reach of stimuli. If he did dance, it was half parody—"second removism"—and he danced only to the offbeat, in a morganatic one to two ratio with the music.

Actually, jive music was the hipster's autobiography, a score to which his life was the text. The first intimations of jive could be heard in the Blues. Jive's Blue Period was very much like Picasso's: it dealt with lives that were sad, stark, and isolated. It represented a relatively realistic or naturalistic stage of development.

Blues turned to jazz. In jazz, as in early, analytical cubism, things were sharpened and accentuated, thrown into bolder relief. Words were used somewhat less frequently than in the Blues; the instruments talked instead. The solo instrument became the narrator. Sometimes (e.g., Cootie Williams) it came very close to literally talking. Usually it spoke passionately, violently, complainingly, against a background of excitedly pulsating drums and guitar, ruminating bass, and assenting orchestration. But, in spite of its passion, jazz was almost always coherent and its intent clear and unequivocal.

Bebop, the third stage in jive music, was analogous in some respects to synthetic cubism. Specific situations, or referents, had largely disappeared; only their "essences" remained. By this time the hipster was no longer willing to be regarded as a primitive; bebop, therefore, was "cerebral" music, expressing the hipster's pretensions, his desire for an imposing, fulldress body of doctrine.

Surprise, "second-removism," and extended virtuosity were the chief characteristics of the bebopper's style. He often achieved surprise by using a tried and true tactic of his favorite comic strip heroes:

> The "enemy" is waiting in a room with drawn gun. The hero kicks open the door and bursts in—*not upright, in the line of fire*—but cleverly lying on the floor, from which position he triumphantly blasts away, while the enemy still aims, ineffectually, at his own expectations.

Borrowing this stratagem, the bebop soloist often entered at an unexpected altitude, came in on an unexpected note, thereby catching the listener off guard and conquering him before he recovered from his surprise.

"Second-removism"—capping the squares—was the dogma of initiation. It established the hipster as keeper of enigmas, ironical pedagogue, a self-appointed exegete. Using his shrewd Socratic method, he discovered the world to be naive, who still tilted with the windmills of one-level meaning. That which you heard in bebop was always *something else*, not the thing you expected; it was always negatively derived, abstraction *from*, not *to*.

The virtuosity of the bebopper resembled that of the streetcorner evangelist who revels in his unbroken delivery. The remarkable run-on quality of bebop solos suggested the infinite resources of the hipster, who could improvise indefinitely, whose invention knew no end, who was, in fact, omniscient.

All the best qualities of jazz—tension, élan, sincerity, violence, immediacy—were toned down in bebop. Bebop's style seemed to consist, to a great extent, in *evading* tension, in connecting, by extreme dexterity, each phrase with another, so that nothing remained, everything was lost in the shuffle of decapitated cadences. This corresponded to the hipster's social behavior as jester, jongleur, or prestidigitator. But it was his own fate he had caused to disappear for the audience, and now the only trick he had left was the monotonous gag of pulling himself—by his own ears, grinning and gratuitous—up out of the hat.

Bebop rarely used words, and, when it did, they were only nonsense syllables, significantly paralleling a contemporaneous loss of vitality in jive language itself. Blues and jazz were documentary in a social sense; bebop was the hipster's Emancipation Proclamation in double talk. It showed the hipster as the victim of his own system, volubly tongue-tied, spitting out his own teeth, running between the raindrops of his spattering chords, never getting wet, washed clean, baptized, or quenching his thirst. He no longer had anything relevant to himself to say—in both his musical and linguistic expression he had finally abstracted himself from his real position in society.

His next step was to abstract himself in action. Tea made this possible. Tea (marihuana) and other drugs supplied the hipster with an indispensable outlet. His situation was too extreme, too tense, to be satisfied with mere fantasy or animalistic domination of the environment. Tea had provided him with a free world to expatiate in. It had the same function as trance in Bali, where the unbearable flatness and de-emotionalization of "waking" life is compensated for by trance ecstasy. The hipster's life, like the Balinese's, became schizoid; whenever possible, he escaped into the richer world of tea, where, for the helpless and humiliating image of a beetle on its back, he could substitute one of himself floating or flying, "high" in spirits, dreamily disassociated, in contrast to the ceaseless pressure exerted on him in real life. Getting high was a form of artificially induced dream catharsis. It differed from *lush* (whisky) in that it didn't encourage aggression. It fostered, rather, the sentimental values so deeply lacking in the hipster's life. It became a *raison d'être*, a calling, an experience shared with fellow believers, a respite, a heaven or haven.

That he was a direct expression of his culture was immediately apparent in its reaction to him. The less sensitive elements dismissed him as they dismissed everything. The intellectuals *manqués*, however, the desperate barometers of society, took him into their bosom. Ransacking everything for meaning, admiring insurgence, they attributed every heroism to the hipster. He became their "there but for the grip of my superego go I." He was received in the Village as an oracle; his language was *the revolution of the word, the personal idiom.* He was the great instinctual man, an ambassador from the Id. He was asked to read things, look at things, feel things, taste things, and report. What was it? Was it *in there?* Was it *gone?* Was it *fine?* He was an interpreter for the blind, the deaf, the dumb, the insensible, the impotent.

With such an audience, nothing was too much. The hipster promptly became, in his own eyes, a poet, a seer, a hero. He laid claims to apocalyptic visions and heuristic discoveries when he *picked up;* he was Lazarus, come back from the dead, come back to tell them all, he would tell them all. He conspicuously consumed himself in a high flame. He cared nothing for catabolic consequences; he was so prodigal as to be invulnerable.

And here he was ruined. The frantic praise of the impotent meant recognition—*actual somewhereness*—to the hipster. He got what he wanted; he stopped protesting, reacting. He began to bureaucratize jive as a machinery for securing the actual—really the false—somewhereness. Jive, which had originally been a critical system, a kind of Surrealism, a personal revision of existing disparities, now grew moribundly selfconscious, smug, encapsulated, isolated from its source, from the sickness which spawned it. It grew more rigid than the institutions it had set out to defy. It became a boring routine. The hipster—once an unregenerate individualist, an underground poet, a guerrilla—had become a pretentious poet laureate. His old subversiveness, his ferocity, was now so manifestly rhetorical as to be obviously harmless. He was brought and placed in the zoo. He was somewhere at last—comfortably ensconced in the 52nd Street clip joints, in Carnegie Hall, and *Life.* He was *in-there* . . . he was back in the American womb. And it was just as unhygienic as ever.

Anatole Broyard, "A Portrait of the Hipster," from *The Scene Before You: A New Approach to American Culture,* Chandler Brossard, ed., (New York: Rinehart and Company, Inc., 1955) 115–119.

"COOL" IN THEORY AND PRACTICE:

Hipsters are much maligned by an unknowing public for being "cool." It should be pointed out, however, that "cool," when used in the Hip sense, does not mean withdrawn, cold, and nonreacting. Cool refers to an attitude which might best be described as poised and self-possessed or unruffled. When a hipster "blows his cool," he loses his poise and succumbs to hysteria, anger, or the prevailing mood of the moment.

A hipster's "cool" is often spoken of as a possession—perhaps a hipster's most cherished possession. One's "cool" enables one to face life as it is and to accept graciously what it has to offer. "Cool" has several subsidiary meanings.

Cool it: Stop it, behave normally, change the subject, leave. "Cool it" is an urgent warning.

Cool yourself, or cool your brains: Relax, stop "coming on."

It's cool: It's all right, or okay. "That's cool with me."

Be cool: Be careful.

Cool that stud: Get rid of him, shut him up.

Is he cool? Does he know what's happening? Will anything we do upset or shock him? Is he a cop?

"Uncool" refers to actions which are socially inappropriate, gauche, foolhardy, or dangerous.

The following list may prove useful.

It is uncool to claim that you used to room with Bird.

It is even less cool to ask, "Who is Bird?"

It is uncool to nod on the street waiting for the light to change.

It is uncool to let anybody know that your uncle is a registered pharmacist.

It is uncool to buddy with a known fink.

It is uncool to ask, "Where'd you get it?"

It is uncool to let anybody use your place as a forwarding address for packages from Mexico.

It is uncool to wear shades after sunset—unless you *should* be wearing shades after sunset, in which case it is uncool to take them off.

Del Close and John Brent, "This is Your Hip Manual," a printed insert in the record album *How to Speak Hip*, (Chicago: Mercury Recording Corporation, (c.1960s).

IN 1950 I WAS IN CHICAGO AT THE CROYDEN HOTEL. That was the hotel all the musicians stayed at. I was rooming with Sammy Curtis. He was a tall guy with a roundish face, rosy cheeks, blonde, curly hair, and he had this lopsided grin; he played the little boy bit. He thought it was charming. He was very talented.

I think we played the Civic Opera House that night. I was featured. I got all the praise and applause, and it was great while it was happening, but after everybody left, there I was alone. I wandered around the town. I went to all the bars. I ended up back at the hotel and went into the bar there. I just had to continue getting loaded; it was a compulsion; I had demons chasing me. The only way I ever got loaded enough, so I would be cool, was when I passed out, fell out someplace, which is what I used to do almost every night. They kicked me out of the bar at about four o'clock in the morning, and I didn't know what to do. There was no place I could get a drink. It was getting daylight, and I couldn't peep in any windows. There was no one on the streets.

I went back up to the room. Sammy was there and Roy King, a tenor player, and Sheila Harris, who's a singer, and some piano player. They were all using heroin. Sammy had been using stuff for a long time, and I knew it, but I never would try it because I knew that the minute I did it would be all over for me. I asked them if they had anything other than stuff, and they didn't. I was so unhappy, and Patti was two thousand miles away, and there was nothing I could do. I had to have something.

Sheila came over to me. She was a good singer who worked with another band. She was about five foot, two, and a little on the chubby side—what they call pleasingly plump. She had nice breasts, large, but nice, and although I've never liked chubby women she was one of the few that turned me on. She had long eyelashes and large eyes, bluish-green. Her face was oval and full, and she had full lips, and her eyebrows were full. Most women in those days plucked their eyebrows, but she had let hers grow, and I liked that. She had long fingers and nice nails. And she was a nymphomaniac. When she looked at a man she was thinking of sucking his cock; that was her thought and she turned you on because you could feel that; everyone could. And you were turned on by the stories. She was a legend among musicians. Whether they had ever made it with her or not they'd all tell stories about balling her. She was purely sensual, but only in a sexual way, no other. No warmth, no love, no beauty. When you looked at her you just saw your cock in her mouth.

She came over to me and offered me some stuff, just to horn it, sniff it. She said, "Why don't you hang up that jive and get in a different groove? Why don't you come in the bathroom with me? I'll show you a new way to go." I was at my wit's end. The only thing I could have done other than what I did was to jump out of the window of the hotel. I think we were on the fourteenth floor. I started to go into the bathroom with her and Sammy saw what was happening and flipped out. He caused a big scene. He said, "I won't be responsible for you starting to use stuff!" But Roy said, "Man, anything would be better than that jive booze scene he's into now. What could be worse? That's really a bringdown." We cooled Sammy out, and me and Sheila walked into the bathroom and locked the door.

When we got in there she started playing with my joint. She said, "Do you want me to say hello to him?" She was marvelous, and she really turned me on, but I said, "Wait a minute. Let's get into this other thing and then we'll get back to that." I was all excited about something new, the heroin. I had made up my mind.

She had a little glass vial filled with white powder, and she poured some out onto the porcelain top of the toilet, chopped it up with a razor blade, and separated it into little piles, little lines. She asked me if I had a dollar bill. She told me to get the newest one I had. I had one, very clean and very stiff. I took it out of my pocket and she said, "Roll it up." I started to roll it up but she said, "No, not that way." She made a tube with a small opening at the bottom and a larger opening at the top. Then she went over to the heroin and she said, "Now watch what I do and do this." She put one finger on her left nostril and she stuck the larger end of the dollar bill into her right nostril. She put the tube at the beginning of one pile, made a little noise, and the pile disappeared. She said, "Now you do that." I closed my nostril. I even remember it was my left nostril. I sniffed it, and a long, thin pile of heroin disappeared. She told me to do the same with the other nostril. I did six little lines and then she said, "Okay, wait a few minutes." While I'm

waiting she's rubbing my joint and playing with me. I felt a tingly, burning sensation up in my sinuses, and I tasted a bitter taste in my throat,
and all of a sudden, all of a sudden, all that feeling—wanting something
but having no idea what it was, thinking it was sex and then when I
had a chance to ball a chick not wanting to ball her because I was afraid
of some disease and because of the guilt; that wandering and wandering
like some derelict; that agony of drinking and drinking and nothing
ever being resolved; and . . . no peace at all except when I was playing,
and then the minute that I stopped playing there was nothing; that continual, insane search just to pass out somewhere and then to wake up
in the morning and think, "Oh, my God," to wake up and think, "Oh,
God, here we go again," to drink a bottle of warm beer so I could vomit,
so I could start all over again, so I could start that ridiculous, sickening,
horrible, horrible life again—all of a sudden, all of a sudden, the demons and the devils and the wandering and wondering and all the frus-
trations just vanished and they didn't exist at all anymore because I'd
finally found peace.

I felt this peace like a kind of warmth. I could feel it start in my
stomach. From the whole inside of my body I felt the tranquility. It
was so relaxing. It was so gorgeous. Sheila said, "Look at yourself in
the mirror! Look in the mirror!" And that's what I'd always done: I'd
stood and looked at myself in the mirror and I'd talk to myself and say
how rotten I was—"Why do people hate you? Why are you alone?
Why are you so miserable?" I thought, "Oh, no! I don't want to do that!
I don't want to spoil this feeling that's coming up in me!" I was afraid
that if I looked in the mirror I would see it, my whole past life, and
this wonderful feeling would end, but she kept saying, "Look at yourself! Look how beautiful you are! Look at your eyes! Look at your pupils!" I looked in the mirror and I looked like an angel. I looked at my
pupils and they were pinpoints; they were tiny, little dots. It was like
looking into a whole universe of joy and happiness and contentment.

I thought of my grandmother always talking about God and inner
happiness and peace of mind, being content within yourself not needing anybody else, not worrying about whether anybody loves you, if
your father doesn't love you, if your mother took a coathanger and
stuck it up her cunt to try to destroy you because she didn't want you,

because you were an unclean, filthy, dirty, rotten, slimy being that no one wanted, that no one ever wanted, that no one has still ever wanted. I looked at myself and said, "God, no, I am not that. I'm beautiful. I am the whole, complete thing. There's nothing more, nothing more that I care about. I don't care about anybody. I don't care about Patti. I don't need to worry about anything at all." I'd found God.

I loved myself, everything about myself. I loved my talent. I had lost the sour taste of the filthy alcohol that made me vomit and the feeling of the bennies and the strips that put chills up and down my spine. I looked at myself in the mirror and I looked at Sheila and I looked at the few remaining lines of heroin and I took the dollar bill and horned the rest of them down. I said, "This is it. This is the only answer for me. If this is what it takes, then this is what I'm going to do, whatever dues I have to pay . . ." And I *knew* that I would get busted and I *knew* that I would go to prison and that I wouldn't be weak; I wouldn't be an informer like all the phonies, the no-account, the non-real, the zero people that roam around, the scum that slither out from under rocks, the people that destroyed music, that destroyed this country, that destroyed the world, the rotten, fucking, lousy people that for their own little ends—the black power people, the sickening, stinking motherfuckers that play on the fact that they're black, and all this fucking shit that happened later on—the rotten, no-account, filthy women that have no feeling for anything; they have no love for anyone; they don't know what love is; they are shallow hulls of nothingness—the whole group of rotten people that have nothing to offer, that are nothing, never will be anything, were never intended to be anything.

All I can say is, at that moment I saw that I'd found peace of mind. Synthetically produced, but after what I'd been through and all the things I'd done, to trade that misery for total happiness—that was it, you know, that was it. I realized it. I realized that from that moment on I would be, if you want to use the word, a junkie. That's the word they used. That's the word they still use. That is what I became at that moment. That's what I practiced; and that's what I still am. And that's what I will die as—a junkie.

Art and Laurie Pepper, *Straight Life: The Story of Art Pepper,* (New York: Schirmer Books, 1979) 82–86.

LIMELIGHT LADIES: THEY SING OUT WHILE THE BANDSMEN SWING OUT
[*Copy beneath publicity photos c. 1945.*]

ADA BROWN
She's a rhythm singer who has the ability to get a smile or a sob into her songs as the mood and music demands. Ada has composed several ultra modern scores and knows her way around among the notes and scales.

LIL GREEN
Speaking of audiences, the Blues Queen says: "When they act cold, I get 'em all hot and bothered with one of those jelly-roll tunes. And when they seem to be in the groove—I cool 'em down with a slow-an'-easy rider."

MARVA LOUIS
. . . is the ex-wife of Brown Bomber Joe Louis. She did not sing in public before her marriage. Marva made her professional debut after separating from the fistic king. She designs most of her own clothes.

PETERS SISTERS
. . . put in their appearance at New York's *Cafe Zanzibar* on a reinforced stage. They dish out almost a thousand pounds of singing, write music and dance, too. The girls carry weight in hop-to-the-jive quarters.

SISTER ROSETTA THARPE
The number of gals who can deliver spirituals so well as to pack 'em in can be counted on one hand. The sister belongs on that hand. Cab Calloway presented her at the old *Cotton Club*. The club-goers listened and loved it.

SARA VAUGHN
Add a dynamic personality to a versatile song style, mix well with plenty of musical training and hard work, bake with vim and vigor, sprinkle generously with oomph, trim to chic lines—and you have Sara.

DINAH WASHINGTON
. . . can handle the blues, on and off the stage, in equal fashion. This Harlem rhythm girl has never been known to "blow her top." Inappro-

priately enough, a composer wrote a tune in her honor: "Blowtop
Blues."

The Big Book of Swing, Bill Treadwell, ed., (New York: Cambridge House Publishers,
1946) 48–49.

IT HAD BEEN THE PRACTICE OF SOME LATER MUSICIANS to work intensively
at the inventive, though feeling has often been buried in displays of virtuosity. Performers such as Tony Parenti, Don Ewell, Paul Lingle, Bob
Helm, Wally Rose, Burt Bales, Turk Murphy, among others, [The *Partisan Review* text lists: "Armstrong, James P. Johnson, Kid Ory, Barney
Bigard, Art Tatum, Earl Hines, Bechet, Jack Teagarden, George Brunis,
Ben Webster, and a good many of the Chicago stylists clustered around
Eddie Condon"] continue to resist corruption; but their ranks are systematically being thinned out by desertions for cushier swing bands,
by sudden collapses of talent, and the normal high death rate among
jazz musicians, whose occupational hazards include heart attacks, mal-
nutrition, and a recurrent pattern of drunkenness and sudden death of
pneumonia in Middle Western cities.

More than a few go on playing well; the difficulties of hearing them
continue to multiply. Manhattan's Fifty-second Street, once as devoted
to night clubs featuring jazz and jam sessions as Grand Street is to wedding gowns or Bleecker Street to salami, makes way for replacements
in the form of office buildings, expensive clubs, business establishments,
and tourist night spots with "intimate" singers and Hawaiian dancing
girls. Four years ago there was at least one night club in New York that
offered first-rate jazz, unwatered and non-poisonous liquor at reasonable prices, and a quiet crowd that did not come there to have their
photographs taken, their caricatures drawn, or to annoy the musicians.
This was the Pied Piper, on Barrow Street, in the Village. For a brief
period, when it first opened, it offered a memorable five-piece group
that included Max Kaminsky, the late Rod Cless on clarinet, Frank Or-
chard on valve trombone, and, as intermission pianist and at the top
of his form, the remarkable, vastly influential, and still underrated James
P. Johnson. There is nothing remotely like the Pied Piper left in New
York. Indifferent music, high prices, poor liquor, or combinations of
this trinity have taken over everywhere. The rash of jazz "concerts" in

such places as Town Hall have not been very satisfactory substitutes. The musicians, along with the more ravaged-looking members of the audience, wear expressions of strain brought on by the absence of a bar and by a milieu too little enclosed. At various times, attempts have been made to present regular programs of good jazz on the air—notably those conducted by Condon and by Rudi Blesh; but from the start their chances of commercial sponsorship were as remote as those of Wallace Stevens's appearing as a regular contributor to Collier's. The networks made short work of both programs.

While jazz persists on record and occasionally elsewhere, the best of it is increasingly nostalgic, depending more and more on a cultist rather than on a popular base; it is almost drowned out by the racket of the large swing and popular bands. These have next to nothing to do with jazz, although they often contain remnants of rather gratuitous jazz in solo work (the best of these bands, Artie Shaw's and Benny Goodman's, are gone). Standard practice today in the search for trademark and novelty is the isolation of some rhythmic pattern, tonal element, or harmonic trickery to vulgarize and thus "build up" a style. Hence "rippling rhythms," slinky piano effects, fixated use of a series of augmented chords, musical statements that are so surfacy that they beg the question of feeling at all. The Stan Kenton band is a good example of tremendous effort going into the creation of such a style, through echo chamber effects and hollow intimations of Debussy and Stravinsky.

Enormously popular just now are the relaxed Cream of Wheat–Gerber Baby Food instrumental trios, usually piano, guitar, and string bass, with one man singing empty little jump tunes. There are dozens of these, all playing at a volume undeviating as a cat's purr. This music had its origin, I would guess, in the dimly lit night clubs of the East Fifties, where it served, and still serves, the purpose of covering up dead spots in the conversation. Like the music that dominated the period in the late 1700s just before the revolutionary music of Glück, it was not originally intended to be listened to at all. Millions now follow it, over the air and on records.

And now, finally, we come to those who play in the latest and extravagantly acclaimed manner variously labeled Be-Bob, bebop, and rebop. Here is a full-fledged cult. Its more orthodox devotees even model their appearance on that of Dizzy Gillespie, bebop's pioneer and bell-wether, a goateed trumpet player who wears a beret, horn-rimmed glasses, and neckties with his own not very appealing countenance painted thereon. Iconoclastic and compulsive types, many bebop cult-ists extend their interests beyond music—to drug-addiction, abstract painting, and the theories (and for all I know the practice) of Wilhelm Reich, philosopher of the orgasm. Some beboppers are interested in the close textual critics of poetry; I learned from a friend whom I believe to be reliable that one such fan announced that Cleanth Brooks is "definitely hip"—a term of warm approval.

The beboppers or hipsters are, however, a great deal more inter-esting than bebop itself. Yet they offer the most insistent testimonies to bebop's superiority to other kinds of music. 'Do you dig Dizzy?' is fast becoming the musician's counterpart to 'Do you speak English?' writes Mr. Mort Schillinger in *Downbeat*, in characteristic razzmatazz style of the swing magazines. "Never before in the history of Jazz has so dynamic a person as Dizzy Gillespie gained the spotlight of acclaim and idolization . . . from the humblest of the unknown to the heights of huzza at which he stands today. With the waxing of Hawk's [Cole-man Hawkins's] *Body and Soul* . . . Jazz has reached a pinnacle of devel-opment. The human imagination has its limitations, just as the human arm or leg, and Jazz had reached the point where the musician's imagi-nation could no longer function effectively without the added stimulus of new horizons for exploitation. There were two alternatives: either Jazz could remain stagnant and in time lose its identity as a highly crea-tive art, or it could develop new facets for the imagination, new stimuli to artistic fabrication. Fortunately it followed the latter course—chose it and assigned the task to Dizzy Gillespie." Mr. Schillinger goes on to remark Gillespie's "genius for substituting and extending chords in un-orthodox but singularly thrilling ways and places [and] Dizzy's entirely original articulation and phrasing, which are hardly describable through the medium of the printed word without recourse to highly technical terminology . . ."

Mr. Rudi Blesh, in a recent piece in the *Herald Tribune*, is more controlled. "Seeming non-sequiturs can be artfully combined to express an integrated idea, and this method, a psychological one, is common in modern music and literature. But the irrelevant parts of bebop are exactly what they seem; they add up to no such unity . . . A capricious and neurotically rhapsodic sequence of effects for their own sake, [bebop] comes perilously close to complete nonsense as a musical expression . . . Far from a culmination of jazz, bebop is not jazz at all but an ultimately degenerated form of swing, exploiting the most fantastic rhythms and unrelated harmonies that it would seem possible to conceive."

I have been listening to bebop on occasion for several years now, and lately, as I started work on this piece, listening with more strict attention; and I can only report, very possibly because of some deeply buried strain of black reaction in me, that I have found this music uniformly thin, at once dilapidated and overblown, and exhibiting a poverty of thematic development and a richness of affectation not only, apparently, intentional, but enormously self-satisfied. Whole-toned progressions and triple-tongued runs are worked relentlessly, far beyond the saturation point. There has been nothing like this in the way of an overconsciousness of stylistic idiosyncrasy, I should say, since the Gothic Revival. Although bebop's defenders reserve as their trump card this music's "element of the unexpected," it is precisely bebop's undeviating pattern of incoherence and limitation that makes it predictable in the extreme, and ultimately as boring as the projects of Gutzon Borglum.

In Paris, where Erskine Caldwell, Steinbeck, Henry Miller, and Horace McCoy are best sellers and "nobody reads Proust anymore," where the post-Picasso painters have sunk into torpor and repetition, and where intellectuals are more cynically Stalinized than in any other city in the world, bebop is vastly admired. Evidently Gresham's and Epstean's laws work with equal severity in other countries besides the United States, although a lot of people are taking Christ's sweet time finding it out.

Weldon Kees [1948], *Reviews and Essays, 1936–55*, James Reidel, ed., (Ann Arbor: The University of Michigan Press, 1988) 194–198.

THE BARTENDER SHOOK HIS HEAD. Either he didn't have any or he didn't trust me. All he did was turn Bessie Smith over.

> *Gimme a pigfoot and bottle of beer,*
> *And I don't care.*

Past times, simpler times, when we went to a bar to drink whiskey instead of staying home to smoke pot. Past days, gone days, when every saloon had a print of Custer's Last Stand donated by the Budweiser Brewery. Old times, Budweiser times, when we called for a boilermaker when we wanted a shot and a beer. Gone times, Schlitz times, when a man would say "I'm taking a count" when he wanted to know how much money he had instead of "I'm reviewing my holdings." Lost times when nothing was easier than to forget an army serial-number. Times that had transpired upon some first-person person's planet before third-person times came along. Times when there had been nothing to get grim about except crapping out three rolls running or having to go to a war. How was it then that the campus fellows, arrived with their blueprints to which the arts must henceforward conform at peril of getting bad grades, felt grim about everything?

Had the big crapout to them been simply in being born? Or had it begun later, and all Daddy's fault too, when he'd forbidden his boy to ride a bicycle for fear of a skinned knee? Had the fathers, out of love, built a picture-window world wherein well-behaved sons could watch others ride no-hands with no risk to themselves? Was Junior so grim about everything because his true self had been left looking out of a picture window? While campus fellows, authentic paperfish authorities, began seeking ways and means of bringing the arts into a picture-window world where the artist would be both safer and richer, certain prebeatnik cats went searching Chicago's South Side for ways and means of passing for black.

Through Richard Wright we had become aware that those who ran the white world had lost the will to act honestly. We had learned from Wright that it is those who have nothing to lose by speaking out who become the ones to speak the truth. And to these, all the horrors of poverty—schizophrenia, homosexuality, drug addiction, prostitution, disease, and sudden death on the gamblers' stairs—were no more remarkable than the sight of a man with a fresh haircut. In the midst of life, where there are nothing but horrors, there is no horror.

Crafty madams and ancient midwives, tenor-sax players and policy-runners, con men, quacks, pimps and tarts, poolroom sharks and intellectuals, all were citizens of a country whose capital was Forty-seventh and Indiana. But only the latter had divorced themselves, intellectually, from Negro life. Talking in phrases picked up in evening courses at the University of Chicago or Northwestern, we knew that the phrases, so high-sounding to their own ears, were as artificial as hair-straighteners and skin-lighteners. We had been made suspicious of the values of the white world by Wright. Our suspicions had been confirmed in war.

Wright had made us aware that the Christianity of the white American middle class had lost its nerve: now we saw it be a coast-to-coast fraud. And the fraud lay in this: that property was more valuable than people. The Negro had come up in America, putting the value of people above that of property simply because he had no property to evaluate.

This fraud, as essential to successful merchandising as making a profit, had by 1948 so pervaded the American white middle class that its ancient image of Jesus Christ had become that of The Young Man On His Way Up whose total purpose was accumulation of securities; and whose morality was confined by the warning: "Don't Get Caught."

By 1948 everything went, in the race through the supermart of publishing, advertising, television, and bond-selling; and Christianity had lent its blessing to the Supermart. The image of America reflected in editorials in *Life*, on TV, in movies, and on the stage, was a painted image that had nothing to do with the real life of these States.

"The horror, gentlemen, lies precisely in this: that there is no horror."

But in Negro music we heard voices of men and women whose connection with life was still real.

Nelson Algren, *Who Lost an American?* (New York: The Macmillan Company, 1963) 140–142.

I REMEMBER THAT THE ONLY WAY MY MOTHER could make me wake up happy was to put on Cootie Williams. I just loved Cootie Williams! Do you know, he played a trumpet in such a way that you could *taste* the notes. Really chewy. Chu Berry I dug. He had that bite, that mouth thing going, like Hawkins did. So it was people like Cootie Williams, Hawkins, Prez, and the real capper was Charlie Parker. Goddamn! That man astounds me to this day! When I listen to his records, I still can't believe it.

I had the great privilege of hearing that man "live" every single night for nearly two years. Because I went to the trouble to go hear him. The blessing was that he was there. I was also very grateful that somehow or other my hearing and my sense of the importance of this man was such that I availed myself of the opportunity.

I was at the U. of Chicago in '51, '52, '53, and '54 and at that time Charles was damn near dead. I really enjoy calling him *Charles* Parker. There is something about "Charlie" that doesn't fit the man. He was Charles. He was dying and none of us realized it.

He was working in a little joint on 63rd Street in Chicago and all of his side-musicians were high-school kids. Just a thrown-together band: a piano, bass, drum, and Parker. That's all. The kids would be eighteen, nineteen, twenty, maybe twentyone . . . If they weren't old enough they would fake their age or something. But really nowhere. I mean the kind of group you would expect to find in an after-hours joint in San Francisco. Really dedicated, really young musicians who knew who the hell Parker was. Boy did they know! They just played their asses off.

And he would come up after a set, oh, I remember him so well! He always wore double-breasted brown suits—God, or a brown double-breasted gabardine coat with blue pinstripe pants and bad shoes, just terrible. The cat just didn't give a fuck how he looked, he just didn't care at all. And his horn always hanging from his neck, and he had these funny walleyes . . . the one eye was high and to the outside . . .

He would come after a set, you know, one of those fantastic tunes [scats "Scrapple from the Apple"] and the kids are trying to stay in there with him, and they are staying as best they can because they know who they are playing with. They know it. (I'd like to run into a couple of those kids now. I bet they are big guys now. Real heavy.) After the set was over—and here was everyone, a bunch of Okies in a Chicago bar giving you so much *crap*. No one was even listening, man . . . just nothing going on . . . there would be maybe eight people there: me and seven pimps and whores. Weird, man, because it was really a down Chicago bar scene. One of the places was called The Beehive. Charles Parker revolved around four joints within six blocks on 63rd Street, which is a famous old jazz street. Apparently he had a good contact for his heroin. That is the reason why he stayed there. Because he had a big name, Jesus, he could have made three or four thousand a week!

You know who he reminded me of? The only person I have ever met that reminded me of Charles Parker was Jack Spicer. They were the same man. They were just hell-bent on self-destruction. They were both six feet plus and heavy. They were big and strong. Jesus, Charles Parker had hands like a fucking farmer! Big hands, He had a working body and it turned all into mind at a terrible price. They were very similar men and they both had the same approach to their art.

Parker used to get up after a set and walk over to the piano player and he would be so sweet . . . his horn hanging from his neck like a big necklace. He was big enough, he was really a strong man, his horn just hung and swung around. He didn't hold it like other guys do. And he leaned over and showed the kid how the chords should have gone. And the kid would sit there like: "oh, yeah, oh yeah . . . of course . . . B flat 7th . . . oh, B 9th minor . . . wow! . . ." And these tremendous tempos he would lay on these poor kids. Tremendous tempos that he would take with great ease and brilliance. . . .

Lew Welch, from *Golden Gate: Interviews with Five San Francisco Poets*, David Meltzer, ed., (Berkeley: Wingbow Press, 1976) 180–182.

Song for Bird and Myself

I am dissatisfied with my poetry.
I am dissatisfied with my sex life.
I am dissatisfied with the angels I believe in.
    Neo-classical like Bird,
    Distrusting the reality
    of every note.
    Half-real
    We blow the sentence pure and real
    Like chewing angels.

"Listen, Bird, why do we have to sit here dying
In a half-furnished room?
The rest of the combo
Is safe in houses
Blowing bird-brained Dixieland,
How warm and free they are. What right
Music."
                    "Man,
                    We
                    Can't stay away from the sounds.
                    We're crazy, Jack
                    We gotta stay here 'til
                    They come and get us."

Neo-classical like Bird.
Once two birds got into the Rare Book Room.
Miss Swift said,
"Don't
Call a custodian
Put crumbs on the outside of the window
Let them
Come outside."
                    Neo-classical
The soft line strains
Not to be neo-classical.
But Miss Swift went to lunch. They
Called a custodian.
Four came.
Armed like Myrmidons, they
Killed the birds.
Miss Munsterberg
Who was the first
American translator of Rilke
Said
"Suppose one of them
Had been the Holy Ghost."

Miss Swift,
Who was back from lunch,
Said
"Which."
But the poem isn't over.
It keeps going
Long after everybody
Has settled down comfortably into laughter.
The bastards
on the other side of the paper
Keep laughing.
LISTEN.
STOP LAUGHING.
THE POEM ISN'T OVER. Butterflies.
I knew there would be butterflies
For Butterflies represent the lost soul
Represent the way the wind wanders
Represent the bodies
We only clasp in the middle of a poem.
See, the stars have faded.
There are only butterflies.
Listen to
The terrible sound of their wings moving.
Listen.
The poem isn't over.

Have you ever wrestled with a bird,
You idiotic reader?
Jacob wrestled with an angel.
(I remind you of the image)
or a butterfly
Have you ever wrestled with a single butterfly?
Sex is no longer important.
Colors take the form of wings. Words
Have got to be said.
A butterfly,
A bird,

Planted at the heart of being afraid of dying.
Blow,
Bird,
Blow,
Be,
Neo-classical.
Let the wings say
What the wings mean
Terrible and pure.

    The horse
    In Cocteau
    Is as neo-classical an idea as one can manage.
    Writes all our poetry for us
    Is Gertrude Stein
    Is God
    Is the needle for which
    God help us
    There is no substitute
    Or the Ace of Swords
    When you are telling a fortune
    Who tells death.
    Or the Jack of Hearts
    Whose gypsy fortune we clasp
    In the middle of a poem.

"And are we angels, Bird?"
    "That's what we're trying to tell 'em, Jack
    There aren't any angels except when
    You and me blow 'em."

So Bird and I sing
outside your window
So Bird and I die
Outside your window.
This is the wonderful world of Dixieland
Deny

The bloody motherfucking Holy Ghost.
This is the end of the poem.
You can start laughing, you bastards. This is
The end of the poem.

[1956]

Jack Spicer, *The Collected Books of Jack Spicer*, Robin Blaser, ed., (Los Angeles: Black Sparrow Press, 1975) 346–348.

AS SOON AS SHE APPEARS, YOUR SPIRITS LIFT. Her body is ample, comfortable, and easily carried on her elegant sprightly feet as she steps up to the microphone, briskly professional yet with a sense of enjoyment like a girl's. In her face shine appraising sardonic almond eyes, the wide generous nose dilates, and the amused lips savor the situation of her presence there among you. About her whole person is an air of absolute indestructibility. And then, with a smack matter-of-fact attack, she starts to sing.

And how she sings! Ella Fitzgerald, if not "the greatest," is certainly the most universal female popular singer of the English-speaking world: universal, that is, by the variety of the songs she sings in ballads and jazz idiom, by the original stylings that she uses in her interpretations, and by the different publics that admire her, ranging, as they do, from juke-box primitives to the Roman-suited hi-fi esoterica with their mine-detector ears. To be, in the mid-twentieth century, an immensely popular artist of the highest caliber is an astonishing achievement, partly explicable by her gifts and partly by her nature, each admirable as the other.

The voice itself, the actual instrument, is not remarkable: a "healthy, rather ordinary voice" is how one of her own sleeve notes describes it, not unkindly. But everything else she has, or has acquired. An inborn sense of rhythm, so strongly felt that she can vary the beat to a preposterous degree without ever for a second losing it. Clear, precise diction, and a sixth sense for pace. Easy, assured and infinitely flexible phrasing, graceful, undulating and vivacious.

Thus equipped, Ella can interpret her songs in the richest possible way. In one sense, she is entirely faithful to the lyricist's and the composer's purpose. She has an intense affection for the words and, above

all, the meaning of each phrase, which she delivers with no conde-
scension whatsoever, without smart twists of intellectualization, and
with no concession towards intrusive sentiment. But in another way,
she departs, or seems to, from the "usual" interpretation of the number—until one remembers that no song exists until it is sung, that it is
the singer who in a real sense partly creates it, and that there are no
"usual" versions of a song at all. For Ella, using her voice as an instrumentalist would his wind or strings, and possessed of a musicianship
of a quality that enables her to transform the melody in a free improvisation, can recreate a song, making it seem, at first hearing, almost "unrecognizable." And not only change the song, but change her voice, or
seem to. It is her chameleon-like self-identification with the mood and
style of the number that leads to the variations of quality in her singing,
ranging from almost hoarse, sharp, exclamatory teenage sounds to entirely mature (but always youthful) middle-register notes of velvety
smoothness.

As one would expect, she is past-mistress of the throw-away technique: understatement may be sustained throughout a song, but without diminishing the urgency, the fluency of communication, the quiet
excitement of the sound. Sometimes the whole conception of a rather
meaningless number (a few too excessive love ballads, for example) is
altered by a total throwaway, and a mad acceleration of speed, so that
instead of falling into bathos by singing the ditty straight, Ella catches
the mood the ballad-writer really intended by a roller-skate delivery of
a sort of berserk enthusiasm, bowling madly along to save the melody
from the death-kiss of a guffaw. Scat, or wordless onomatopoeic sound,
often mildly indecent, she sings as nobody else quite can—delightfully
and entirely convincingly. Singers' gimmicks are clipped to an absolute
minimum: for instance, the slight catch in the throat in the middle of
a word (much abused by her numberless imitators); the almost inaudi-
ble tremolo in certain sustained notes; and the occasional smoky shiver
when she rises to the treble clef.

Reflected in these splendid sounds is a no less splendid personality.
What is she most like to hear, to look at, to imagine? At moments, certainly, like Mom, a thoroughly reassuring character, but a Mom of a
particular kind: that rare and admirable species who turn an amused

eye upon the young, and would tolerate from them just simply anything at all. For instance, when Ella has made us understand the real sense of an apparently familiar song, her attitude seems like that of an amiable and clear-witted schoolmarm teaching esteemed and very bright young people: with no patronage, and with affection and a lively interest. It is thus, too, that while nothing could be less morbid, and more normal, than her song, her style has a certain sexlessness, a sense of disembodiment from physical entanglements that is replaced by a general vague elation. She even, at times, contrives to guy sex, entirely without heaviness, in the manners of expert practitioners in this knife-edge art like Mae West, Sinatra, Marilyn Monroe and Groucho Marx. Yet nothing could be further from the bland inverted pallor of the now very popular Lesbian-type singers. She has, in short, an extremely light oblique touch emotionally, combined with a direct stylistic general frontal attack.

It is also the voice of a great lady with a wonderfully crazy streak to her: the *grande dame* presence with undercurrents of entirely uninhibited, unselfconscious mayhem. Often, in her songs, she seems most graciously to descend the stairs half way . . . then leap on the banisters and slide the rest, though arriving always entirely the right way up at her destination. You can't describe her, really, as an "actress," because the sense of a "performance" in the usual way is altogether lacking. She's so good you only have to listen, it is the voice that acts. Nor, unless you see her, does her voice sound particularly "colored"—just as she seems any age between sixteen and forty (which is close on what she really is), so does her voice sound as if it might belong to either race.

In a word (or two), her outstanding characteristics are her radiant bonhomie as a human being and, as a performer, her agile, swinging, easy, unornamental delivery, conveying a variety of moods of which the finest one is lyrical, glowing with warmth and light. The all-enveloping sensation that her music gives is of a relaxed acceptance of life—acceptance, not advocacy; and her criticism is confined to a mildly cocked eyebrow, or a sigh. To hear her is to be given, in the most telling and pleasurable form, that particular gift of the spirits that is the great gift of jazz, in its more positive moods, to your frowning, cross-patch age.

Colin MacInnes [1961], *England, Half English*, (London: The Hogarth Press, 1986) 130–133.

Chaloff

In an instant the world seems fairly made of wood.
Balsa wood, and air. And song consists in passing
nothings around on a deck. The Pacific Ocean rests
upon a peak, and Boston is a bay. Honey dumps the flood,
burying the furlong granite ear. A multi-lunged, galumphing
chain of events stirs and stows the static—
mops, churns, hooks, and levels out.
Downstairs smells of polish remover.
In early autumn a butterfly kisses the goof.
He is able: "I once knew how to do this."

Motion was the first miracle,
followed by a bird act.
While it shines on the pointed hush's shameless order of mention,
a piano's gravity will see to acquiring a proper knife.
In tingles I catch the blandished coffee's murmur on a string
hearing sowbugs scamper over flannel sheets.
You must soothe beasts first to be funk.

What's new? Maybe Chaloff wasn't. Anyhow, in Egyptian
Gardens his chorus recalls their dancing like a nut.
Night the one color of a vocalist's shirt
embosses coasters from its incline of a sort,
although Lower Slobovia is no way a state of music.
But such aloof floes make mockery of the continuous present.
Against the nub, the nebulous, his glazed twig
wiffles, woos, and wails,
striding an important pressure the dew blapped.
Which twig holds night?
Who's only catastrophic?
The world and its cracks?
Wish, occlusion, force,
a practice out of fondest samplings, which fitfully bent beads.

[1984]

Bill Berkson, *Lush Life*, (Calais, Vermont: Z Press, 1984) 42–43.

A NOTE ON BOP

In Bop, especially in its drums which almost purely color and are colored by time itself, there is the sense that sheer continuance gets articulated. Momentum as seduction, in which the "one" of that ever first beat tends very soon to lose its "e." And the shaping of the always initial impact becomes the highest of enveloping tasks.

Awareness of all the room that exists within a single beat, and just exactly which point in that space you want to occupy, though the room itself may be moving at a very high rate of speed. At the time. Bop's fascination with extremes of tempo reveals its major involvement with the realms of time. Time and Changes, Bop's two keystones, nothing more basic.

The feel is that time has a precise center. Like tight-roping on a moving pulley clothesline, you're always trying to keep up midway between the poles. It really gets that sharply physical. As a drummer you're holding time's cutting edge in your right hand (ride cymbal), a simultaneity of holding and shaping. You occupy the center of the sonic sphere, the world, and ride it and bear it, inviolable (why heroin is Bop's perfect chemical). And everything that happens there happens once and at once. Once and Ounce, Groove and Chord, Wave and Particle: the Complementarity of Bop.

Bop's connections with poetry are too synesthesiac to be descriptively fixed. Perhaps there is a renewal of the urge toward a longer more supple line. And the continual sense of the image *in motion*, never static, acted out and acted upon. Kerouac pointed to Lee Konitz "who inspired me in 1951 to 'write the way he plays'." Then again Cecil Taylor (moving over a thinner place in the Bop Continuum) once remarked that he wanted to "try to imitate on the piano the leaps in space a dancer makes." And Jean-Luc Godard last night on television spoke of his movies as "the train, not the station, because I am no longer waiting."

Touch is essential. Can you touch time? Consider Kenny Clarke's "magic cymbal" which he "kept level" and "when somebody would sit in on drums and use his set, it would sound like the top of a garbage can, but when he played on it, it was like fine crystal."

Time is a substance if you hear you can get on and ride. I have always found metric feet awkward as a base for my lines. Rather the unceasing teem of that top cymbal at the back of my room.

Max Roach is imprinted on my nervous reflex. I sit at my desk help-lessly tapping out his snare and bass exchanges between thoughts. Sometimes I feel the space between people (voices) in terms of tempos. The rush of an idea, a Blakey press-roll. That characteristic Roy Haynes snare & sock-cymbal figure a definitely constructed image, perhaps over to one side but more important than the main action, a sort of very bright cam. Klook's brushes a landscape in my sleep.

Then there is the famous door of Elvin Jones: "The length of my solos doesn't mean anything. When I go on for so long, I am looking for the right way to get out. Sometimes the door goes right by and I don't see it, so I have to wait until it comes around again. Sometimes it doesn't come around at all for a long long time."

These days I ask myself again and more acutely the relation (if there is one?) between language forms and the wordless shapes of time. Per-haps there is no direct exchange. All I can be sure of is that I am able to possess them both within one body and one mind.

Clark Coolidge [1980] (personal correspondence with the author).

JAZZ IS A DIFFERENT FRATERNITY ALTOGETHER, a wholly different kind of music making. It has nothing to do with composed music and when it seeks to be influenced by contemporary music it isn't jazz and it isn't good. Improvisation has its own time world, necessarily a loose and large one since only in an imprecisely limited time could real improvi-sation be worked up to; the stage has to be set, and there must be heat. The percussion and bass (not the piano; that instrument is too hybrid and besides, most of the players have just discovered Debussy) func-tions as a central-heating system. They must keep the temperature "cool," not cool. It is a kind of masturbation that never arrives anywhere (of course) but which supplies the "artificial" genesis the art requires. The point of interest is instrumental virtuosity, instrumental person-ality, not melody, not harmony, and certainly not rhythm. Rhythm doesn't exist really because no rhythmic proportion or relaxation exists. Instead of rhythm there is "beat." The players beat all the time merely to keep up and know which side of the beat they are on. The ideas are instrumental, or, rather, they aren't ideas because they come after, come from the instruments. Shorty Rogers's trumpet playing is an example of what I mean by instrumental derivation, though his trumpet is really a deep-bored bugle-sounding instrument which reminds me of the keyed bugles I like so much and wrote for in the first version of *Los Noces*. (Hearing Mr. Rogers play this instrument in Los Angeles last year perhaps influenced me to use it in *Threne*. His patterns are instrumental: half-valve effects with lip glissandos, intervals and runs that derive from the fingers, "trills" on one note, for example, G to G on a B-flat instrument—between open and first-and-third fingers—etc.)

As an example of what I have said about timing, I can listen to Shorty Rogers's good style with its dotted-note tradition, for stretches of fifteen minutes or more and not feel the time at all, whereas the weight of every "serious" virtuoso I know depresses me beyond the counter-action of equanil in about five. Has jazz influenced me? Jazz patterns and, especially, jazz instrumental combinations did influence me forty years ago, of course, but not the idea of jazz. As I say, that is another world. I don't follow it but I respect it. It can be an art of very touching dignity as it is in the New Orleans jazz funerals. And, at its rare best, it is certainly the best musical entertainment in the U.S.

Igor Stravinsky, *Stravinsky: In Conversation with Robert Craft*, (Harmondsworth, Middlesex, England: Penguin Books, 1962) 128–130.

THIS IS OUR MANIFESTO

Helmets off helmets off:
We've lost!
The companies are scattered. The companies, battalions, armies. The great armies. Only the hosts of the dead, they still stand. Stand like measureless forests: dark, purple-coloured, full of voices. But the guns lie like frozen dinosaurs with rigid limbs. Purple with steel and ambushed fury. And the helmets they are rusting. Take your rusty helmets off: we've lost.

In our dixies thin children now fetch milk. Thin milk. The children are purple with frost. And the milk is purple with poverty.

Never again shall we fall in to a whistle and say "Yessir" to a bellow. Guns and sergeants bellow no more. We shall weep, spit and sing as we will. But the song of the roaring tanks and the song of the edelweiss we shall sing no more, for the tanks and the sergeants rage no more, and the edelweiss has rotted away to the sing-song of blood. And no general calls us "Thou" before the battle. Before the terrible battle.

We shall never again have sand in our teeth with fear. (No sand of the steppes, no Ukrainian sand and none from Cyrenaica or Normandy—nor the bitter angry sand of our homeland!) And never again the hot mad feeling in brain and belly before the battle.

Never again shall we be so happy, to feel another beside us. Warm and there and breathing and belching and humming—at night on the advance. Never again shall we be as happy as gipsies about a loaf of bread and five grams of tobacco and two armfuls of hay. We shall never march together again, for from now on all march alone. That is good. That is hard. No longer to have the stubborn grumbling other man beside you—at night, at night on the advance. Who hears everything too. Who never says anything. Who stomachs everything.

And if at night a man must weep, he can do so again. For he need no longer sing—with fear.

Now jazz is our song. Excited, hectic jazz is our music. And the hot mad frantic song, through which the drums race, catlike, scratching. And sometimes still the old sentimental soldiers' bawl, with which anguish was outscreamed and with which mothers were denied. Terrible male chorus from bearded lips, sung into the lonely twilight of dug-out and goods-train, over-pitched by the mouth-organ's tinny tremolo:

Virile song of men—did no one hear the children bawling away their fear of the purple maw of the guns?

Heroic song of men—did no one hear the hearts sobbing when they sang upside, the grimy, the crusty, the bearded, the lousy?

Song of men, soldiers' bawling, sentimental and high-spirited, virile and deepthroated, valiantly bawled by the youngsters, too: Does none hear the cry for mother? The last cry of man, the adventurer? The terrible cry: Upidee?

Our upidee and our music are a dance over the abyss that yawns at us. And that music is jazz. For our hearts and our heads have the same hot-cold rhythm: excited, crazy and hectic, unrestrained.

And our girls, they have the same hot beat in their hands and their hips. And their laughter is hoarse and brittle and hard as a clarinet. And their hair, it crackles like phosphorous. It burns. And their heart has a syncopated beat, savage and sad. Sentimental. Our girls are like that: like jazz. And the nights are like that, the girl-jangling nights, like jazz: hot and hectic. Excited.

Who will write us new laws of harmony? We have no further use for well-tempered clavichords. We ourselves are too much dissonance.

Who will cry a purple cry for us? Who a purple deliverance? We have no further use for still life. Our life is loud.

Wolfgang Borchert, *The Man Outside: The Prose Works of Wolfgang Borchert*, David Porter trans., (London: Calder and Boyars, 1947) 245–247.

IN 1938, [ERIC] VOGEL PLAYED TRUMPET in a dixieland combo with the Paskus brothers on guitar and drums, Bramer on piano, and Kolek on clarinet. They worked semi-pro jobs around Brno, Czechoslovakia, and Vogel had one of the largest collections of jazz records in the country. He was proud to know enough English to read the occasional issue of *Down Beat* which came his way. They were too involved with jazz to worry about politics.

When the Germans invaded on 15 March 1939, the doorbells of Jews began to ring: "Gestapo!" Vogel's turn came: "*Aufmachen!*" The man standing there in an SS uniform and a swastika on his arm had been listening to one of their jam sessions a few weeks earlier. "Oh, it's you," he said. "Well don't worry."

Vogel lost his engineering job to a Christian. He continued to sell arrangements to Bubek Bryen's band. Some he transcribed from American records, Chick Webb's "Squeeze Me" for example. Soon Jews were banned from theatres, movies, coffee houses and nightclubs and an 8 P.M. curfew was announced. So much for live music.

Vogel wore a yellow star on his lapel. The Jews of Brno were crowded into a ghetto. When his family was forced to share a two-room apartment with two other families, he practiced trumpet, muted in a closet, and continued arranging. Rehearsing the Bryen band one evening, he discovered it was one hour past curfew when two Gestapo officers arrested him in the middle of "Boogie Woogie Blues."

They took him to headquarters. By chance his SS friend from the jam session was there. "I have a personal account to settle with this pig Jew," he said to his colleagues. "Leave him to me." This may seem cock-eyed, but Vogel says the officer then took him home, borrowed some jazz records and books about jazz music and that was the end of it.

When the Nazis confiscated Jewish-owned musical instruments, Vogel soaked his valves in sulfuric acid to keep anybody from playing musical military marches on a jazz trumpet. Arranging was impossible without a piano.

He worked registering Czech Jews in a "technical bureau" until—he never could figure this out—he was ordered to organize a jazz course. Not asked, not permitted—ordered. He recruited a teaching staff. Forty students applied. Waiting for instruments, the teachers gave courses in jazz theory and history. He managed to get hold of twelve recordings of "St. Louis Blues," played by twelve different groups, to illustrate how spontaneous interpretation counts more than composi-tion. Every improviser is a composer, he said. He compared jazz mu-sicians to painters, who are free to fill the canvas with subjective visions; while classical musicians, like photographers, must always shoot in focus.

Most of the pupils were elderly classical string players who had to be retrained on reeds and brass. After several weeks, the ensemble sounded better than he expected. It was time to find a name. He had liked the expression "killer diller" he once found in *Down Beat*, though he had no idea what it meant. Since the name of his Jewish community was Kehila, he called his band the "Kille Dillers."

A thousand Jews were being shipped to unknown destinations every two weeks and on 25 March 1942, it was the Kille Dillers' turn: "You may take with you not more than thirty pounds of baggage." Ma-chine-guns covered them as they boarded a waiting train. When the morning sun rose they were surprised to discover they were headed west, not east. They were prodded from the station to Theresienstadt by a pack of armed, snarling men.

Theresienstadt was an old fortress surrounded by a deep moat with a population of about 3,000 civilians plus a few thousand soldiers. The civilians were evacuated, the town sealed by a heavy guard. He met some musicians from Prague but there were no instruments so "the only mu-sic was vocal."

Wait a minute. It is impossible to let that go by. What did they sing? "Blue and Sentimental"? "Nobody Loves You When You're Down and Out"? This tale was getting hairy. I lost my first kilo.

They discovered a battered piano in an attic, some old horns were smuggled in. They played muted because entertainment was banned. Then, suddenly, it was not only permitted, but ordered. A committee for "entertainment in your free time" [Freizeitgestaltung] was formed. The Germans were renovating Theresienstadt into a model ghetto to disprove rumors about slave labor and gas chambers. A Red Corps committee was expected.

All surfaces received a fresh coat of paint. New musical instruments arrived, ensembles were organized. Some of the best musicians in Europe were in that ghetto. On 8 January 1943, Vogel wrote a letter to the Freizeitgestaltung asking permission to start a jazz band called the Ghetto Swingers. Permission was granted.

Clarinetist Fritz Weiss, "without any doubt one of the best jazz musicians of pre-war Europe," could also arrange and soon there was a library of twenty arrangements. Musical staves had to be drawn by hand on blank paper. Vogel taped five pencils together to save time. He arranged the band's theme song: "I Got Rhythm." Still basically an amateur with little reading experience, having trouble keeping up, Vogel was "politely asked to play third trumpet and not too loudly."

Martin Roman, once pianist with the famous Marek Weber band, was appointed leader. Vogel writes:

> The Ghetto Swingers was quite a good band. We played with swing and feeling, mostly in the style of Benny Goodman. Closing my eyes now, I can almost hear Goodman emanating from Weiss' clarinet. There was Nettl, piano; Schuman, drums; Goldschmidt, guitar; Lubensky, bass; Vodnansky, alto saxophone; Donde, tenor saxophone; Kohn, Chokkes and Vogel, trumpets; Taussig, trombone and Weiss on clarinet.

A guitar player named Vicherek had recently been convicted of having "defiled musical culture" by singing Louis Armstrong's scat vocal on "Tiger Rag" in public. And yet there the Ghetto Swingers were playing the same music in the same sort of camp to which Vicherek had been sent for playing it outside.

When the Red Cross commission (two Danes, one Swiss) arrived, the symphony orchestra played in the main square and the Ghetto Swingers were swinging in the cafe. Handed sardines, under-nourished children were ordered to complain: "Oh, not sardines again."

A movie was shot to document the "good life" in Theresienstadt. The Ghetto Swingers appear several times. The film crew from Prague was impressed with the band and the band was flattered. The film includes sporting events, concerts and vaudeville and took several weeks to shoot. The band began to believe the propaganda. Perhaps the swinging, intense music they were playing had something to do with it. The carefully orchestrated Nazi illusion of freedom and security in Theresienstadt took the form of reality in their minds. They planned for the post-war future, when they would stay together and tour the world.

As soon as the Red Cross and the film crew left, on 28 September 1944, the Ghetto Swingers went on the road to Auschwitz. Fritz Weiss was gassed upon arrival: ". . . our beloved and wonderfully gifted Fritz Weiss, one of the best jazz musicians Europe ever had."

From photographs, Fritz Weiss appears to resemble Artie Shaw more than Goodman. He is handsome and virile and you can guess from his engaged stance and determined embouchure that he probably played well. The Ghetto Swingers are on a bandstand in a park, wearing white shirts and neat neckties. It resembles a summer jazz festival.

In Auschwitz, Vogel was pushed towards a hill. An SS officer on top pointed either left or right. Waiting at the bottom, an elderly guard asked Vogel: "What did you do in Theresienstadt?"

"I played in a jazz band."

"Just what we need here. When you come to the top of the hill tell the officer you are in perfect health and take ten years off your age."

Vogel went left; the gas chambers were to the right. Before falling asleep in the barracks he watched a Dutch Jew who had finked on other Jews tortured to a slow death by inmates. The next day, the prisoners were ordered outside to be counted. They stood foodless for hours in a snowstorm. The weak passed out or were led away. Vogel was beaten by young trustees in striped pajamas.

After an SS man commanded: *"Musiker, vortreten,"* (musicians, step forward), he punched Vogel in the stomach for the hell of it and said follow me. In barracks two, Vogel was astonished to find several surviving Ghetto Swingers. They embraced and kissed. In a few hours he was dressed in a sharp band uniform. He had shoes, food, cigarettes. He was introduced to "the two German mass-murderers" who were in charge of the camp, one of whom, Willy, asked what instrument he played.

"Trumpet."

"We already have two," Willy groaned.

Vogel froze; he knew the price of redundancy in these places.

But Willy was a music lover. "I'll get you a trumpet even if I have to sell a bottle of whiskey for it."

Thirty musicians played symphonies, operas and jazz without written music twelve hours a day for the guards, one of whom said: "You guys are good. There was a wonderful Gypsy band here for six weeks. They were good too but they went up the chimney."

Vogel writes: "We had some good players among us and we made good music"—until leaving by freight train not chimney, four weeks later. "During the voyage, we sang vocal versions of the music we had been playing, like Lambert-Hendricks-Ross would do later."

Arriving in the Heinkel aircraft factory, which was running low on slaves, somebody told an officer: "We are musicians. We were in the Auschwitz choir." He was beaten; music was not mentioned again, though an inspector who remembered Martin Roman from the Marek Weber band did what he could to ease their workload.

Vogel jumped off a gondola car headed for the final solution in Dachau and managed to reach the forest. He was starving and the Allies were close so he took a chance crawling out when he saw an automobile. Nuts! Luftwaffe officers. But they knew they were soon going to need all the good karma they could get and they gave him bread and directions to the nearby village of Petzenhausen, where he was fed hot black coffee and potatoes and hidden in a barn.

He rubbed his eyes in disbelief when he saw what was printed in large letters on the side of the first American jeep to enter the village: "BOOGIE WOOGIE."

Mike Zwerin, *La Tristesse de Saint Louis: Jazz Under the Nazis,* (London: Quartet Books, 1985) 24–29.

Free Jazz, Fusion, JAZZaK and ReTro-JazZ

The post-Bop Era of the fifties and sixties was marked by regional and ideological disputes—West Coast (cool) versus East Coast (hot), "soul/funk" (hot) versus Third Stream (cool). By the middle sixties these had become further polarized by another war, urban unrest (racial division expressing itself most notably in Martin Luther King, Jr. [cool] and Malcolm X [hot], the Civil Rights movement, and the Watts rebellion), and the political involvement of white middle-class college students in various "liberation" movements at home and abroad. Assassination bullets shattered the rigid tranquillity of TV sit-coms, broke through the shield, pouring forth a roar of disruptive images from Viet Nam, college campuses, ghettos, as well as paranoiac fantasies and conspiracy films and novels. Social institutions built to support the Cold War economy began eroding; the government went into convulsions; ultimately a President was forced to resign from office rather than be impeached. While rock 'n' roll became the official pop music, a major symbolic field for actualizing (and activating) a consumership coming into majority, jazz radicalized itself through the energetic deconstructive/reconstructive works of Ornette Coleman and the oceanic scalar passion of John Coltrane. In Free Jazz a utopian moment was seized upon and declared. It opened a cultural horizon and boundary. Like Bebop, it was another attempt to reclaim jazz as a black art form and discourse; musicians formed organizations, began self-producing records, formed alliances with other black and white cultural workers, and many were incorporated into the shifting curricula of universities trying to reflect and accommodate the social upheavals of the period. Black arts movements energized urban culture, developed multimedia events in which jazz, poetry, and dance, all expressing a re-mythologized Black History, released (and realized) a flowering of African-American art more extensive and ongoing than the brief Harlem Renaissance.

Counter currents of jazz as profession (akin to stockbroking or orthopedic surgery) became more rigorously incorporated into educational institutions. Much of what was wild and boundary-breaking in Free Jazz (potentially liberating, problematizing, or instantly clarifying) was tamed, standardized by the new wave of computer-spawned music technologies. Here technician (in terms of "chops") met and fused with technocrat. Fusion blended rock/pop hooks, beat, amplifier sound, and thickened them with advanced jazz harmonies, poly-rhythms, and instrumental facility. The hybridization of rock and jazz was colonized by the ECM therapeutic discs produced by Manfred Eicher, followed by the mellow jello of Windham Hill's acoustic relaxants. In a sense, ECM and Windham Hill were the white side of the Free Jazz movement: modal, free form, extended exploratory solos and ensemble playing, articulating the Reagan/Bush era of soundtrack, sound bite, and surfaces reflecting Yuppie faces and mystique; a solipsistic, apolitical escalator to status, capital and material accumu-lation. A period of rapidly diminishing options offered by super-gluey media conglomerates busily smoothing out difference, defiance, or questions. (A further facet of middle-class colonialism can be ascribed to the merchandising of "world music" and the fusionary efforts at subordinating ethnomusics into company-store dial tone.)

Beneath the exalting chaos of Free Jazz was a white perception of jazz and black political power linked to ghoulish and incendiary conclu-sions. The generational framing of Philip Larkin's white flag in the face of the newer jazz is contrasted with equally protective rhetoric from radical white poet John Sinclair. Jazz magazines projected estab-lishment difficulties with the movement; negative (often hysteric) criticism decried the defacing of established norms and forms, ex-pressed anxiety about mixing politics and art (as if that never existed) and worry about "Black Power." Critics attacked the unrestrained creative "energy" unleashed in performance as much as they challenged revisionary practices of performing. Free Jazz defenders and party hacks were as strident in asserting the multiple revolutions the music affirmed; some favored the revolutionary political aspects, others ad-vocated a homemade Afrocentrism (currently reshaped by many rap-pers), while others bypassed both in favor of embracing avant-garde status and proselytizing for the "classical" content of jazz. Power relations were challenged, rearranged, abandoned, as the seventies slow-burned into the eighties and the retreat of Free Jazz and the arising of neo-con Jazz.

—DM

ABOUT THE TIME I STARTED LISTENING TO ROCK in the mid-Sixties, I stopped listening to jazz. I was fed up with the bad vibes, the arrogance, hostility, and craziness of the jazz scene. Guys getting knifed to death at the pimp bar in Birdland. Hysterical Jewish managers right out of the old Berlin cabarets. Arrogant spades sticking it up every white man's ass. The tone of that day was set by Miles Davis. He consummated its contempt. Every black musician modeled himself after Miles, working behind shades, turning his back on the audience, walking off the stand when he wasn't soloing, and receiving the press with all sorts of booby traps ranging from put-ons and lies to outright threats of violence.

Jazz was sick to death in those days. Some of the musicians, like Bud Powell or Charlie Mingus, were simply crazy. Bud was an electro-shock zombie who had been brought back to New York from Paris by Oscar Goodstein, the owner of Birdland. He could barely get his hands together to play his old stuff. The last time I saw him work, he had a couple of scared-looking kids on bass and drums. Somebody asked him, "Who are those two little twerps?" "I dunno," mumbled Bud. "We never been introduced."

Mingus was another story. A huge man mountain, always smoldering with paranoia and weight pills, he sometimes erupted with terrifying violence. One night in the Village he spotted a man walking into the club with two old sabers tucked under his arm. Divining instantly that this elderly antique dealer was an assassin, Charlie lunged wildly toward the man's table and seized one of his swords. Tearing the curved blade out of the sheath and brandishing it maniacally, he sent hundreds of customers screaming and scrambling for their lives.

It was easier for a white man to put up with the stupor of Powell or the physical menace of Man Mountain Mingus than it was to withstand the withering contempt of Davis. Miles was a soul man, a sound, a black Bogey. He was also an insufferable prick. Posturing onstage in his shades, continental suits and banty-weight boxer's physique, he played the role of the jazz genius. "Miles could spit in his horn and it would get five stars in *Down Beat*," quipped one A&R man. Actually, the spitting was more likely to be aimed at the audience.

Putting down the house was one of the classic mannerisms of the be-bop musician. Miles had studied the art with the masters. Yet the

contempt that rolled off a real genius like Charlie Parker had a very
different feel than the posturing of Monsieur. Miles was a paper panther. His power was almost entirely the power of the press. No matter
how hard he hit the bag at Gleason's, his trumpet tone remained the
puniest in jazz. He could never do a Buddy Bolden and "call the children home" by sticking his horn through a ballpark fence. Miles stuck
his horn right into the mike—and even amplified it hardly had the
punch of a champion.

What Miles did possess in superlative degree was the art of mime.
He was jazz's Marcel Marceau. With a single gesture he could signal
an attitude; with a single note, precipitate a deep mood. Listening to
him was like watching Balinese shadow puppets. Everything was a dark
profile, a tenebrous outline, a stylized stretch-and-dip that closed into
itself with ritualistic finality.

When Miles was a jazz kid with Charlie Parker, his role was that
of femme foil to Bird's aggressively thrusting horn. The classic picture
of the pair shows a heavy-shouldered Parker hunching forward while
beside him trembles a skinny kid whose body is bent back in a supple
S-curve. Like Frank Sinatra, who commenced his career a softly croon-
ing femme-man, then turned into a middle-aged belter, Miles Davis had
to go through a change of life before he could become the musical embodiment of black power.

It took me many years to figure out how bop could have killed jazz
when bop was obviously the greatest thing that ever happened to jazz.
Eventually I realized that bop was a terminal product, that Charlie
Parker had taken jazz to the end of the line. Though Parker was hailed
as a revolutionary and his music treated as the jazz of the future, the
truth was precisely the opposite: bop had simply one-upped the jazz
of the swing era, leaving its materials, techniques and conventions essentially unchanged. Even in his most daring forays, the great Yardbird
had remained firmly locked within the circular walls of theme-and-vari-
ation forms. Round and round he had gone, pouring out brilliant ideas,
tossing off dazzling phrases, suggesting rhythms, harmonies and coun-
terpoints that no one had ever dreamed of in this little world. But all

his creative brilliance had been poured into one of the narrowest and most constrictive of musical forms.

When Bird got through with jazz, he had exhausted its traditional resources: nobody could play faster, think more ingeniously or further sophisticate jazz rhythm. A whole generation would con Bird's exercise book, assimilating his ideas to the common stock; but while they did so, the art of jazz stood still. Worse, it fell into a state of crisis trying to find a new direction in which to grow.

Part of the hang-up of the fifties, therefore, was simply the struggle to break out of this bind; that accounted for the experiments with classical music and the alliances between improvising soloists and structurally sophisticated arranger-composers. The other basic problem was the bleaching out of the jazz essence, a process which had begun with Parker's radical musicalization of jazz. Bird and Diz were steeped to the lips in jazz essence. They never had to worry about "soul." Their epigoni, however, were men of a different stamp. Instead of abstracting their music from the black experience, they abstracted it from the playing of the bop abstracters. The result was a Whiteyfication of jazz leading eventually to the spectral sophistication of Paul Desmond of the Dave Brubeck band.

Loss of the black essence meant not only a weakening of jazz's emotive force; it meant a loss of homogeneity and purity in the jazz idiom. Jazz is an art of taste. Everything the musician hears must be tested against a mental touchstone, a black Kaaba that dictates this *is* or this *is not* jazz. Lots of things that were not jazz originally have been brought into alignment with the jazz tradition, but many more have been rejected. By the early fifties it was becoming harder and harder to know what would work as jazz. Men were toying with Afro-Cuban, Arabic, Spanish, and other folk essences. They were attracted by Impressionism and atonalism. They were into remote periods like the Baroque. How could anyone speak convincingly in such a quotation-ridden tongue?

The answer came in the mid-fifties with the funky, hard bop regression. Musicians like Horace Silver, Bud Powell, Thelonious Monk and Charlie Mingus began to play music that was strongly flavored with traditional blues and gospel sounds. All these men were black and their

embrace of the Negro roots was given a political or social interpretation. Fundamentally, however, their motives were musical; they were
simply getting back to basics.

Albert Goldman, *Freak Show: The Rocksoulbluesjazzsickjewblackhumorsexpoppsych Gig and
Other Scenes from the Counter-Culture*, (New York: Atheneum, 1971) 300–302, 304–306.

WHAT I AM DOING, I suppose, is demonstrating that when I was asked
to write these articles I was patently unfitted to do so and should have
declined. The reason I didn't was that I still thought of myself as a jazz
lover, someone unquestionably on the wavelength of Congo Square,
and although I knew things had been changing I didn't believe jazz itself
could alter out of all recognition any more than the march or the waltz
could. It was simply a question of hearing enough of the new stuff: I
welcomed the chance to do so, feeling confident that once I got the
feel of it all would be made clear. Secondly, I hadn't really any intention
of being a jazz *critic*. In literature, I understood, there were several old
whores who had grown old in the reviewing game by praising everything, and I planned to be their jazz equivalent. This isn't as venal as
it sounds. Since my space was to be so limited, anything but praise
would be wasteful; my readers deserved to be told of the best of all
worlds, and I was the man to do it. It didn't really matter, therefore,
whether I liked things at first or not, as I was going to call them all
masterpieces.

But there came a hitch. When the records, in their exciting square
packages, began obligingly to arrive from the companies, the eagerness
with which I played them turned rapidly to astonishment, to disbelief,
to alarm. I felt I was in some nightmare, in which I had confidently
gone into an examination hall only to find that I couldn't make head
or tail of the questions. It wasn't like listening to a kind of jazz I didn't
care for—Art Tatum, shall I say, or Jelly Roll Morton's Red Hot Pep-
pers. It wasn't like listening to jazz at all. Nearly every characteristic of
the music had been neatly inverted: for instance, the jazz tone, distinguished from 'straight' practice by an almost-human vibrato, had entirely disappeared, giving way to utter flaccidity. Had the most original
feature of jazz been its use of collective improvisation? Banish it: let
the first and last choruses be identical exercises in low-temperature uni-

son. Was jazz instrumentation based on the hockshop trumpets, trombones and clarinets of the returned Civil War regiments? Brace yourself for flutes, harpsichords, electronically-amplified bassoons. Had jazz been essentially a popular art, full of tunes you could whistle? Something fundamentally awful had taken place to ensure that there should be no more tunes. Had the wonderful thing about it been its happy, cake-walky syncopation that set feet tapping and shoulders jerking? Any such feelings were now regularly dispelled by random explosions from the drummer ('dropping bombs'), and the use of non-jazz tempos, 3/4, 5/8, 11/4. Above all, was jazz the music of the American Negro? Then fill it full of conga drums and sambas and all the tawdry trappings of South America, the racket of Middle East bazaars, the cobra-coaxing cacophonies of Calcutta.

But, deeper than this, the sort of emotion the music was trying to evoke seemed to have changed. Whereas the playing of Armstrong, Bechet, Waller and the Condon groups had been relaxed and expansive, the music of the new men seemed to have developed from some of the least attractive characteristics of the late thirties—the tight-assed little John Kirby band, for instance, or the more riff-laden Goodman units. The substitution of bloodless note-patterns for some cheerful or sentimental popular song as a basis for improvisation (I'm thinking of some of the early Parker) was a retrograde step, but worse still was the deliberately-contrived eccentricity of phrasing and harmonies. One of the songs I remember from my dance-music childhood was called 'I'm Nuts About Screwy Music, I'm Mad About Daffy Tempos,' and I've often meant to look it up in the British Museum to see whether the rest of the lyric forecast the rise of bop with such uncanny accuracy. This new mode seemed to have originated partly out of boredom with playing ordinary jazz six nights a week (admittedly a pretty grueling way of making a living), and partly from a desire to wrest back the initiative in jazz from the white musicians, to invent 'something they can't steal because they can't play it.' This motive is shallow and *voulu*. Worst of all is the pinched, unhappy, febrile, tense nature of the music. The constant pressure to be different and difficult demanded greater and greater technical virtuosity and more and more exaggerated musical non-sequiturs. It wasn't, in a word, the music of happy men. I used to think that anyone hearing a Parker record would guess he was a drug addict, but no one hearing Beiderbecke would think he was an alcoholic, and that this summed up the distinction between the kinds of music.

What I was feeling was, no doubt, a greatly-amplified version of the surprise many European listeners felt when, after the war, records of Parker and his followers began to arrive across the Atlantic. "America has gone mad!" wrote George Shearing on reaching New York during this period (it didn't take him long to follow suit), and whereas Shearing was (presumably) taking only Parker and Gillespie on the chin, I was taking everything up to 1961—Monk, Davis, Coltrane, Rollins, The Jazz Messengers, the lot. I was denied even the solace of liking this man and disliking that: I found them all equally off-putting. Parker himself, compulsively fast and showy, couldn't play four bars without resorting to a peculiarly irritating five-note cliché from a prewar song called "The Woody Woodpecker Song." His tone, though much better than that of some of his successors, was thin and sometimes shrill. (I fancy, however, that Parker was improving at the time of his death, possibly as a result of meeting Bechet in France—Bechet was always ready to instruct the young.) The impression of mental hallucination he conveyed could also be derived from the pianist Bud Powell, who cultivated the same kind of manic virtuosity and could sometimes be stopped only by the flashing of a light in his eyes. Gillespie, on the other hand, was a more familiar type, the trumpeter-leader and entertainer, but I didn't relish his addiction to things Latin-American and I found his sense of humor rudimentary. Thelonious Monk seemed a not-very-successful comic, as his funny hats proclaimed: his *faux-naif* elephant-dance piano style, with its gawky intervals and absence of swing, was made doubly tedious by his limited repertoire. With Miles Davis and John Coltrane a new inhumanity emerged. Davis had several manners: the dead muzzled slow stuff, the sour yelping fast stuff, and the sonorous theatrical arranged stuff, and I disliked them all. With John Coltrane metallic and passionless nullity gave way to exercises in gigantic absurdity, great boring excursions on not-especially-attractive themes during which all possible changes were rung, extended investigations of oriental tedium, long-winded and portentous demonstrations of religiosity. It was with

Coltrane, too, that jazz started to be *ugly on purpose:* his nasty tone would become more and more exacerbated until he was fairly screeching at you like a pair of demoniacally-possessed bagpipes. After Coltrane, of course, all was chaos, hatred and absurdity, and one was almost relieved that severance with jazz had become so complete and obvious. But this is running ahead of my story.

The awkward thing was that it was altogether too late in the day to publicize this kind of reaction. In the late forties battle had been joined in the correspondence columns between the beret-and-dark-glasses boys and the mouldy figs; by the early sixties, all this had died down. Setting aside a qualification or two I should like to make later, one can say only that to voice such a viewpoint in 1961 would have been journalistically impossible. By then Parker was dead and a historical figure, in young eyes probably indistinguishable from King Oliver and other founding fathers. There was nothing for it but to carry on with my original plan of undiscriminating praise, and I did so for nearly two years. During this time I blocked in the background by subscribing to *Down Beat* again (there were none of the FRISCO CHIRP'S VEGAS DEBUT headlines I remembered from my schooldays), and read a lot of books. I learned that jazz had now developed socially and musically: the post-war Negro was better educated, more politically conscious and culturally aware than his predecessors, and in consequence the Negro jazz musician was more musically sophisticated. He knew his theory, his harmony, his composition: he had probably been to the Juilliard School of Music, and jazz was just what he didn't want to be associated with, in the sense of grinning over a half dozen chords to an audience all night. He had freed his music as a preliminary to freeing himself: jazz was catching up with the rest of music, becoming chromatic instead of diatonic (this was the something fundamentally awful), taking in other national musical characteristics as the American Negro looked beyond the confines of his own bondage. Practically everyone was agreed about all this. It was fearful. In a humanist society, art—and especially modern, or current, art—assumes great importance, and to lose touch with it is parallel to losing one's faith in a religious age. Or, in this particular case, since jazz is the music of the young, it was like losing one's potency. And yet, try as I would, I couldn't find anything to enjoy in the things I was sent, despite their increasing length—five, seven, nine minutes at a time, nothing like the brilliant three-minute cameos of the age of 78s. Something, I felt, had snapped, and I was drifting deeper into the silent shadowland of middle age. Cold death had taken its first citadel.

And yet again, there was something about the books I was now reading that seemed oddly familiar. This *development,* this *progress,* this *new language* that was more *difficult,* more *complex,* that required you to *work hard at appreciating it,* that you *couldn't expect to understand at first go,* that needed *technical and professional knowledge* to evaluate it *at all levels,* this *revolutionary explosion* that *spoke for our time* while at the same time being *traditional* in the *fullest,* the *deepest* . . . of course! This was the language of criticism of modern painting, modern poetry, modern music. Of *course!* How glibly I had talked of modern jazz, without realizing the force of the adjective: this was *modern* jazz, and Parker was a modern jazz player just as Picasso was a modern painter and Pound a modern poet. I hadn't realized that jazz had gone from Lascaux to Jackson Pollock in fifty years, but now that I realized it, relief came flooding in upon me after nearly two years' despondency. I went back to my books: "After Parker, you had to be something of a musician to follow the best jazz of the day." (Benny Green: *The Reluctant Art.* London: MacGibbon & Kee, 1962.) Of course! After Picasso! After Pound! There could hardly have been a conciser summary of what I don't believe about art.

The reader may here have the sense of having strayed into a private argument. All I am saying is that the term 'modern,' when applied to art, has a more than chronological meaning: it denotes a quality of irresponsibility peculiar to this century, known sometimes as modernism, and once I had classified modern jazz under this heading I knew where I was. I am sure there are books in which the genesis of modernism is set out in full. My own theory is that it is related to an imbalance between the two tensions from which art springs: these are the tension between the artist and his material, and between the artist and his audience, and that in the last seventy-five years or so the second of these has slackened or even perished. In consequence the artist has become over-concerned with his material (hence an age of technical experiment), and, in isolation, has busied himself with the two principal themes of modernism, mystification and outrage. Piqued at being neglected, he has painted portraits of both eyes on the same side of the nose, or smothered a model with paint and rolled her over a blank canvas. He has designed a dwelling-house to be built underground. He has written poems resembling the kind of pictures typists make with their machines during the coffee break, or a novel in gibberish, or a play in which the characters sit in dustbins. He has made a six-hour film of someone asleep.

He has carved human figures with large holes in them. And parallel to this activity ("every idiom has its idiot," as an American novelist has written) there has grown up a kind of critical journalism designed to put it over. The terms and the arguments vary with circumstances, but basically the message is: don't trust your eyes, or ears, or understanding. They'll tell you this is ridiculous, or ugly, or meaningless. Don't believe them. You've got to work at this: after all, you don't expect to understand anything as important as art straight off, do you? I mean, this is pretty complex stuff: if you want to know how complex, I'm giving a course of ninety-six lectures at the local college, starting next week, and you'd be more than welcome. The whole thing's on the rates, you won't have to pay. After all, think what asses people have made of themselves in the past by not understanding art—you don't want to be like that, do you? And so on, and so forth. Keep the suckers spending.

The tension between artist and audience in jazz slackened when the Negro stopped wanting to entertain the white man, and when the audience as a whole, with the end of the Japanese war and the beginning of television, didn't in any case particularly want to be entertained in that way any longer. The jazz band in the night club declined just as my old interest, the dance band, had declined in the restaurant and hotel: jazz moved, ominously, into the culture belt, the concert halls, university recital rooms and summer schools where the kind of criticism I have outlined has freer play. This was bound to make the reestablishment of any artist-audience nexus more difficult, for universities have long been the accepted stamping-ground for the subsidized acceptance of art rather than the real purchase of it—and so, of course, for this kind of criticism, designed as it is to prevent people using their eyes and ears and understandings to report pleasure and discomfort. In such conditions modernism is bound to flourish.

I don't know whether it is worth pursuing my identification of modern jazz with other branches of modern art any further: if I say I dislike both, in what seems to me the same way, I have made my point. Having made the connection, however, I soon saw how quickly jazz was passing from mystification ("Why don't you get a piano player? and what's that stuff he's playing?") to outrage. Men such as Ornette Coleman, Albert Ayler and Archie Shepp, dispensing with pitch, harmony, theme, tone, tune and rhythm, were copied by older (Rollins, Coltrane) and young players alike. And some of them gave a keener edge to what they were playing by suggesting that it had some political relation to the aspirations of the Black Power movement. From using music to entertain the white man, the Negro has moved to hating him with it. Anyone who thinks that an Archie ("America's done me a lot of wrong") Shepp record is anything but two fingers extended from a bunched fist at him personally cannot have much appreciation of what he is hearing. Or, as LeRoi Jones puts it, "Listening to Sonny Murray, you can hear the primal needs of the new music. The heaviest emotional indentation it makes. From ghostly moans of spirit, let out full to the heroic marchspirituals and priestly celebrations of the new blackness."

By this time I was quite certain that jazz had ceased to be produced. The society that had engendered it had gone, and would not return. Yet surely all that energy and delight could not vanish as completely as it came? Looking round, it didn't take long to discover what was delighting the youth of the sixties as jazz had delighted their fathers; indeed, one could hardly ask the question for the deafening racket of the groups, the slamming, thudding, whanging cult of beat music that derived straight from the Negro clubs on Chicago's South Side, a music so popular that its practitioners formed a new aristocracy that was the envy of all who beheld them, supported by their own radio stations throughout the world's waking hours. Perhaps I was mistaken in thinking that jazz had died; what it had done was split into two, intelligence without beat and beat without intelligence, and it was the latter which had won the kind of youthful allegiance that had led me to hammer an accompaniment to Ray Noble's "Tiger Rag" when I was 12 or 13.

Beat jazz was gone to seed, just as "modern jazz" was: B. B. King or Or-
nette Coleman? A difficult choice, and if I were to come down (as I
should) on the side of the former, it wouldn't be under the illusion that
I was listening to the latterday equivalent of Billie Holiday and Teddy
Wilson, Pee Wee Russell and Jess Stacy, or Fats Waller and his
Rhythm.

Philip Larkin, *All What Jazz: A Record Diary, 1961–1971*, (New York: Farrar, Straus,
& Giroux, 1985) 18–25.

> What I would like to see is artists owning as much of them-
> selves as possible. Or most people.
> —George Russell, *Jazz & Pop*, April 1970

I really can't see much need for "reviewing" these records, at least not
until enough people are listening to this music—these musics—that
we can carry on an intelligent and knowledgeable discussion of the specific records, that is, until enough people are thoroughly *familiar* with
the body of music, or musics, of which these records are part. *Familiar*,
as in *family*. So I have to see my task as creating or producing some effective *propaganda* for this music, or again, these musics, and these specific
records, in the hopes that people can read what I write here and be
moved somehow to procure copies of these records, take them home
with them and introduce the music to their families, and let it become
part of their lives. Because people are going to have to get to this music
sooner or later, and the sooner the better—not only for the individual
musicians and bands involved, but for the good of the whole people,
if you can relate to that. Because this is liberation music, self-determination music, music that will help you, inspire you to transform yourself, yourselves, and to work to bring about the transformation of the
social order which keeps so many of us, and so many more of our brothers and sisters, oppressed, hungry, and beaten down.

Now, I could talk about the music, but I want you to listen to it
for yourselves, so I will restrict myself primarily to talking about the
context in which the music is made, the extramusical aspects of the music
(extramusical only in the sense that you will not be able to *hear* what
I'm talking about here on the records when you listen to them, except

as these things fully *inform* the music and make the music *possible*—you dig?). What I have to talk about is the human context of the music, then—the social and political realities which shape the music and which, equally, are shaped *by* the music. Because the music cannot be separated, must not be separated, except at the peril of the musicians and their audience and at the peril of the whole social order finally. The music may be strong in itself, it may hold, it may charge the listener, sure, but once the musician is separated from the music, once the music becomes less than the *first term* of his life (her life), once the listener becomes less than the first (equal) term of the music and the musicians equally, then what the people get is less than what they deserve, and there is something wrong with the whole structure of that society in which the music is produced—it becomes, or comes to be, less than what it was *meant* to be, if you can relate to that.

Because music is the thing that gives us breath and strength, that sustains us and keeps us alive, and we live for the music, it lives and breathes for us, and when something else happens in there, when something disrupts the flow of the music through the musicians to the people, when those relations (*that* relation, really) are disrupted or corrupted, then the people are being cheated, and the musicians are being cheated, and the natural balance of the life of the people is destroyed. As it is so much today anyway, which is what we are trying to put a stop to now, which is what this music and these words, and the musicians' lives and our lives too, are dedicated and committed to stopping, this destruction of the balance of our lives. And what I want to say is that we have to start with the first things, the primary things, like our breath, our daily acts and gestures, and we have to integrate ourselves with the universe from our cells on out; we can't separate ourselves from our words, acts, or gestures, or from our music, or we are doomed. It has to start there, inside the skin, and the relations have to be maintained all the way out, through whatever other bodies or things that come into our lives.

Because if we are going to talk about liberation, we have to talk about liberation in the total sense, and we have to see that (1) there is no freedom that does not start at the root to grow out free—or you can't talk about being free, or sing about being free, without *being* free, and without manifesting that freedom *throughout* your activity equally; and (2) one person can't be free until all people are free. We have to learn these things as we can, because we are quite purposefully taught differently, but what is important is that we *are* learning, and the music is helping us learn about freedom. Liberation music, self-determination music, the two terms are coterminous, they define each other—and they help us define ourselves, as the music does. This music is meant to liberate you, just as it liberates the musicians as they play it, just as their own personal and collective liberation is the productive force of the music itself—these are free musicians, and they can make free music, and they can get this music to you to help you free yourselves so you can join with them then to help free the rest of the people.

Now, as we have been taught by other liberation fighters, we cannot deal with personal or cultural freedom without talking about and dealing with economic freedom, or the people's control of the means of production . . .

. . . The musicians' lives and their economic work (not just their musical work) have much which is of use to us in all we do. Because we have to change this world, and it is most important for us that we learn *how* to move—i.e., *how* to do that which we know must be done, that which *we ourselves* must do. And we can learn that from these men, we can learn varying approaches to the problem of self-determination for the artist and for all people—from the way in which Herbie Mann, an individual artist who is probably more interested in his own welfare than in wide social issues, has created his own production company so he can produce and market recordings of his (and Roy Ayers' in this instance) and retain maximum control over the ultimate product; to the *whole thing* that Sun Ra has made of his original impulse for musical creation, the way he has kept a band together for twenty years, has produced his own records, has kept full control of the music and everything associated with it in the hands of himself and his musicians, and all of this without even the most minimal remunerative consideration!

These men are harbingers, some of the most beautiful and persuasive harbingers, of the New Order, and their activity points a way for all of us to explore. They have solved, or have at least begun to solve, the problem of separation—of the musicians' separation from the music, of the music's separation from the people it is meant for, of the musicians' separation from the means of production. One of the most beautiful things about this music—as exemplified by these albums—is the way the music is so close to the lives of the musicians, so close that it *can't* really be separated, so close that it can help destroy separation everywhere. Stanley Crouch says it best in his killer liner notes for the Horace Tapscott album (*The Giant is Awakened*):

> But the most important thing to understand is that these men are as new as this music, their lives and their music are not separate. They don't, like so many others, stop being warm as soon as they get from behind their instruments, don't rein up all the strength and knowledge they play with some cracker style shuck corny super hip "attitude" off the band stand. And that's the message, as Walter Lowe would say, "A way to live." Or as Horace says: "The relationship between you and me as men is the first thing, the piano is something else: I just use it for certain things."

Right on, Horace.

But that's not all of it, either—there's one more thing I have to get in here, and that is that music, as the musicians' lives, is *revolutionary* music, music of the highest and positive CHANGE effect—it is the highest energy music, the freest, the most natural, the most *inspirational* music there is—not just these records, I mean, but the music or musics of which these recordings are just a small and representative part: because we have to talk about Cecil Taylor, we have to talk about Pharoah Sanders, we have to talk about Albert Ayler and Archie Shepp and Joseph Jarman and Roscoe Mitchell and Marion Brown and Sunny Murray certainly, we have to talk about Richard Abrams and Alice Coltrane and Charles Moore and Gato Barbieri and Gunter Hampel, we have to talk about the Jazz Composers Orchestra, we have to talk about the whole range and scope of this music (these musics), and we have to see that the whole thing is more than just the music, we have to talk about selfdetermination for all peoples, we have to talk about the Black

Panther party, and the National Liberation Front of South Vietnam and the People's Republic of China, and the Cuban Living Revolution and the rising Youth Nation in Amerika and throughout the postindustrial world, we have to talk about the incredible force of high-energy rock and roll, we have to talk about the killer blues that gave birth to these musics in this land, we have to talk about oppressed people and their total human liberation, we have to talk about what Stanley Crouch says. "Human closeness, Natural Intimacy, the Natural Closeness of Human Beings, the Spiritual Principle beyond machines and madness is what playing (like this) teaches you, is what listening (to this music) to learn will let you know . . . You can learn from the music because it's there to teach you, to put everybody close to himself or herself and every other self worth being close to"—which is *all selves,* when you get down to it. We have to deal with *everything* in its natural context and destroy separation on *every* level, and what I am trying to say is that this music—and I am *not* claiming too much for it—this music will drive us to do that if we let it.

John Sinclair, *Music and Politics,* (New York: The World Publishing Co., 1971) 33–38.

JAZZ 1968

If it's bullshit, put
the name on it,
call it bullshit .
    What's happening is
    the opening of it
    up, change up & go
take all the chances, if you
get good enuf at it, you

        can't make no mistakes
    It's a fiction & a diction

    : what you got is freedom .
Is it dull? You did it   .

                [1975]

Paul Blackburn, *The Collected Poems of Paul Blackburn,* Edith Jarolim, ed., (New York: Persea Books, 1985) 551.

AS WELL AS GOODNESS, BEAUTY, AND INNOVATION, (Coltrane's) music is characterized . . . by a curious conflict between the static (the modes) and movement (the rapid succession of notes). More precisely, it is movement "towards" an idea that is expressed in the title of one of his records, "Ascension."

Although like many others, before and after him, he chose elements from other cultures, it was to enrich his creation with elements that he experienced and used positively, as an affirmation to put in the place and position of an established culture, which, at no time, did he wish to attack.

He was an explorer in a triple sense. He was a musical explorer, who discovered, and knew how to combine and vitalize, elements from various cultures. The choice of the modal was, as well as a means of escaping from established musical routines, an ideological preference: the international language of the music of colored peoples. He was a Surrealist exploring content and boundaries, in a musically active introspection that must provide knowledge about the individual man and about man in general, offering the audience a universe in which the beautiful is close to "nature," and therefore "truer" which leads to a third way, that of spiritual exploration, towards an "elsewhere." It is at this point that his career takes on the dual appearance of a hopeless search for a sort of paradise—of mystical life—and of a marathon, which is human in its urgency, and in the circumstances of an unbearable social reality, and very far from the serenity of religious initiation.

One must, it seems, interpret the combination of static elements (the use of modes and establishment in a "sound") and dynamic elements (movement, both physical and emotional), as the meeting of a religious search and a social pursuit, the second being as real as the first, though unconscious. The normal mystical career is too obviously a process of passive discovery for this inventive search, with all its movement and intensity, to claim such an interpretation.

We are reminded that the term *Beat* Generation means both "beaten" by society and a search for *beatitude* and rhythm (beats), the latter symbolizing vitality. Coltrane, whose mysticism I have no desire to deny, probably lived all three dimensions of this definition; without denying through hate earlier ways of life or creation, he replaced them by a *new culture*, a search for truth, even more than for beauty.

In a very divided profession, Coltrane was always ready to help young musicians or fellow-players. Indeed, he was more "social" than political and even declared himself, in a very clear way, to be apolitical on the most burning issue:

> I don't know by what criteria you can differentiate a black musician from a white musician; in fact, I don't think there are such criteria.

Many free jazz musicians, and not only whites, share this position, including one of Shepp's old partners, the black trumpeter B(ill) Dixon:

> I don't know whether you can say that [the new music] is black, white, or colorless. Which is obvious when I play (and if I am black), I play from so-called black experience . . .

Either on purely professional grounds, or because of a certain sort of humanism, many musicians have declared themselves to be against conscious politicization.

. . . Karl Berger, a free jazz musician of German origin, defines latent politicization thus:

> If there is a chance of finding a form of human union in the world, our music is the beginning of it. Music is my politics, my religion, my philosophy.

Others go so far as to admit religious commitments (among many others, Steve Lacy, in this respect a very moderate man, claims to have adopted the *Tao Teh Ching* ["The Way of Life"] by Lao-Tsu as his Bible and guide for everyday living . . .)

From a musical point of view, Coltrane, who is regarded as a free jazz musician only from his final period, was above all an innovator, a solitary soloist, pursuing his own ways of improvisation without responding to or expecting musical responses from his fellow-players. Those players created an atmosphere by following parallel itineraries of improvisation. They have each, in their own way, developed a type of improvisation that is largely autonomous, very "free" in this sense.

On stage, the musician behaved with introspective concentration, playing until he was exhausted; the result was spectacular, but in no way contrived. Much has been said of the hypnotic fascination that developed, through the energy projected into the music and by the repetitive aspects of the music. A record can never recreate to the same extent the hypnotic quality achieved by a long, live session.

Although Coltrane sometimes shocked his audiences by leaving the stage abruptly, without acknowledging applause, or by a certain lack of organization at the end of pieces, he does not seem to have behaved in a hostile way.

Unlike the politically oriented musicians, Coltrane and those like him, although, musically, extremely radical, were concerned not so much to destroy as to develop. The hypnotic fascination that he himself felt and wanted to communicate is not strictly of an artistic order, but he provides no further information as to what is expressed in a search that has been described, somewhat over-hastily, as purely mystical. Like a whole series of other musicians—and in particular the founder of a musico-religious sect, Sun Ra—he wished to create a sort of living utopia, a deep study of which should explain with precision the factors linked with a given social situation.

Alfred Willener, *The Action-Image of Society: On Cultural Politicization*, A. A. Sheridan Smith, trans., (New York: Pantheon Books, n.d.) 247–250.

TED FOX: *You've said that Coltrane really taught you things about music. In what way? You've also said he kept you involved in jazz.*

BOB THIELE: It wasn't that he kept me involved in jazz. He brought me to what, in that period, was the "new jazz" or "new black jazz." The critics were giving it all sorts of names. Another classification at the time was "avant-garde." For his second album for Impulse, we decided to record live at the Village Vanguard. I was apprehensive, a little nervous about doing it. I had not known Coltrane before then. I had heard some of his records. He was turning jazz music around. So I met him. You know, there was no reason to have meetings before making the recordings because we were merely recording whatever he played; it wasn't a question of selecting certain tunes to be played. We decided to record, I believe, all three nights of his [stand at the Vanguard]. But it was just at that initial stage, during those three nights, that I got to know him. He happened to be very warm, very friendly, and very quiet. He certainly wasn't outgoing. He was, as I recall it, reticent to talk about anything. But we hit it off. I mean, sometimes these things happen. I've grown up with musicians. I deal with musicians. I relate to them, I guess. And we got along fine, as I began to spend more and more time with him, and we had our various meetings as to what should be used for an album, and where we should record, and what musicians to use.

It was during this period that he was explaining to me what he was trying to do musically. Initially, all I knew when I heard some of the music, being an old-time swinger, was that it sounded as though he was literally leaving the chords. When he was improvising, it just didn't hit me right. But I have a hunch that part of it was that he felt he could go further. I mean, I've really thought about it quite a bit; he explained everything to me, why he was playing the way he played, and how he felt music could go. He always felt restricted playing within the chord, staying within the chords of, say, a Cole Porter song. He was the first guy who really took vamps, and played endlessly on three chords. But those vamps were just devastating. They were truly exciting. I think what I'm trying to lead up to is that it happened naturally. You know, you can go to school and have someone explain a subject to two students, and one bombs out while the other just goes, bam, right along with it. Because I know other producers my age who, to this day, look at me like I'm nuts. They can't understand how I can listen to that music or why people buy it. Yet some of these fellows made some of the finest recordings in the history of classic jazz. And then the curtain came down [on traditional jazz] and it never went any further.

What did Coltrane say to you to convince you other than just playing?

He explained it technically, as to why one would leave the chords. "Who says there has to be a restriction on what you play?" And the more I listened, the more it sounded natural to me.

. . . You can be technical until you throw up, but how many people ask you, "What is jazz?" or "How do you know when you're listening to jazz?" I'm sure you've heard it before. Some of those classic jazz producers know Fats Waller's line, "If you have to explain it, then you don't

know what it is." There's no way to explain it. I believe that somehow
it's inbred in America, in the people as they grow up. All popular music
stems from jazz. Gershwin and composers like that wrote because they
heard jazz musicians. They went to Harlem and heard jazz bands. The
songwriters of our day were really writing rhythmic popular songs. The
song "Margie" swings if Coltrane or Coleman Hawkins plays it. They
were writing a form of popular music that definitely had roots in jazz.
What can you say? Either you feel it or you don't feel it.

Ted Fox, *In the Groove: The People Behind the Music*, (New York: St. Martin's Press,
1985) 192–194.

To John Coltrane

After the rain, the valley opened its mouth
and a few doves flew out and then disappeared,
rising so high we couldn't see them anymore

After the rain, a voice began singing, off
somewhere within the stunning aroma of kisses
that the fields gave up, flaring with brightness

After the rain, the air was spanking fresh,
angels came and sat floating in it, and the doves
nestled within their gossamer pockets

After the rain, the combo started to play, and
we walked out through the wet grass, barefoot,
likewise naked as you began to sing your song

After the rain, Elvin took his muscular prayer,
McCoy's fingers flashed upon the shimmering keys, and
Jimmy Garrison put his hand on your shoulder

After the rain, there was a tuneful peace that grins,
a falcon edged closer to its unconcerned prey, and
the day floats on, blissful as the tenor of your love

[June 6, 1976]

Jim Brodey, *Judyism*, (New York: United Artists, 1980) 28.

Elegy (For Bill Evans, 1929–1980)

Music your hands are no longer here to make
Still breaks against my ear, still shakes my heart.
Then I feel that I am still before you.
You bend above your shadow on the keys
That tremble at your touch or crystallize,
Water forced to concentrate. In meditation
You close your eyes to see yourself more clearly.

Now you know the source of sound,
The element bone and muscle penetrate
Hoping to bring back beauty.
Hoping to catch what lies beyond our reach,
You hunted with your fingertips.

My life you found, and many other lives
Which traveled through your hands upon their journey.
Note by note we followed in your tracks, like
Hearing the rain, eyes closed to feel more deeply.
We stood before the mountains of your touch.
The sunlight and the shade you carried us
We drank, tasting our bitter lives more sweetly
From the spring of song that never stops its kiss.

Bill Zavatsky, liner note on *You Must Believe in Spring,* by Bill Evans, (Burbank: Warner Bros. Inc., 1981).

"AN IMAGE: LEE KONITZ WITH STRING QUARTET" arranged by Bill Russo. I bet a lot of arrangers wanted to cop the Lee Sound, especially in the later Forties when he had that silk pencilpoint going. String quartet allows use of individual voices, separates out the strands of what usually became a snooze in cotton wadding (Bird with Strings, etc.). Russo's liner-notes show that he seems to well understand the problems of such a set-up ("understandable to string musicians and yet compatible with a partial use of jazz vocabulary"), and is out front about his intent ("distinctly & purposely a non-jazz composition using superimposed jazz improvisation"). Konitz lends himself to these strings well, but they never allow any full-out blowing, tend to be a mite gingerly in the transitions. I always was fond of Russo's (& Bill Holman's) arrangements for Kenton, in fact used his SWEETS as themesong for an FM jazz show I used to jock in Providence late fifties. Ah, Kenton . . . What to do with that vast WHELK! All his massed brass surely stirred (especially live) in my teen years, before I knew any better (?) Will he end up remembered as the Flying Dutchman of Jazz? That was an orchestra all right, too bad it was seldom a band.

> "He can take care of himself even though he goofs and does
> April in Paris from inside out as if the tune was the room he
> lived in and was going out at midnight with his coat on"
> —Jack Kerouac "following Lee Konitz" in VISIONS OF CODY

Thinking about that fascinating Konitz long-line thing, just why did he back off?, etc. And it does seem a mid-life tendency with many or most. With Konitz it seems to stem from the hassle and detachment from Tristano and K's retreat to California in the early Sixties when he lived in Palo Alto (appropriately?) and took outside gigs and did a little teaching. And, as he said later, "just noodled around," took few gigs, evidently stopped thinking of himself as a pro musician for two or three years. In fact there's always this nature of his personality that doesn't quite admit to being a working-pro player, self-effacing shy "kid" who can't completely believe in the strength of his abilities. Along with which goes an openness, a great curiosity about all kinds of music —I once saw him sitting back in the shadows blowing long held tones with LaMonte Young at the Metropolitan Museum. Also a strictness of discipline and will to study out everything he might think to play, or have played. An inner model of seriousness along with a doubt that he'll ever quite make it or come up to pure level. And then there's the story (he told in interview) about how he got the call to come back and play with a Tristano group at the Half-Note in 1964 and was actually afraid and delayed, goofed so he was (partly on purpose) a couple of days late for the gig. Somewhere in there he must have laid back and looked at what he'd been doing and felt that he didn't quite understand it, the long line maybe moving too fast for meditative thought?, and he could see places where he had once played too many ready licks (those acrobatic trilling figures), so wanted to come down from sheer momentum heights and analyze and take it all apart, thus the broken-off shorter "implying" phrases ever after. There's his remark in another interview (1980, I think) where he says one should be able to "justify" every note one plays and not just go along with a bag of recyclable phrases. But, it could be that the converse of all this is the fact that that same momentum can carry you to places/phrases you never could have gotten to otherwise. Think, too, of those Kerouac long lines where you know he didn't know where he would end up but kept the momentum going, rushing to find out. There seems a great tendency for certain musicians to worry about "mere virtuosity," and of course that *is* that danger of slickness where you end up a boring veneer-product of your own half-forgotten desires (Oscar Peterson for example). But! It seems to me there's nothing more utterly charging than that long-line held up on sheer drive-of-moment taking all corners at an instancy. No doubt it takes great psycho-physical energies to maintain, tend to drain off a bit by middleage. Though I don't think that's the main problem, more a thought problem. Konitz says he went back and listened to his recorded output, probably forming there a desire for greater succinctness, abstracted rhythm. I know, looking back at my own old work (I tend to avoid), there comes a point where everything seems to be in quotes, and it all tumbles out into weighted fragments so you begin to think how maybe you might totally consciously produce the perfect phrases, etc. getting it all backasswards (I think). Art seems to come best from getting oneself in to a state of great mental alertness compounded of sheer high momentum (no thoughts of falling) and subconscious ability to keep an amazing number of elements suspended ready at the milli-second to be placed in time. Wow. Anyway, I believe in that great high *sustain*, pick-up on the fly, ability to shine and wing when in doubt, *everything* up for grabs, a half-conscious corner-pocket genius that can never be taught to anybody completely or explained even to oneself. So, Konitz (I'm imagining) comes out of these reconsideration years with an almost wisdom-of-the-mountaintop view and makes the run for concision and meditative discontinuous flow. Funny thing though is that there was a period (just out of the Kenton band when he made those dates with the Mulligan quartet, 1953) when he had the concision *and* the momentum too! I still can't believe how that fantastic jumping-ahead-of-the-barlines thing he has going so seamlessly then, sometimes finishing with the next chord a bar or two before that chord came up, never got picked up on or developed, even by him. In the gaps between his leaps, where most listening musicians must've gulped and wondered if it'd all fall apart, you can hear ghost echoes of all kinds of long lines twisting in & through, almost like those Bach violin sonatas where he's working with phantom counterlines. No doubt Konitz came out of the Kenton brassworks with greater strength of sound (he even says this somewhere, though the LennieBirds were putting him down for joining Stan at all), and certainly his tone was never more amazing, a shine as if amber were one of the heavy metals. I wonder if that phrasal barjumping came at all out of a consideration of Mulligan's tendency toward a two-beatish 4/4. Did that open holes for him to dodge around in and play with the meter? Then in 1954 (the Storyville album livetracks, plus that Pennsylvania Avenue track on the Timespan album) he still had the long line going perfectly. Some impossible lengths woven into forward slings on These Foolish Things. A high-pressure fluidity of line, the one that Kerouac said inspired him to write like Konitz played. Ceaseless sinuosities and carvings of space, riding the line onwards 'round any possible corner, hearingman's reach. The very impossibility of it all making a vacuum/hollow that must be entered. Talk about passion! Ah, the poems that could be written . . .

Clark Coolidge (from personal correspondence with the editor).

MY LIFE. THIS IS THE STORY OF MY LIFE. It's high time it were written. The little memory I've got left is going. Everything gets mixed up in my head. Last names and first names, dates and places. The music is all that remains, the music of my seventy years. Copy it out on these scraps of paper: I only wish I could. The machines they've got today can't bring anything back to life. Player pianos chewing away at music rolls. Ragtime, roughtime. They've lost the secet of high fidelity. Cylinders are the last word in turn-of-the-century technique. And all they cut on them are the fashionable ditties. If I could just go over the lovely choruses of yesteryear, one by one. Put them on paper, like illuminations. So they wouldn't disappear with me. They were what I lived in. They where what I lived for. As far back as I can remember, in the furthest reaches of my old age, when I used to listen to Billy Taylor. No, David Taylor. No, Cecil Taylor. I can still see him leaning over the piano keyboard. Lost in the belly of the instrument. Scratching the chords with his fingernails. It was pure and it was melodious. Occasionally, he would also touch the keys with his fingers. At the time, I never suspected he was creating a new art. Yet he soon had countless disciples. The most conservative ones turned all their attention to the sound board. They strewed it with small objects: corks, nails, coins. It was what they called a pre-paired piano. But the most daring ones were fascinated by the keyboard with its black and white geometry. So they sat down and figured out what it symbolized. History was on their side. For half a century, playing the piano consisted mostly of pressing down keys. That devil Taylor, what a posterity he's had! At the same period there was Archistecp, Tchi-Cagee, Ivenszenson, Elbert Taylor . . . or rather Albert Ayler. (Better give up on the first names, my memory's playing tricks on me.) Ayler was the hardest of all to follow. An innovator, a voice of protest. Like all the fellows in the ghetto. But he was a rare type. Nobody understood Ayler. His immediate influence was nil, I have to admit that. It's only been felt very recently, as far as I can tell. And yet the ghetto's world-wide protest has died out. Even if they still do protest today, it's gotten awfully folksy. Back in those days people thought Ayler's music was a kind of absolute mockery. They were reading too much into it. Actually, he was already playing in the spirit of the Gay Nineties. A remarkable forerunner: he even respected the sour notes that have become the rule lately. Fifty years behind his time, has anybody done better? And Ornette! It's true that in those days no one really knew how to play the violin. But he put everything he had into it! Those rondos he sawed out with that mischievous bow of his were a foretaste of the closed grooves of *musique concrete*. We discovered the sound objects and its acid freshness. How restful that music was, in which everything kept coming back over and over again. Ornette, where are you now? What happened to those high notes you could get out of your trumpet? They were so smooth, so sensitive, so sciatic that we forget the mad modernism of Moffett, alias the Skunk, your drum-

mer. Oh! the world we lived in lacked unity no doubt. Alongside the
dreamers and the terrorists, the giants of show business began to loom
over the horizon. Louis, Ella, Sinatra. Strong bonds began to form between the music and the general public. And the bigger the public grew,
the fonder it became of pop songs. Who appreciated the wild ecstasy
of Cottrell . . . no, Coltrane? The genuine, original fans like myself. But
the masses wanted lyrics that were easy to follow and a tune they could
hum. This was the price that had to be paid to get out of the ghetto.
In this respect, Louis, Ella, Sinatra managed to imitate other, already
established singers who had very different conceptions. In those days,
teen-age audiences showed their enthusiasm by clapping their hands.
It's a well-known fact that uninhibited clapping in time to music is
caused by a degeneration of psychomotor cells in the adolescent. This
phenomenon of juvenile regression to the animal state can still be seen
today in the carvin' contests. It was customary to send a delegation of
clappers on stage. Sometimes a whole group of them were sent up there
rigged with cumbersome instruments, electric guitars that had a certain
charm (unfortunately, they've been supplanted by the banjo). The clap-
per delegate would sing, or pretend to. What he sang didn't count; all
that mattered was the pitch of excitement which he could help the
crowd to reach. So long as he swung his hips well, who cared whether
he sang on key? At the opposite pole, Louis, Ella, Sinatra wanted singing to be musical. They advocated a more elaborate kind of song, occasionally more literary, and tried to give it an artistic rendition. A man
named Chayrles, or Raych, I'm not sure which anymore, had already
foreseen this change of direction. It was irreversible, for the youngsters
soon lost all their influence. The pop song acted as a connecting link
and promoted the rise of a concert industry that thrived until just before
the dark days of Wall Street . . . But at the same time it wasn't uncom-
mon for the producer to pay a musician like Rollins tens of thousands
to disrecord an album that hadn't sold. I, at least, had bought it, and
so had a few other nuts like me. That was my claim to fame. And the
way I got my kicks. The supremacy of the long-playing record went
unchallenged in those days. Everyone derived benefits from this, artist
and customer alike. Often a number would cover an entire side. A half-

dozen records took care of your whole afternoon. They didn't stint on blowing in those days. There was a tendency to go to excesses, like Mingus, or to be torrential, like Cannon Ball. A degree of moderation appeared with the M. J. Q., who prefigured the cool era, soon to be followed by the great Lester's presidency. Miles, who had dropped out of sight, made a brilliant comeback by associating with the crack penmanship of Grandpa and his rowdy grandson to disrecord the Capitol series. He went on to finish his career alongside Bird, the great man of that golden age. Ah! Parker! Monk! Gillespie! and his beret! Minton's . . . that was the end of a world. I sob as I write those names. What do they mean today? Those who bore them are gone now, they belong to the future, it has swallowed them up forever. My memory is those heroes' last refuge! . . .

Andre Hodeir, *The Worlds of Jazz*, Noel Burch, trans., (New York: Grove Press, 1972) 51–55, 56–57.

On Dewey Redman's Ascending Zither, I Rose Unarmed
in Vast Intelligent Light

On Dewey Redman's ascending zither, I rose unarmed
    in vast intelligent light, the likes
        of which
I've scarcely ever seen before. Feeling the tremble
    of falling through flesh, the color
        of space, whistling, in-
                haled gentleness
taking one through a rhapsody of windy breezes, down
through slithery quarters, where silken light invades
    the pretty Martian winter fields of yellow
        quartz, magnified piss
          stains
              of immortal Fire
              that quivering, takes a firm
     hand
       in

the moving spirit whispering nebulae haze, flowing,
flowering with blond drowsy unlimitable distance.

And magnificent Change.

Jim Brodey [1975], *Judyism*, (New York: United Artists, 1980) 12.

I STARTED PLAYING BECAUSE I HEARD THE CALL. It's an artistic calling. The
first question is if you *hear* it, and the second question if you *heed* it. And
I heard the call, I heard the jazz, and I went for it. And all other con-
siderations were less determinant than that. It was as straightforward
as that. When I heard Duke Ellington I was about 12 or 13 years old
and wow! It was a knockout. Then after a few years trying to play the
piano I heard Sidney Bechet playing a Duke Ellington tune, "The
Mooche," and it clicked. I heard the connection between composer, soloist, the orchestral style . . . but mostly it was about the nature of jazz,
so I had to go and see what was happening. That's how I heard the
call. I also heard Art Tatum and I flipped, I gave up the piano. Then
I heard Louis Armstrong, then Miles Davis. Each thing you hear de-
termines the direction that you go. You just follow the music, and if
you follow the music you can go *anywhere*. It even brought me to Paris.
I've been following the music since then. I've gone wherever it takes me.

But I wasn't so confident back then, I didn't know what I was doing.
I was in the dark. But I smelled something, I heard something, I felt
something, I thought something . . . But I didn't know what I was doing, I didn't know where I was going, I didn't know what was involved.
Music is just out there, and you have to leap, take a chance, go off the
ledge, off the edge.

Steve Lacy, quoted in "The Man with the Straight Horn" by Richard Scott in *The
Wire*, # 100:15 (London: *The Wire Magazine Ltd.*, 1992).

BOOKS ON PARADE

This list of books is arranged to correspond somewhat with the anthology's sections; obviously, such figures as Armstrong, Ellington, Benny Carter, Basie, and so on, straddle time zones, equally present in the Free Jazz era as they were in the Jazz Age. I've bracketed an asterisk to indicate a book I found valuable; in other cases, I have added blurb decor about books and authors of outstanding merit.

General Histories, Collections

Abe, Katsuji, et al. *Jazz Giants: Visions of the Great American Legends* (New York: Billboard, 1988).

Baker, Houston A., Jr. *Blues, Ideology, and African-American Literature: A Vernacular Theory* (Chicago: University of Chicago Press, 1984).

Balliett, Whitney. *American Musicians: 56 Portraits in Jazz* (New York: Oxford University Press, 1986). [One of the premier white jazz journalists.]

————. *American Singers: Twenty-Seven Portraits in Song,* expanded edition (New York: Oxford University Press, 1988).

————. *Barney, Bradley, and Max: Sixteen Portraits in Jazz* (New York: Oxford University Press, 1989).

Berendt, Joachim-Ernst. *The Jazz Book: From New Orleans to Rock and Free Jazz* (New York: Hill and Wang, 1975).

Berendt, Joachim-Ernst. *Jazz: A Photo History* (New York: Schirmer, 1978). [*]

Blesh, Rudi. *Shining Trumpets: A History of Jazz* (New York: Knopf, 1958).

Bogle, Donald. *Toms, Coons, Mulattoes, Mammies, and Bucks: An Interpretive History of Blacks in American Films* (New York: Viking, 1973). [First-rate trailblazing work.]

Carruth, Hayden. *Sitting In: Selected Writings on Jazz, Blues and Related Topics* (Iowa City:

University of Iowa Press, 1986).

Clifford, James. *The Predicament of Culture: Twentieth-Century Ethnology, Literature, and Art* (Cambridge: Harvard University Press, 1989). [Challenging work by an anthropologist; pertinent for its assessment and critique of modernist and postmodern white high cultural uses of blackness and "primitivism."]

Collier, James Lincoln. *The Making of Jazz: A Comprehensive History* (Boston: Houghton Mifflin, 1978).

Cripps, Thomas. *Slow Fade to Black: The Negro in American Film, 1900–1942* (New York: Oxford University Press, 1977). [*]

Crouch, Stanley. *Notes of a Hanging Judge: Essays and Reviews, 1979–1989* (New York: Oxford University Press, 1990). [A vigorous polemicist, elegant writer, and challenging cultural and jazz critic.]

Dale, Rodney. *The World of Jazz* (New York: Exeter, 1982).

Dempsey, Travis. *An Autobiography of Black Jazz* (Chicago: Urban Research Institute, 1983).

Eberly, Philip K. *Music in the Air: America's Changing Taste in Music, 1920–1980* (New York: Hastings, 1982). [*]

Eisenberg, Evan. *The Recording Angel: The Experience of Music from Aristotle to Zappa* (New York: McGraw-Hill, 1987). [*]

Ellison, Ralph. *Shadow and Act* (New York: Random House, 1964). [By the author of *The Invisible Man*, undoubtedly one of the major postwar American novels, this collection includes memorable essays on Charlie Christian and other jazz figures.]

Emery, Lynne Fauley. *Black Dance in the United States: 1619–1970* (Salem: Ayer, 1972).

Feather, Leonard. *The Book of Jazz* (New York: Horizon Press, 1957).

———. *The Encyclopedia of Jazz* (New York: Horizon, 1955).

———. *The Encyclopedia of Jazz in the Sixties* (New York: Horizon Press, 1967). [British-born musician, producer, composer, also a prolific author, record reviewer, liner note writer brings these skills together in assembling his ongoing encyclopedias. Besides being noted for his attempts at integrating jazz, Feather's been an active advocate for women in jazz.]

Feinstein, Sascha, and Yusef Komunyakaa, eds. *The Jazz Poetry Anthology* (Bloomington: Indiana University Press, 1991).

Finkelstein, Sidney. *Jazz: A People's Music* (New York: Da Capo, 1975 reprint of 1948 edition). [Early Left overview of jazz as history and social process.]

Gates, Henry Louis, Jr. *The Signifying Monkey: A Theory of African-American Literary Criticism* (New York: Oxford University Press, 1989).

Gelatt, Roland. *The Fabulous Phonograph: 1877–1977* (New York: Macmillan, 1977). [Still the best general cultural history of the impact of the recording industry on American life.]

Giddins, Gary. *Riding on a Blue Note: Jazz and American Pop* (New York: Oxford University Press, 1981).

Gioia, Ted. *The Imperfect Art: Reflections on Jazz and Modern Culture* (New York: Oxford University Press, 1988.) [A knowledgeable, thoughtful meditation on the difficulties and epiphanies within jazz and writing about jazz.]

Gleason, Ralph J., ed. *Jam Session: An Anthology of Jazz* (New York: Putnam, 1958).

Goffin, Robert. *Jazz: From the Congo to the Metropolitan* (New York: Doubleday, 1944). [According to *Esquire* editor Arnold Gingrich: "Goffin was the first serious man of letters to take jazz seriously enough to devote a book to it . . . after that came Panassie . . . and Delaunay, . . . In other words, it took this Belgian, Goffin, and the two Frenchmen . . . to get us Americans to sit down and listen to jazz . . ."]

Gold, Robert S. *Jazz Lexicon* (New York: Knopf, 1964). [*]

Gottlieb, William P. *The Golden Age of Jazz* (New York: Da Capo, 1987). [*]

Grimes, Kitty. *Jazz Voices* (London: Quartet Books, 1983).

Hammond, John. *John Hammond on Record* (New York: Summit Books, 1977). [Modest memoir by silver-spoon civil libertarian and jazz fan who produced major records by major artists like Billie Holiday, Charlie Christian, Bessie Smith, up to Bob Dylan and George Benson.]

Harris, Rex. *Jazz* (Harmondsworth: Penguin Books, 1952).

Hentoff, Nat. *The Jazz Life* (New York: Dial Press, 1961).

———. *Jazz Is* (New York: Random House, 1976).

Hinton, Milt, and David G. Berger. *Bass Lines: The Stories and Photos of Milt Hinton* (Philadelphia: Temple University Press, 1988). [An insider's memoirs; an accomplished photographer's document of his jazz life.]

Hobsbawm, Eric. *The Jazz Scene*, revised and expanded edition (New York: Pantheon Books, 1992). [Essential study, augmented with the inclusion of the noted historian's later jazz criticism.]

Hodeir, Andre. *Jazz: Its Evolution and Essence* (New York: Grove Press, 1956). [First book translated into English by a postwar French musician/intellectual, infusing jazz criticism with unexpected historical, philosophical, structural concerns.]

———. *Toward Jazz* (New York: Grove Press, 1962).

———. *The Worlds of Jazz* (New York: Grove Press, 1972). [The last work of Hodeir I've seen. He spins off into a kind of Derridean free-form loopiness that's both touching and tackily insular.]

Horricks, Raymond, and others. *These Jazzmen of Our Time* (London: Gollancz, 1959).

Hughes, Langston. *The First Book of Jazz* (New York: Franklin Watts, 1955). [Introductory text written for children by a major American poet.]

Jones, Leroi (Amiri Baraka). *Blues People: Negro Music in White America* (New York: Morrow, 1963). [Wake-up call by a major African-American poet, playwright, radical.]

Keepnews, Orrin. *The View from Within: Jazz Writings, 1948–1987* (New York: Oxford University Press, 1988). [Uneven but important gathering by record producer Keepnews, noted for his work with Thelonious Monk, Bill Evans, Sonny

Rollins, and other major players of the fifties and sixties New York jazz scene.]

Keepnews, Orrin, and Bill Grauer. *A Pictorial History of Jazz: People and Places from New Orleans to the Sixties* (New York: Crowell, 1975). [*]

Keil, Charles. *Urban Blues* (Chicago: University of Chicago Press, 1966).

Larkin, Philip. *All What Jazz: A Record Diary, 1961–1971* (New York: Farrar, Straus & Giroux, 1985).

Lees, Gene. *Meet Me at Jim & Andy's: Jazz Musicians and Their World* (New York: Oxford University Press, 1988).

Leonard, Neil. *Jazz: Myth and Religion* (New York: Oxford University Press, 1987). [*]

Levine, Lawrence W. *Black Culture and Black Consciousness: Afro-American Folk Thought from Slavery to Freedom* (New York: Oxford University Press, 1977). [An invaluable background text by a noted American cultural historian.]

Locke, Alain. *The Negro and His Music* (Washington: Associates in Folk Education, 1936). [Essay by important Harlem Renaissance writer and theorist.]

Marchand, Roland. *Advertising the American Dream: Making Way for Modernity* (Berkeley: University of California Press, 1985). [Important study; links jazz as a modernist emblem, showing its uses in print and radio advertising. One of the fullest histories of the rise of advertising as a major cultural force.]

Meeker, David. *Jazz in the Movies: A Guide to Jazz Musicians, 1917–1977* (New Rochelle: Arlington House, 1977). [Available in an updated reprint published by Da Capo; this is fun but often one would like more plot information on what look like intriguing or bizarre flicks.]

Morris, Ronald. *Wait Until Dark: Jazz and the Underworld, 1880–1940* (Bowling Green: Bowling Green University Popular Press, 1980). [Important area of jazz history, culture, and economics.]

Murray, Albert. *Stomping the Blues* (New York: McGraw-Hill, 1976). [A rich feast of verbal virtuosity; a fusionary work blending Melville and Ellington into a rhapsodic survey of African-American art.]

Nanry, Charles, with Edward Berger. *The Jazz Text* (New York: Van Nostrand, 1979). [A sociological approach to jazz as subject and history.]

Ostransky, Leroy. *Understanding Jazz* (Englewood Cliffs: Prentice-Hall, 1977).

———. *Jazz City: The Impact of Our Cities on the Development of Jazz* (Englewood Cliffs: Prentice-Hall, 1978). [*]

Panassie, Hughes. *The Real Jazz* (New York: Smith and Durrell, 1942). [An early and important French assessment of American jazz; serious yet laced with buried or exposed romantic racism.]

Reisner, Robert G. *The Jazz Titans* (New York: Doubleday, 1960).

Roberts, John Storm. *Black Music of Two Worlds* (New York: Praeger, 1972).

Rubin, William, ed. *Primitivism in 20th Century Art: Affinity of the Tribal and the Modern* (New York: Museum of Modern Art, 1984). [Necessary companion to "Histories of the Tribal and Modern" in the Clifford book above.]

Sargeant, Winthrop. *Jazz: A History* (New York: McGraw-Hill, 1964).

Sidran, Ben. *Black Talk* (New York: Da Capo, 1971).

Simon, George T., ed. *Esquire's World of Jazz* (New York: Crowell, 1975). [*]

Starr, Frederick. *Red and Hot: The Fate of Jazz in the Soviet Union* (New York: Oxford University Press, 1983). [A fascinating and ultimately stirring history of how jazz was received, emulated, died for, reborn for, in the darkening utopia of revolution, Stalinism, and post-Stalinism.]

Stearns, Marshall W. *The Story of Jazz* (New York: Oxford University Press, 1956).

———. and Jean Stearns. *Jazz Dance: The Story of American Vernacular Dance* (New York: Schirmer Books/Macmillan, 1968). [Significant history; scholarly and readable.]

Stewart, Charles, and Paul Carter Harrison. *Chuck Stewart's Jazz Files* (London: Quartet, 1985).

Symes, Peter. *Focus on Jazz* (New York: St. Martin's, 1988).

Taylor, Billy. *Jazz Piano: History and Development* (Dubuque: Brown, 1982). [Useful overview by prominent jazz pianist and educator.]

Terkel, Studs. *Giants of Jazz* (New York: Crowell, 1957).

Tirro, Frank. *Jazz: A History* (New York: W. W. Norton, 1977).

Ulanov, Barry. *A History of Jazz in America* (New York: Viking Press, 1952).

Voigt, John. *Jazz Music in Print and Jazz Books in Print* (Boston: Hornpipe, 1982).

Walton, Ortiz M. *Music: Black, White and Blue* (New York: Morrow, 1972). [An overlooked book, reclaiming and politicizing the black struggle within jazz and jazz culture. Sometimes uneven, it nevertheless retains energy and purpose.]

Williams, Martin T. *The Jazz Tradition*, second revised edition (New York: Oxford University Press, 1993). [Still an excellent critical introduction to jazz; originally published in 1959.]

———. *Jazz Changes* (New York: Oxford University Press, 1992).

———. *Jazz in Its Time* (New York: Oxford University Press, 1989).

Young, Al. *Things Ain't What They Used to Be: Musical Memoirs* (Berkeley: Creative Arts, 1987).

———. *Bodies and Soul: Musical Memoirs* (Berkeley: Creative Arts, 1981). [Often evocative occasional essays, reviews, reminiscences by noted poet-novelist.]

Classic Jazz and the Jazz Age

Albertson, Chris. *Bessie* (New York: Stein and Day, 1972). [The most complete biography of Bessie Smith to date.]

Anderson, Jervis. *This Was Harlem: A Cultural Portrait, 1900–1950* (New York: Farrar, Straus & Giroux, 1981). [*]

Armstrong, Louis. *Swing That Music* (New York: Longmans, Green, 1946).

———. *Satchmo: My Life in New Orleans* (New York: Prentice-Hall, 1954). [Incomparable memoir of Armstrong's formative years.]

Barker, Danny. *A Life in Jazz*, ed. by Alyn Shipton (London: Macmillan, 1986). [*]

Bechet, Sidney. *Treat It Gentle* (New York: Hill and Wang, 1960). [The first portions of this memoir are absolutely dazzling.]

Berlin, Edward. *Ragtime: A Musical and Cultural History* (Berkeley: University of California Press, 1980). [*]

Berton, Ralph. *Remembering Bix: A Memoir of the Jazz Age* (New York: Harper & Row, 1974). [*]

Bigard, Barney. *With Louis and the Duke; Autobiography of a Jazz Clarinetist*, ed. by Barry Martyn (New York: Oxford University Press, 1986). [*]

Blesh, Rudi, and Harriet Janis. *They All Played Ragtime* (New York: Oak Publications, 1966).

Bradford, Perry. *Born with the Blues: Perry Bradford's Own Story, the True Story of the Pioneering Blues Singers and Musicians in the Early Days of Jazz* (New York: Oak Publications, 1965). [*]

Brunn, H.O. *The Story of the Original Dixieland Jazz Band* (Baton Rouge: Louisiana State University Press, 1960). [*]

Buerkle, Jack, and Danny Barker. *Bourbon Street Black: The New Orleans Black Jazzmen* (New York: Oxford University Press, 1974). [*]

Carmichael, Hoagy. *The Stardust Road* (New York: Rinehart, 1946). [One of the quintessential romantic memoirs of the Jazz Age.]

Charters, Samuel. *Jelly Roll Morton's Last Night at the Jungle Inn: An Imaginary Memoir* (New York/London: Marion Boyars Publishers, Inc., 1984). [Charters, a pioneering blues scholar, record producer, poet, attempts to embody Morton talking at the end of his life.]

Collier, James Lincoln. *Louis Armstrong: An American Genius* (New York: Oxford University Press, 1983).

————. *Duke Ellington* (New York: Oxford University Press, 1987).

Cowley, Malcolm. *Exile's Return* (New York: Viking, 1956). [*]

Ellington, Edward "Duke". *Music Is My Mistress* (New York: Doubleday, 1973). [Often criticized by fans and critics for what it leaves out, I was able to read it as a sequence of prose poems and thus enjoyed the work immensely. Ellington was a suave trickster, a dazzlingly veiled persona whose occasional writings gathered as his autobiography are actually more revealing than credited.]

Erenberg, Lewis A. *Steppin' Out: New York Nightlife and the Transformation of American Culture, 1890–1930* (Chicago: University of Chicago Press, 1981). [First-rate study, readable and astute.]

Foster, George "Pops." *The Autobiography of . . .* (as told to Tom Stoppard) (Berkeley: University of California Press, 1971). [*]

Hadlock, Richard. *Jazz Masters of the Twenties* (New York: Macmillan, 1966). [An excellent and intelligent study.]

Handy, W. C. *Father of the Blues: An Autobiography* (New York: Macmillan, 1941).

Haskins, Jim. *The Cotton Club* (New York: Random House , 1977).

Huggins, Nathan. *The Harlem Renaissance* (New York: Oxford University Press,

1971). [Major pioneering work; written with great style.]

——, ed. *Voices from the Harlem Renaissance* (New York: Oxford University Press, 1976). [Excellent collection of Harlem Renaissance writing.]

Kaminsky, Max, with V. E. Hughes. *My Life in Jazz* (New York: Harper & Row, 1963).

Kellner, Bruce. *Carl Van Vechten and the Irreverent Decades* (Norman: University of Oklahoma Press, 1968). [*]

Leib, Sandra. *Mother of the Blues: A Study of Ma Rainey* (Boston: University of Massachusetts Press, 1981).

Leonard, Neil. *Jazz and the White American: The Acceptance of a New Art Form* (Chicago: University of Chicago Press, 1962). [Ground-breaking historical and social analysis.]

Lewis, David Levering. *When Harlem Was in Vogue* (New York: Knopf, 1978). [*]

Lomax. Alan. *Mr. Jelly Roll: The Fortunes of Jelly Roll Morton, New Orleans Creole and 'Inventor' of Jazz* (New York: Duell, Sloane and Pearce, 1950). [No matter what, an unforgettably fascinating work. Texas folklorist Lomax transcribed Morton in his last years at the Library of Congress and then fashioned a biographical narrative out of the material. Morton's complex revisionary inventiveness is further thickened through Lomax's concept of the 'real' Morton. The Library of Congress acetates have been periodically pirated or reissued on records and are equally irresistible.]

Manone, Wingy, with Paul Vandervoot. *Trumpet on the Wing* (New York: Doubleday, 1948).

Marquis, Donald M. *In Search of Buddy Bolden: First Man of Jazz* (Baton Rouge: Louisiana State University Press, 1987). [Thorough scholarly reconstruction of the legendary actuality of Bolden's life.]

Mezzrow, Milton "Mezz," with Bernard Wolfe. *Really the Blues* (New York: Random House, 1946). [Undervalued novelist and culture critic Wolfe turned Mezzrow's garrulousness into the quintesssential proto-hipster epic, replete with propulsive vernacular rhythms, putting into place the archetype embodied by postwar Jewish intellectuals, hipsters, beatniks, and their struggle with race, the body, transgression.]

Ogren, Kathy J. *The Jazz Revolution: Twenties America and the Meaning of Jazz* (New York: Oxford University Press, 1989). [Excellent historical-cultural study; rich in detail.]

Ondaatje, Michael. *Coming Through Slaughter* (New York: W. W. Norton, 1977). [A poet-novelist's imaginary biography of Bolden.]

Osgood, H. O. *So This Is Jazz* (Boston: Little, Brown, 1926). [*]

Reed, Ishmael. *Mumbo Jumbo* (New York: Doubleday, 1970). [Reed's meta-fiction of the Cotton Club era is a non-stop engine of invention and virtuosity.]

Rose, Al. *I Remember Jazz: Six Decades Among the Great Jazzmen* (Baton Rouge: Louisiana State University Press, 1987).

Sargeant, Winthrop. *Jazz: Hot and Hybrid* (New York: Arrow Editions, 1938).

Schuller, Gunther. *Early Jazz: Its Roots and Development* (New York: Oxford University Press, 1968). [Essential work.]

Seldes, Gilbert. *Seven Lively Arts* (New York: Sagamore Press, 1957 reprint of 1924 edition). [One of the first American advocates of popular culture criticism.]

Shaw, Arnold. *The Jazz Age: Popular Music in the 1920s* (New York: Oxford University Press, 1987).

Smith, Willie "The Lion," with George Hoefer. *Music on My Mind: The Memoirs of an American Pianist* (New York: Doubleday, 1964). [Vibrant memoir of a major New York stride pianist.]

Sudhalter, Richard M., and Philips R. Evans with William Dean-Myatt. *Bix, Man and Legend* (New York: Arlington House, 1974). [The ultimate fan's book: photographs, a comprehensive discography; obsessive and overwhelmingly informative.]

Turner, Frederick. *Remembering Song: Encounters with the New Orleans Jazz Tradition* (New York: Viking, 1982). [*]

Van Vechten, Carl. *Nigger Heaven* (New York: Knopf, 1926). [The twenties ur-text of romantic racism.]

Whiteman, Paul, with Mary Margaret McBride. *Jazz* (New York: J. H. Sears, 1926). [The Great White Father of jazz mediated through McBride's radio-personality-chat style.]

Williams, Martin T. *Jazz Masters of New Orleans* (New York: Macmillan, 1967).

Pre-Bop Swing

Berger, Morroe. *Benny Carter: A Life in American Music.* 2 volumes. (Metuchen: Scarecrow Press, 1982). [*]

Blesh, Rudi. *Combo: U.S.A.* (New York: Chilton Books, 1971).

Büchmann-Møller, Frank. *You Just Fight for Your Life: The Story of Lester Young* (New York: Praeger, 1990). [The most thorough biographical study of Young to date, though not necessarily the best written.]

Calloway, Cab, with Bryant Rollings. *Of Minnie the Moocher and Me* (New York: Crowell, 1976). [*]

Chilton, John. *Billie's Blues: The Billie Holiday Story, 1933–1959* (London: Quartet Books, 1975). [Essential supplement to the above; exacting and accessible writing.]

Collier, James Lincoln. *Benny Goodman and the Swing Era* (New York: Oxford University Press, 1989). [*]

Condon, Eddie, and Thomas Sugrue. *We Called It Music: A Generation of Jazz* (New York: Henry Holt, 1947). [Lively insider's look at revivalist jazz and small group swing practiced in Manhattan from the middle thirties to late forties.]

Dance, Stanley. *The World of Duke Ellington* (New York: Scribner's, 1970). [An oral history of a major American composer in conversations with musicians, managers, fans, progeny, bookers, and the maestro himself.]

————. *The World of Earl Hines* (New York: Scribner's, n.d.). [*]

————. *The World of Swing* (New York: Scribner's, 1974). [*]

Delaunay, Charles. *Django Reinhardt* (London: Cassell, 1963). [To date, the only biography in English. Like other jazz comets, Reinhardt lived and created propelled by inexplicable energy and faith. His particular genius had considerable influence on American jazz and Western Swing guitar.]

Goodman, Benny, with Irving Kolodin. *Kingdom of Swing* (New York: Stackpole, 1939). [Whiteman's successor as "King of Swing"; interesting text to deconstruct.]

Hodes, Art, and Chadwick Hansen, eds. *Selections from the Gutter: Portraits from the Jazz Record* (Berkeley: University of California Press, 1977). [Musician and fan writings from *Jazz Record*, illuminated by the bright vernacular style of Hodes, an immigrant blues-based pianist ensconced in the Chicago jazz scene.]

Holiday, Billie, with William Dufty. *Lady Sings The Blues* (New York: Doubleday, 1956). [Contested autobiography; often criticized for taking "liberties" with truth and history, yet terrifically readable.]

Jewell, Derek. *Duke: Portrait of Duke Ellington* (New York: Norton, 1977).

Kater, Michael H. *Different Drummers: Jazz in the Culture of Nazi Germany* (New York: Oxford University Press, 1992). [Serious cultural history, despite an often academic writing style. Fills out the occasionally overwrought writing of Zwerin in the next, related, title.]

Porter, Lewis. *Lester Young* (Boston: Twayne Publishers, 1985). [Valuable musicological study.]

Porter, Lewis, ed. *A Lester Young Reader* (Washington: Smithsonian Institution Press, 1991). [Invaluable anthology of critical writing on Young; transcripts of interviews with Young.]

Russell, Ross. *Jazz Style in Kansas City and the Southwest* (Berkeley: University of California, 1971). [Exemplary history of the Kansas City renaissance of the forties that put into play such luminaries as Lester Young, Ben Webster, Charlie Parker, Mary Lou Williams.]

Schuller, Gunther. *The Swing Era: The Development of Jazz 1930–1945* (New York: Oxford University Press, 1989). [The second volume of Schuller's authoritative musicological reading of jazz.]

Shaw, Arnold. *The Street That Never Slept: New York's Fabled 52nd Street* (New York: Coward, McCann & Geoghegan, Inc., 1971). [Anecdotal history of a major venue for small swing and Bebop artists; insights into milieu.]

Shaw, Artie. *The Trouble with Cinderella* (New York: Farrar, Straus and Young, 1952). [A surprising writing performance by a major Swing Era figure; one of the better jazz autobiographies.]

Simon, George T. *The Big Bands* (New York: Macmillan, 1967). [*]

Smith, Jay D., and Len Guttridge. *Jack Teagarden: The Story of a Jazz Maverick* (London: Cassell, 1960). [The only full-scale biography of the distinctive trombone virtuoso and singer.]

Stewart, Rex. *Jazz Masters of the Thirties* (New York: Macmillan, 1972). [Wonderful essays by a significant member in the Ellington band; an influential player with a decided flair for writing.]

Wells, Dicky, as told to Stanley Dance. *The Night People* (Boston: Crescendo Publishers, 1971). [*]

Zwerin, Mike. *La Tristesse de Saint Louis: Jazz Under the Nazis* (London: Quartet Books, 1985). [*]

Crazy and Cool

Brossard, Chandler, ed. *The Scene Before You: A New Approach to American Culture* (New York: Henry Holt and Company, 1955). [Essential anthology of critical essays grappling with postwar alienated hipsterism, racism, cultural marginality, by lively stylish writer/intellectuals.]

Bruce, Lenny. *The Essential Lenny Bruce.* John Cohen, ed. (New York: Ballantine Books, 1968).

Carr, Roy, Brian Case, and Fred Dellar. *The Hip: Hipsters, Jazz and the Beat Generation* (London: Faber & Faber, 1986). [Postmodern scrapbook of fifties culture; contemporary illustrations, album covers, photos, advertising, and scattered essays on subjects like Slim Gaillard, Chet Baker, clothing, etc.]

Cerulli, Dom, Burt Korall, and Mort Nasatir, eds. *The Jazz Word* (New York: Ballantine, 1960). [Spotty anthology of jazz-related writing, hipster theory, and beat finger-snapping; interesting historical memento of paperback exploitation of cultural trends.]

Chambers, Jack. *Milestones 1: The Music and Times of Miles Davis to 1960* (Toronto: University of Toronto, 1983).

————. *Milestones 2: The Music and Times of Miles Davis Since 1960* (Toronto: University of Toronto, 1985). [Each volume builds a biographical context around Davis' record dates.]

Cole, Bill. *Miles Davis: A Musical Biography* (New York: Morrow, 1974). [*]

Crow, Bill. *Jazz Anecdotes* (New York: Oxford University Press, 1990).

————. *From Birdland to Broadway: Scenes from a Jazz Life* (New York: Oxford University Press, 1992).

Davis, Miles, with Quincy Troupe. *Miles* (New York: Simon and Schuster, 1989). [Troupe transcribes Davis at the height of his celebrity as both jazz hero and pop icon. Its obsessive dissing bothered white critics and fans.]

Easton, Carol. *Straight Ahead: The Story of Stan Kenton* (New York: Morrow, 1973). [*]

Feather, Leonard. *Inside Bebop* (New York: J. J. Robbins, 1949).

Gioia, Ted. *West Coast Jazz: Modern Jazz in California, 1946–1960* (New York: Oxford University Press, 1992). [First-rate critical history.]

Gitler, Ira. *Jazz Masters of the Forties* (New York: Macmillan, 1966). [Excellent study.]

———. *Swing to Bop: An Oral History of the Transition in Jazz in the 1940s* (New York: Oxford University Press, 1985). [*]

Goldberg, Joe. *Jazz Masters of the Fifties* (New York: Macmillan, 1965). [*]

Goldman, Albert. *Ladies and Gentlemen — Lenny Bruce!* (New York: Random House, 1971). [Goldman reaches heights of hipster Elizabethan fervor recounting postwar subcultures of burlesque, night clubs, drugs, and jazz.]

———. Freak Show: *The Rocksoulbluesjazzsickjewblackhumorsexpoppsych Gig and Other Scenes from the Counter-Culture* (New York: Atheneum, 1971). [*]

Hawes, Hampton, and Don Asher. *Raise Up Off Me: A Portrait of Hampton Hawes* (New York: Coward, McCann, Geoghegan, 1974). [Pianist/novelist Asher's lean and careful reworking of Hawes' story remains a memorable book.]

Marsh, Graham, and Glyn Callingham, eds. *California Cool: West Coast Jazz of the 50s and 60s: The Album Cover Art* (San Francisco: Chronicle Books, 1992).

Mingus, Charles. *Beneath the Underdog: His World as Composed by Mingus*, Nel King, ed. (New York: Knopf, 1971). [Another rare autobiography. Distilled from a rumored thousand pages, one wonders what was left out. Mingus is an oceanic writer of great passion, rage, slyness, angry dignity.]

Nutall, Jeff. *Bomb Culture* (London; MacGibbon & Kee, 1969). [Postwar British poet's analysis of jazz and pop culture.]

Pepper, Art, and Laurie Pepper. *Straight Life: The Story of Art Pepper* (New York: Schirmer Books/Macmillan, 1973). [One of the great autobiographies, as much for the jazz life as for Pepper's powerful descriptions of prison, where he spent a good third of his life on drug charges.]

Priestly, Brian. *Mingus: A Critical Biography* (New York: Da Capo, 1984). [*]

Reisner, Robert G. *Bird: The Legend of Charlie Parker* (New York: Citadel Press, 1962). [Fascinating gathering of oral history by immediate contemporaries of the Bebop scene remembering Parker. What emerges is a "legend" in the process of formation. Everyone knew a completely different Parker; events are described and redescribed from opposite readings. No matter what, everything and anything Parker did was deeply significant and worthy of continual telling and retelling.]

Rexroth, Kenneth. *World Outside the Window: Selected Essays. . . .* Branford Morrow, ed. (New York: New Directions, 1987). [Fine sampler of maverick poet-critic's range, including essays on jazz and poetry.]

Rosenthal, David H. *Hard Bop: Jazz and Black Music, 1955–1965* (New York: Oxford University Press, 1992). [*]

Russell, Ross. *Bird Lives! The High Life and Hard Times of Charlie (Yardbird) Parker* (New York: Charterhouse, 1973). [The only complete biography of Parker. As the title indicates, a mixed blessing. Russell, an L.A. record store owner and producer/owner of Dial Records, was an insider, yet often loses critical perspective in explaining the unimaginable Parker genius and person. Like many hagiographies, it's absorbingly readable, edged in fiction-like mannerisms of dialogue and description. His roman à clef, *The Sound*, on the other hand, is, despite Kerouac, one of the best fictional attempts at writing the Bebop culture.]

———. *The Sound* (New York: Dial, 1961). [*]

Spellman, A.B. *Four Lives in the Bebop Business* (New York: Pantheon Books, 1966). [Especially valuable for the essays on Herbie Nichols and Cecil Taylor.]

Wilson, John S. *Jazz: The Transition Years, 1940–1960* (New York: Appleton-Century-Crofts, 1962). [*]

Free Jazz, Fusion

Bailey, Derek. *Musical Improvisation: Its Nature and Practice in Music* (Englewood Cliffs: Prentice-Hall, 1980). [A sustained set of reflections and interviews provoked in part by the British author/guitarist's participation in the European Free Jazz movement.]

Baraka, Amiri, and Amina Baraka. *The Music: Reflections on Jazz and Blues* (New York: Morrow, 1987). [*]

Baraka, Amiri. *The Leroi Jones/Amiri Baraka Reader*, ed. by William J. Harris (New York: Thunder's Mouth Press, 1991). [*]

Cole, Bill. *John Coltrane* (New York: Schirmer Books, 1976). [*]

Coryell, Julie, and Laura Friedman. *Jazz-Rock Fusion: The People, the Music* (New York: Delta Books, 1978). [Interviews and photographs of "fusion" musicians on the eve of their ascendancy.]

Davis, Francis. *In the Moment: Jazz in the 1980s* (New York: Oxford University Press, 1986). [*]

Kofsky, Frank. *Black Nationalism and the Revolution in Music* (New York: Pathfinder Press, 1970). [Heavy-hitting and heavy-handed polemic noted for its interviews with Coltrane and Elvin Jones.]

Litweiler, John. *The Freedom Principle: Jazz After 1958* (New York: Morrow, 1984). [*]

Mackey, Nathaniel. *Bedouin Hornbook* (Lexington: Callaloo Fiction Series, 1986). [Brilliant vision of the jazz spirit.]

Neal, Larry. *Visions of a Liberated Future: Black Arts Movement Writings*, Michael Schwartz, ed. (New York: Thunder's Mouth Press, 1989). [*]

Rivelli, Pauline, and Robert Levin, eds. *The Black Giants* (New York: World Publishing, 1970). [Essays and musician interviews emphasizing the black avant-garde.]

Simosko, V., and B. Tepperman. *Eric Dolphy* (Washington: Smithsonian Institution Press, 1974). [*]

Simpkins, Cuthbert Ormond. *Coltrane* (New York: Herndon House, 1975).

Sinclair, John, and Robert Levin. *Music and Politics* (Cleveland: World Publishing Co., 1971). [Encapsulates two ideological grounds around jazz and politics of the Vietnam era: Levin, measured, analytical; Sinclair, intuitive and loud, visionary.]

Tate, Greg. *Flyboy in the Buttermilk* (New York: Fireside/Simon and Schuster, 1992). [*]

Williams, Martin. *Jazz Masters in Transition, 1957–1969* (New York: Macmillan, 1970). [*]

Wilmer, Valerie. *As Serious as Your Life.* (London: Alison & Busby, 1977). [*]

——. *Jazz People* (Indianapolis: Bobbs-Merrill, 1970). [*]

——. *The Face of Black Music* (New York: Da Capo, 1976). [*]

PERMISSIONS

Every effort has been made to identify the holders of copyright of previously published materials included in this book. The publisher apolo-
gizes for any oversights that may have occurred; any errors that may
have been made will be corrected in subsequent prints upon notifica-
tion to the publisher. Grateful acknowledgment is made to the following for permission to reprint copyrighted material:

Starr, Sandra Leonard. Copyright © 1988 by Sandra Leonard Starr. Reprinted by permission of Sandra Leonard Starr.

Stravinsky, Igor. From *Conversations with Igor Stravinsky*, by Igor Stravinsky and Robert Craft. Copyright © 1958, 1959 by Igor Stravinsky. Also published under the title *Stravinsky: In Conversation with Robert Craft*.

Taylor, Roger L. From *Art, An Enemy of the People*. Copyright © 1978. Reprinted by permission of the author.

Townsend, Charles R. From *San Antonio Rose: The Life and Music of Bob Wills*. Published by University of Illinois Press. Copyright © 1976 by the Board of Trustees of the University of Illinois.

Treadwell, Bill, editor. From *The Big Book of Swing*. Copyright © 1946 by Cambridge House Publishers, NY.

Vechten, Carl Van. From *Nigger Heaven* by Carl Van Vechten. Copyright © 1926 by Alfred A. Knopf, Inc. and renewed 1954 by Carl Van Vechten. Reprinted by permission of the publisher.

Vian, Boris. Copyright © 1982 by Christian Bourgois Editeur. Reprinted by permission of Christian Bourgois.

Welch, Lew. From *Golden Gate: Interviews with Five San Francisco Poets*. Copyright © 1976 by David Meltzer. Reprinted by permission.

Wentworth, Harold and Stuart Berg Flexner. Excerpts from *The Dictionary of American Slang* by Harold Wentworth and Stuart Flexner. Copyright © 1960, 1967, 1975 by Harper & Row, Publishers, Inc. Reprinted by permission of HarperCollins Publishers Inc.

Whiteman, Paul. From *So This is Jazz*. Copyright © 1926.

Whitmore, Stanford. Excerpt from *Solo*, copyright © 1955 and renewed 1983 by Stanford Whitmore, reprinted by permission of Harcourt Brace & Company.

Wieners, John. "1930 Jazz" Copyright © 1967 by John Wieners. Reprinted from *Cultural Affairs in Boston: Poetry & Prose 1956–1985* with the permission of Black Sparrow Press

Willener, Alfred. From *The Action-Image of Society: On Cultural Politicization*. Copyright date unavailable. Reprinted by permission of Routledge.

Williams, William Carlos. From *Interviews with William Carlos Williams*. Copyright © 1976 by New Directions Publishing Corporation.

Zavatsky, Bill. Copyright © 1981 by Bill Zavatsky. Reprinted by permission of Bill Zavatsky. Originally appeared in liner note on *You Must Believe in Spring* by Bill Evans (Burbank: Warner Bros. Inc., 1981).

Zwerin, Mike. "La Tristesse de Saint Louis" from *Jazz Under the Nazis* by Mike Zwerin, pages 24–29. Copyright © 1985 by Mike Zwerin. Reprinted by permission of William Morrow & Co., Inc.

INDEX OF ANTHOLOGIZED MATERIAL

ABOUT THE EDITOR

DAVID MELTZER began his literary career during the Beat heyday in San Francisco, reading poetry to jazz accompaniment at the famous Jazz Cellar. He is the author of *The Secret Garden: The Classical Kabbalah; Birth: Hymns, Prayers, Documents, Myths, Amulets;* and *Death: An Anthology of Ancient Texts, Songs, Prayers, and Stories,* as well as many books of poetry, including *Arrows: Selected Poetry 1982–1992.* He teaches in the Humanities and graduate Poetics programs at the New College of California. He lives in the Bay Area with his wife, Tina, and his son, Adam.

Cover design: Sharon Smith
Cover and hand lettering: Ward Shumaker
Text design and production: David Peattie
Text type: Adobe Centaur and Minion
Editing and proofing: Will Powers and Tom Hassett
Printing and binding: Haddon Craftsmen, Inc.